CARL VAN DOREN
A MAN OF IDEAS

BY ROBIN K. FOSTER

Armillary Press
Arlington, Virginia

Excerpts from *Three Worlds* by Carl Van Doren, copyright © 1936 by Carl Van Doren. Used by permission of Viking Books, an imprint of Penguin Publishing Group, a division of Penguin Random House LLC. All rights reserved.

Excerpts from *Benjamin Franklin* by Carl Van Doren, copyright © 1938 by Carl Van Doren, renewed © by Margaret Van Doren Bevans, Anne Van Doren Ross, and Barbara Van Doren Klaw. Used by permission of Viking Books, an imprint of Penguin Publishing Group, a division of Penguin Random House LLC. All rights reserved.

Excerpts from *Jane Mecom* by Carl Van Doren, copyright © 1950 by Carl Van Doren. Used by permission of Viking Books, an imprint of Penguin Publishing Group, a division of Penguin Random House LLC. All rights reserved.

Excerpts from the following titles: *The Roving Critic* © 1923 by Carl Van Doren; *What is American Literature* © 1935 by Carl Van Doren; *Many Minds* © 1924 by Carl Van Doren; *Sinclair Lewis, A Biographical Sketch* © 1933 by Carl Van Doren; *Patriotic Anthology* © 1941 by Carl Van Doren; and unpublished works and letters are reprinted by permission of Susan Klaw.

"In Memoriam" by Mark Van Doren reprinted by permission of Adam Van Doren.

Cover image: sketch of Carl Van Doren by Hugo Gellert, 1923

Book design by Tara Mayberry, TeaBerryCreative.com

Copyright © 2018 by Robin K. Foster

All rights reserved, including the right to reproduce this book or portions thereof in any form whatsoever.

ISBN: 978-0-692-18921-4
Library of Congress Control Number: 2018911064

Armillary Press
Arlington, Virginia
Printed in the United States of America

ALSO BY ROBIN K. FOSTER

➤—·—◄

The Age of Sail in The Age of Aquarius;
The South Street Seaport and the Crisis of the Sixties

To Stan, who shares my own desire *TO KNOW*

And in memory of Lois Foster Rather,
fellow Biographer on the Trail

A biographer looks into his heart as a poet does.

–CARL VAN DOREN

CONTENTS

Carl Van Doren Chronology...xi

Introduction 1

1 The Glory of Great Verse...13

2 A Man of Ideas...49

3 The Man Who Knew Everybody................................... 103

4 Shifting Materials 127

5 The Roving Critic... 147

6 Biographer on the Trail...159

7 The Americanism of Carl and Mark Van Doren.......... 187

8 Following His Head.. 197

9 Following His Heart 227

10 Under the Useful Tree..267

11 Such Noble Patterns..307

Author's Note..317

Endnotes 321

Bibliography...333

Abbreviations in Notes 339

My deep appreciation, gratitude, and friendship go out to Susan Klaw, who opened up the Van Doren family home at Cornwall to me, my inquisitive eye, and my biographer's heart. Spending time at Carl and Irita Van Doren's country home made all the difference in the world to this *Biographer on the Trail*. Thank you, Susan.

And thank you to Ellen Harkness, who shared memories of her aunt Elizabeth Marion with me.

Special thanks to Princeton University's Rare Books and Special Collections, which houses the Carl Van Doren Papers, and to Sandra Bossert and Brianna Cregle in Princeton's Manuscript Reading Room; to Washington State University Library's Manuscripts, Archives, and Special Collections, which houses the Elizabeth Marion Saunders Papers; Cornell University Library's Rare Books and Manuscripts, home to the Hendrik Willem Van Loon Papers; and The Library of Congress, which holds the Irita Van Doren Papers as well as numerous radio recordings I listened to in the course of my research. These invaluable collections, as well as the always helpful and knowledgeable staff who tend to the archives and their researchers, are the bread-and-butter for any Biographer on the Trail. While digital access to source material has opened up the research process in both speed and scope, brick-and-mortar archives, libraries, and museum collections remain, and will forever be, a researcher's Mecca. What it is to hold a handwritten letter, a typed manuscript with penciled notes in the margin, a telegram, a yellowed photograph, an envelope with its tell-tale red Air Mail stamp...! *Ah, the past is not always a foreign country; sometimes it's right in front of you. And it's breathtaking.*

And thank you to Stan, my husband but also my comrade-in-arms in all things history, literature, art, knowledge, life. *Pleased with how the match was scored*, indeed.

→—·—←

CARL VAN DOREN
CHRONOLOGY

SEPT 10, 1885	Carl Clinton Van Doren born Hope, Illinois
1907	A.B. University of Illinois
1911	Ph.D. Columbia University
1911-'30	Professor of English, Columbia University
1912	Marries Irita Bradford
1915, '17, '20	Daughters Anne, Margaret, and Barbara born
1917-'21	Managing Editor, *The Cambridge History of American Literature*
1919-'22	Literary Editor, *The Nation*
AUG '19	"On Studying Biography"
1921	"Revolt from the Village"
1921	*The American Novel*
1922	*Contemporary American Novelists, 1900-1920* "The American Rhythm"
1922-'25	Literary Editor, *Century*

1923	*The Roving Critic*
1924	*Many Minds; Critical Essays on American Writers*
1925	*Other Provinces* *American and British Literature Since 1890*, ed.
1926-'34	Editor, The Literary Guild of America
1926	*The Ninth Wave*
DEC '26	"Why I am an Unbeliever"
1930	*Swift*
1933	*Sinclair Lewis; A Biographical Sketch* *American Literature: An Introduction*
1935	*An Anthology of World Prose*, ed.
1936	Divorced from Irita
1936	*Three Worlds*
1937	"The American Imagination"
1938	*Benjamin Franklin*
FEB 1939	Marries Jean Wright Gorman
1939	Wins Pulitzer Prize for *Benjamin Franklin*
1939	*An Illinois Boyhood*
1940	Editor, The Readers Club

1941	*Secret History of the American Revolution: An Account of the Conspiracies of Benedict Arnold and Numerous Others Drawn from the Secret Service Paper*
1941	*The Patriotic Anthology; Introduced by Carl Van Doren*
1943	*Mutiny in January: The Story of a Crisis in the Continental Army*
FEB 1945	Divorced from Jean
1945	*Carl Van Doren: The Viking Portable Library*
1946	*American Scriptures*, ed. with Carl Cramer
OCT 1946	Meets Elizabeth Marion at Reed Conference
1948	*The Great Rehearsal: The Story of the Making and Ratifying of the Constitution of the United States*
1950	*The Letters of Benjamin Franklin & Jane Mecom*, ed.
JUL 18, 1950	Dies in Connecticut following heart attack
1950	*Jane Mecom, The Favorite Sister of Benjamin Franklin* (published posthumously)

INTRODUCTION

I have long been captivated by this country's golden age of literary criticism. Most of the books that live on my shelves date to the 1920s, '30s, '40s, and '50s, an era when literary and cultural criticism flourished in an intellectual climate that was decidedly public. During this golden age, when literary achievement was considered to be a family tradition, the Van Doren literary dynasty began a legacy that has all but faded from the American cultural scene. We no longer admire great *men of letters*. We don't even know who those men or women might be. That is primarily because America no longer has a public niche for the *Intellectual*. With few notable exceptions, our intellectuals now toil in obscurity in research universities and publish books clearly meant for other scholars. Any understanding of a common intellectual culture eludes us. One of the twentieth century's most prolific intellectuals, Carl Van Doren, became a scholar to satisfy his personal curiosity, became a teacher to earn a living, but wrote to fulfill a restless instinct.

Carl Van Doren can best be described by what is today clearly an anachronism: the man of letters. This moniker simply no longer exists. Certainly, we have men and women held in high intellectual esteem: certain university professors or leaders of intellectually-minded foundations; literary geniuses; popular writers of national significance. But the *man of letters* is gone. Richard Posner wrote on the decline of the public intellectual across the last century, and points to the rise of the modern university and the trend towards specialization of knowledge across all realms of intellectual work as the major causes of this decline. The public intellectual was someone often schooled in the nation's top universities but not necessarily so, and moved beyond the constraints of the ivory tower in order to write for a more generalized American audience; the public intellectual who wrote about general matters of culture and public concern and often used the medium of literature to reveal his erudition and elucidate his ideas; the public intellectual who was then increasingly disregarded by the ivory tower that reared him, as universities heightened their demand for specialization and began collecting only those academics who carved out for themselves a very specific (often esoteric) niche.

This man—or, less often woman: she did, however, exist—belongs to the nineteenth and early twentieth centuries. He lives there still in the archives, in preserved correspondence, in long-forgotten documents, in his original words and essays. And so if I am going to write a biography on the man who wrote the seminal biography on Benjamin Franklin and won the Pulitzer Prize for it in 1939; who was the author of a great many books, essays, magazine articles, literary criticism, and radio broadcasts; who was husband, father, treasured friend, and correspondent, it is to the archives I go.

Carl Van Doren, distinguished man of letters of that golden age, did not wish to be biographied dully. Naturally, one would assume that any person who might one day have a biography written about him would want an interested writer to create an interesting narrative. But on this point Carl Van Doren was quite clear. When a former student approached the Pulitzer Prize winning author about writing his biography, Van Doren confided to a friend that this "dull" former student would surely write an even duller biography. Van Doren rejected the offer. Fast-forward seventy-odd years and no long-form biography on one of this country's most esteemed historian/writer/biographer/literary critic/man-of-letters has ever been written. Van Doren did not want to be dully biographied. And I, a historian and writer with a long-time interest in this twentieth century man of letters, get it. Who wants to read a dull biography? Who wants to write one?

Of course, when I began this pilgrimage into the archives, I was not aware of Van Doren's dread at the thought of being the subject of a "dull" biography. That came several months into my research, with a sentence buried in a letter Van Doren wrote to friend and fellow writer Elizabeth Marion. Just a sentence that a bleary-eyed historian reading through decades of correspondence could surely overlook. Poring through the personal correspondence of persons long deceased is, to put it simply: *fascinating*. The work, however, is slow going; partly because it is so fascinating and you do not want to miss a word, partly because handwritten correspondence can be really difficult to decipher. The initial sense of voyeurism one experiences quickly fades when one remembers this collection of many, many, many linear feet of correspondence was not preserved by accident. Indeed this trove, and others like it, was quite purposefully saved. These fortunate letters were *not* mailed to their intended recipients with the specific instructions to burn after reading (because many public persons have long requested exactly that). No, these letters were preserved for some future interested party to read. Because it is clear, once you start digging around in the archives, that certain information *has* been lost, destroyed, or left out; usually related to that one particular thread you really need, or want, to clarify. The extant collection was clearly meant to be read, by some future historian or biographer, no doubt. Preferably not a dull one.

Dear Reader, Is this a challenge to a future would-be biographer? Carl Van Doren stated quite clearly that he did not want a dull biography written about him. But is dullness, like beauty, in the eye of the beholder? What were Van Doren's standards, exactly, when it comes to good writing? The writer and critic felt that cleverness and dullness were recognizable facets of one's personality. A dull man would most certainly produce a dull biography, but a clever and astute person could, quite likely, write an interesting one. We know Van Doren found the subtle, intimate aspects of an individual's story much more interesting and compelling than the "many subjects that are supposed to be more suitable to history, with all its damned traditional dignity." The biography should not be simply academic, although the research and writing must be scrupulous. Van Doren, we know, was no fan of the wheel of academia that turned only for itself, nor of academics who wrote jargon-filled language solely for other academics. The biography certainly should not be dull. So that particular proposal, in 1950, by a former student turned would-be biographer, was out of the question.

Yet, Van Doren *did* want to be biographied some day, we can be sure. The extant collection of his personal and professional correspondence, his diaries and notes, his contracts and lecture scripts, his original manuscripts, magazine articles, award certificates, and family photographs, were very specifically donated to the Princeton University Library archives and placed under the immediate stewardship of Van Doren's good friend, Julian Boyd. Van Doren left behind invaluable fodder for an *interesting* biography. This much is clear.

The first rule of archival research is this: you never know what you're going to get. You don't know where the research will take you. It's best not to have too many preconceived ideas about your subject or hold fast to a particular angle you intend to take when you begin to write your story. Lives are complicated, turns-of-events should be counted on, and you need to be open for that. How does a man's life conform, in lived reality, to his expectations? Van Doren's comment to Elizabeth Marion regarding the dull student who would surely write a dull biography indicates to *this* historian that Van Doren had higher aspirations for his life story than one of mediocrity. Indeed, I might easily have overlooked this one line in one of hundreds of letters—most of them, mercifully, typed rather than hand-written—in a file marked "Elizabeth Marion," which I also might have overlooked...because I wasn't initially searching for personal correspondence.

My idea was to examine the body of work of this literary icon who wrote prolifically across the 1920s, '30s, and '40s for publications like *The Nation, Century, Scribner's, Atlantic Monthly, The New Republic,* the *Saturday Review, Bookman,* and *Good Housekeeping;* was the author of many books of American and literary history and won the Pulitzer Prize; was a literary editor; wrote the introductions to over one hundred books written by other authors; presided over the selections of mail-order book clubs including the Literary Guild of America and the Readers Club; gave lectures on issues of historical and cultural significance at public libraries, women's clubs, and historical societies across the country; recorded radio broadcast promotional pieces for U.S. war bonds; believed in a federated world government and worked with *Americans United for World Government*; and was written about in *Time* and *Life* magazines. And as I was waiting one day for a requested box of materials to be delivered to me at Princeton University Library's rare books and manuscript reading room, I was offered a box of correspondence that was immediately available. The Elizabeth Marion correspondence. Which changed everything.

This is detective work, when you get right down to it. I am a pilgrim in the archives, journeying to that sacred place—the archive—for fundamental reasons of curiosity, both intellectual and spiritual. This is my holy place, and I am travelling to a time and place in the not-too-distant past which is yet vastly different from my own world. I get lost in that time and place, spending hours in archival reading rooms, which tend to be smallish and windowless, although not always. The Library of Congress's main reading room is distracting in its architectural and artistic splendor. I am reminded of Annie Dillard, who, writing about her own process, advised writers to seek *a room with no view*, so that one would not be distracted by the proximal world. Fortunately,

I wasn't trying to write my story in that magnificent space at the Library of Congress; I was there searching for clues.

There are going to be some dead-ends in the process. Sometimes a hint or a bit of innuendo can never be fully fleshed out or corroborated. Sometimes the information you uncover is downright contradictory to some other piece of information. Sometimes you have to let a thread go, because you can't be certain enough to be credible. Academically-trained as I am (my Ph.D. is in American Studies), I have no sabbatical or research grant to provide me with assistants who will do the grunt work. The grunt work is the work of the pilgrim. As Carl Van Doren himself wrote in his autobiography, "Only love can carry [one] through the labor that goes into a book." As I conduct my trek from archive to archive, from the Princeton University Library Rare Books and Manuscripts reading room; to the archives at Washington State University; to Cornell University Library; to the glorious Library of Congress' main reading room and its less structurally grandiose but nevertheless invaluable tertiary reading rooms located in the adjacent Madison Library; to Carl Van Doren's summer home in Connecticut, I transcribe handwritten scrawl into legible notes; I listen to reel-to-reel recordings of 1940s' radio shows; I read through decades of personal correspondence, lecture circuit contracts, Van Doren's original essays and articles. I inhabit his recorded world and I try to know the parts of his life that are knowable because they were recorded for posterity.

Much of what we can know about the life and work of Carl Van Doren we glean though his personal correspondence with friends and family, most of whom were fellow writers. In his autobiography, Van Doren wrote that writers do not have to meet regularly face-to-face in order to know each other deeply and establish relationships, but rather "Their writings are conversations, and when they meet they go on talking from where they left off reading." Van Doren left behind a trove of correspondence with fellow writers such as Sinclair Lewis, Theodore Dreiser, Willa Cather, H. L. Mencken, Mary Hunter Austin, Elinor Wylie, Robert Frost, and Carl's brother and fellow Pulitzer Prize winner Mark Van Doren.[1]

Van Doren's autobiography *Three Worlds,* written in 1936 when he was fifty years old and only fourteen years before his death, is invaluable as well. Among all of the literary hats he donned, Van Doren wrote that he was primarily a *biographer*, and that "a biographer looks into his heart as a poet does." This connection between the work of the biographer and the poet is significant, as Van Doren's early attempts at writing poetry were quickly snubbed out. He knew, he recalled in *Three Worlds*, that his poetry simply wasn't good enough. Nor were his attempts at fiction going to cut it. After his novel *The Ninth Wave* received meager critical and commercial acclaim, Van Doren accepted Sinclair Lewis's remarks that a good novelist "had to feel strong attraction or antipathy at sight for people or he could not represent them with necessary force." Van Doren acknowledged he had too much "Dutch indifference" to succeed there.

Poetry and novel-writing aside, Van Doren's successes as a biographer, historian, essayist, and literary critic marked a golden era of literary and cultural criticism across the 1920s, '30s, '40s and up to his death in July, 1950. The final message from Van Doren's autobiography is brilliant, humble, astute. His assured and measured voice speaks to readers of his immediate future and to our own time:

> You who may be reading this book tomorrow or the day after tomorrow will wonder why I could not foresee the events which lie between us and which you will think ought to have been plain to me. I strain my eyes into the dark and make out nothing: wars, dictatorships, revolutions, recoveries, compromises... I think that the general spirit of America is putting behind it a dull confusion and beginning to free its great energies. But this may be wishes which I mistake for facts. I may have looked into the wrong American heart for a sign of what was happening to America. You know, and I do not. I have told you only what I know about these times.[2]

And that's the point of writing a biography: to uncover what one person's life can tell us not only about his life, but about his times. *A biographer looks into his heart as a poet does.* Leslie Fielder, essayist and somewhat-contemporary of Van Doren's, wrote that a good essay "contains not only revelations of the self, but the society in which the self is defined. The crown and climax of the essay is literary criticism," because literature is man's "subtlest and loveliest means of ordering and understanding his life." So as I sift through the archives for evidence that will help me to know the life and times of Carl Van Doren, my pilgrimage moves beyond my inquiry into this particular man of letters and into the whole of American cultural life.[3]

Historian by training, biographer and critic by trade, poet in his heart, Van Doren knew that we need to understand the past in order to more clearly see our own present circumstances. "A knowledge of history and literature is indispensable in affairs," he wrote. Our own times are troubling. The past is not simply a foreign country; sometimes the past is a refuge. We look at the past from the present state of our own world, a world that invariably colors our perceptions of past lives, past events. Van Doren wrote, "The biographer is an organism, not a machine. While he is resolving somebody else's life, he is living a part of his own." This reality tends to get lost when a reader picks up a biography or other work of history. For the sake of objectivity, the biographer attempts to remain mostly absent from the very work he or she is creating. But let's be clear: every writer leaves countless notes and pages on the cutting room floor, and what does make it into the book is very much determined by the biographer's own interests.

We all start from somewhere, and how successfully we deliver the story, and where we bring our reader, very much depends on how much poetry goes into that process. Indeed, Mark Van Doren once said, "you can't write about anything without lending it your own terrific life." I began writing this biography intent on illuminating the *golden age of literary criticism* through the work of one man who brought literature and cultural criticism to the American public.

What I found was much more. What I found was a life.

CHAPTER 1

→ · ←

THE GLORY OF GREAT VERSE

The last book Carl Van Doren wrote was published a few months after his death in 1950. *Jane Mecom, The Favorite Sister of Ben Franklin* grew out of Van Doren's larger work on the full correspondence between Franklin and his youngest sister Jane. In describing *Jane Mecom*, Van Doren wrote of the life-long correspondence between the pair, stressing the impact their correspondence had on our larger understanding of the great statesman and his lesser-known sister:

> Their love and their letters, reaching back and forth between them, bound them together in the longest comfortable friendship either of them ever had. Without the letters, the love might have been lost sight of. It shines in all his words, whether he

advised or consoled or teased her. Within her range, and in her own bright, ardent, impetuous, sometimes faulty idiom, she wrote almost as well as he, with a touch of flavor and distinction in every line. Their correspondence is the conversation of a wise man and a sensitive, emotional woman, about the things that mattered to them jointly, through all the changes of their differing fortunes, for more than sixty years. That correspondence, much of it long buried, now comes to light in words as true and colors as lively as they ever were. Jane Mecom adds a new grace to Benjamin Franklin. He mirrors and interprets her. Hereafter neither brother nor sister will stand alone in the world's memory, *for neither can be fully known or truly remembered without the other.*[4]

This is a tribute to the power of archival research, if ever there was one. The long-hidden private correspondence between the esteemed statesman/philosopher/inventor and his cherished sister reveals a human sensibility in Franklin—and in Jane Mecom as well, whom we might otherwise know nothing about—that, without this trove of letters, would have remained unknowable. The story of Jane Mecom's life, and those parts of Benjamin Franklin's life that are illuminated by reading their letters, is a gift to history in and of itself, an advancement in the scholarship on one of our nation's most fascinating citizens. What's more interesting to *this* biographer, however, is the fact that Carl Van Doren wrote these words while he was in the midst of what I can only describe as a love story. Without Van Doren's own archived correspondence, *his* "love might have been lost sight of. It shines in all his words, whether he advised or consoled or teased her. Within her range, and in her own bright, ardent, impetuous, sometimes faulty idiom, she wrote almost as well as he, with a touch of flavor and distinction in every line. Their correspondence is the conversation of a wise man and a sensitive, emotional woman, about the things that mattered to them jointly, through all the changes of their differing fortunes. Hereafter neither...will stand alone in the world's memory, *for neither can be fully known or truly remembered without the other.*"

The woman, in Van Doren's case, was Elizabeth Marion, a writer of some minor success whom Van Doren met in 1946 at the Conference of Writers on the Northwest at Portland's Reed College. Before she was thirty, Elizabeth Marion had authored three novels: *The Day Will Come* (1939); *Ellen Spring* (1941); and *The Keys to the House* (1944). She was born in Spokane in 1916 and was raised on the family farm near Spangle, Washington. Elizabeth Marion lived in Spangle, and later Fairfield, with her parents and her five younger siblings (her brother Elliot, just a year younger than Elizabeth, died in 1938) and her many cats, was working on a new manuscript and held a seasonal secretarial position with a state Congressional office. Van Doren, by this time a Pulitzer Prize-winning author and widely respected biographer and literary critic, had been invited by his friend Victor Chittick at Reed College to serve as the featured guest of the conference. A *New York Times* article on the event described Elizabeth Marion as the youngest participant in the conference, who led a "sincere and moving little talk groping for the artist's essential purpose." To Elizabeth, the Reed Conference was *the most wonderful* writers conference there ever was. The participants and the setting bedazzled and bewitched her to the point of giddiness.

Van Doren immediately took a shine to Elizabeth Marion and so began, when the younger writer sent a letter to Van Doren at his home in New York City, a correspondence that would last the rest of Carl's life. In her first letter, dated November 16, 1946, Elizabeth Marion thanked Mr. Van Doren for the copy of his recent book, *Carl Van Doren: The Viking Portable Library*, that he had sent her. Of Van Doren's chapter on Willa Cather, Elizabeth gushed,

> It is a fine lesson in writing, that chapter...and sets a goal so high one can't help having a shot at it...it illuminates fiercely, to me, how life is so—not the same, universal? In the world, and how its backgrounds vary in the parishes...I shall read Elinor Wylie this winter, because of your chapter about her, which makes her seem so much more wonderful, as person and poet, than the single poem and the dingy footnote in the literature books we had in school. (Nov. 16, 1946)[5]

Ambivalent about being the focus of attention by so great a man of letters as Mr. Carl Van Doren, Elizabeth Marion was both terrified and star-struck. It had been three years, after all, since she had written anything "fit to print." At the same time, she was thrown into a state of pure literary admiration for Van Doren's work. If she had previously read any of his essays or books, she did not say. However, upon reading the *Portable Library*, she was hooked.

> You never write a sentence that is not simplicity itself, and never a phrase that is not beautifully uncommonplace... and I—I know just enough to prevent my remarking it looks so easy! the results look easy... (Nov. 16, 1946)[6]

Van Doren's letter to Elizabeth Marion arrived a few weeks later, in which his tone, on the whole, was protective and paternal. He offered himself as a mentor to the young writer, as she trudged daily through her writing and attempted to navigate the always-maddening publishing process.

> ...But go ahead writing the book, when you get ready, and write only such letters to admirers as you have to. If you have no binding contract with your publishers, I wish you would let me see the ms of that next novel and let me see about getting it published to the best advantage. (I never before suggested this to

any writer, and it makes me feel rather impertinent.) And if you ever feel the need of an assistant-father in New York, you can count on me to be always available, as my own daughters can and do. (Dec. 10, 1946)[7]

It didn't take long for Carl Van Doren and Elizabeth Marion to become increasingly familiar and comfortable with one another, "fast friends" you could say. He could write cryptically and between-the-lines, while she was never at a loss for words when describing the goings-on in her mind and in her rural part of the world. The life of the mind was tantalizing to both writers. The two began to engage in playful banter almost from the first. Playing with words is pure fun for those who write for a living, and the thrill of finding a kindred spirit who enjoys words and sentences and double-entendre and literary references as much as you do is priceless. This was certainly the case for Carl Van Doren and Elizabeth Marion. The year of their meeting was 1946, with a continent and thirty years between the two writers, and yet they found in each other a growing affection, both intellectual and spiritual. Van Doren, a man for whom a woman had to be intelligent to be truly interesting, felt this right from the start. He wrote to Elizabeth, "There is some similarity in our wave-lengths, says he proudly. I shall not be politely obscure again."[8]

Van Doren, hoping to open the doors to an academic assignment for Elizabeth, reached out to Chittick in search of a staff position at Reed College.[i] Hinting to Elizabeth that he was engaged in a little behind-the-scenes plotting on her behalf, Van Doren wrote to Chittick, eagerly suggesting to his former graduate student that he ought to bring Elizabeth Marion to Reed.

> If Reed College has any essential creative flair, it will contrive some scheme by which she can stay on there, for a year or so, on the staff, in some capacity or other that will support her. Don't tell me she has only a high school education. It's more than Franklin or Lincoln had. The gal is full of genius. She is authentic Northwest and wants to go on living there, without benefit of New York or Hollywood. She will be worth as much to your writers as Frost meant to Amherst...So get to work on this hunch, which you have probably already had. (Dec. 23, 1946)[9]

The appointment was not to be, and Van Doren was less than pleased. For her part, Elizabeth Marion hinted that she would rather write than talk about writing, and the matter was dropped. A handful of letters into their correspondence, Van Doren wrote

. . . .

i   Van Doren and Chittick met at Columbia in 1917, while Chittick was a graduate student and Van Doren served as his mentor. When Chittick asked if Van Doren would read some of his early chapters, Van Doren happily replied that he "shall never be too busy for dissertations." Chittick later had trouble finding a publisher for his finished work (which went on to become the seminal study of Thomas Chandler Haliburton and was praised as the best of all Canadian literary biographies) to which Van Doren commiserated, "Curse all publishers! You will join me in that."

of the birth of another granddaughter, of a meeting with his friend the writer James Thurber, and some pleasantries about Edmund Wilson (the two writers were not exactly friends). He relished in telling Elizabeth about a book by the Irish poet W.B. Yeats, his dear friend and poet Elinor Wylie, and a French film he saw which he wished he could have escorted Elizabeth to. Van Doren admitted that he had been fond of her ever since "my eyes lighted on you." He "babbled" on about his granddaughter, but did not want Elizabeth to think that he made a habit of gushing about his children or grandchildren. No, he only got this personal with "whole men and women," who, he acknowledged, were few and far between. "You seem to me as complete as they come: animal, intellectual, and spiritual, if you don't mind a straightforward tribute as I suppose you don't."[10]

For her part, Elizabeth Marion was a tad star-stuck over Van Doren's literary acquaintances. Far removed from the nation's literary scene in New York, she admitted that she loved the fact that Van Doren was personally acquainted with "the elder Yeats," writing to him of her admiration:

> Sometimes I feel as if any minute I'll begin to mutter in my beard that you bear a striking resemblance to the Man Who Knew Everybody...probably there isn't anything miraculous in your knowing practically everybody I can pluck out of my library, but it seems so, once in awhile... (Feb. 11, 1947)[11]

To a young writer like Elizabeth Marion, Carl Van Doren might very well have been the Man Who Knew Everybody. While Elizabeth Marion had some success with the publication of her three novels, she was having trouble focusing on her next project. Still, books and their authors were critical to her daily existence. The tiny room in her family's farm house that served as her office was jam-packed with books—stacks of books—and miscellaneous gadgets and piles of paper and her father's camera equipment. No matter what was going on in the material world around her, books were a refuge, in which a lovely "isolation of the body is made beguiling and worthwhile by this invasion of minds, a veritable parade of them, who have no knowledge of this little backwater, who live in a livelier place altogether, but who shine brighter to me <u>because</u> they're so distant...books do that for me, more than anything else...all the minds, sparkling and mysterious and more everlasting than souls, leaving their welcome testaments on the bookshelves..."[12]

Meanwhile, Van Doren had spent a career situated smack in the middle of New York's literary world, which, for all intents and purposes, was the nation's literary world. Van Doren worked closely with literary greats Sinclair Lewis, Theodore Dreiser, James Thurber, Elinor Wylie, H.L. Mencken, Robert Frost, and Mark Van Doren. He had written countless essays of literary criticism as well as articles in popular magazines, edited two literary magazines, was an esteemed judge on monthly book club panels, appeared on radio broadcasts, had written well over one hundred book introductions, served on committees with distinguished Americans like Eleanor Roosevelt, Archibald MacLeish, and Robert Frost, and had won the Pulitzer Prize. The New York literary world was a small circle indeed, and Van Doren's essays of literary criticism covered everybody who was anybody. The literati lived in the same Greenwich Village neighborhood in New York and summered together on nearby farms in rural Connecticut. Carl Van Doren lived and worked during the nation's golden age of literary criticism and to Elizabeth Marion, he was indeed the Man Who Knew Everybody.

Carl Clinton Van Doren was born in 1885 in Hope, Illinois. Like many pioneers, Carl's great-great-grandfather Luther Tillotson had migrated west from his birthplace in Farmington, Connecticut in the early decades of the 1800s. Decades before newspaperman Horace Greeley would entreat the nation to "Go west, young man, and grow up with the country," Luther Tillotson packed up his few belongings and headed west to Hamilton County, Ohio. In just a few years Tillotson and his wife Priscilla Buell packed up again and headed westward still, this time settling in Warren County, Indiana. Their oldest son, Ephraim Buell Tillotson, was born there, in Warren County in 1811, and later married Polly Ann Cronkhite. The couple had twelve children (many of whom died in childhood) and in 1854 continued westward to Hope, Illinois, settling what was to become known as the "old Tillotson homestead." The grown children of Ephraim Buell and Polly Ann themselves settled close to the family homestead, where land on the open prairie was cheap, farming was the American way of life, and progress seemed as inevitable as Manifest Destiny. The Tillotson clan remained, for the most part, near the homestead for a generation or two, before a new wave of wanderlust swept grandchildren all points East and West.

Of Ephraim and Polly Ann's twelve children, the oldest was Sarah Ann Tillotson, who married Edward Ostrander Foster (Edward Ostrander Foster was the grandfather of *this* author's grandfather). Those newlyweds settled in nearby Armstrong, where Edward was farmer/postmaster and both were Sunday school teachers at the local Methodist church. Ephraim and Polly Ann's second child, Rebecca Tillotson, married Jeremiah King Butz in 1859 and set up housekeeping near the Tillotson homestead in Hope, where Jeremiah was a farmer and Becky was a charter member of the Hope Christian Church. Becky was Carl Van Doren's "Republican and radical" grandmother. Jeremiah was, conversely, a Whig and conservative. The couple managed to work out their differing political views early on, or at least agreed to disagree. Carl Van Doren described Hope in 1860 as an open prairie; the Tillotsons were prairie people. By 1885, when Carl was born, "the community was as settled in its virtues and vices as if it had been there a thousand years." Family lore tells of a New England Tillotson who, migrating to New York, married a woman of the Five Tribes. Van Doren remembered, "My great-grandfather Tillotson looked almost as much Indian as Puritan, austere and proud." At a large family reunion in the summer of 1918, the extended Tillotson clan gathered near Danville, Illinois. Van Doren's cousin Otto E. Henry composed and recited a poem of Tillotson family history to mark the occasion:[13]

> It is said, you know, that the first Mr. T.
> To arrive in this country from across the sea
> Was a member of that brave little Pilgrim flock
> That landed from the Mayflower on Plymouth Rock.
> And in after years, so the story goes,
> Another Mr. T. was led to propose
> To a dusky maid of the Aborigines,
> Regardless of the effect on family trees.
>
> Our worthy grandshire, Mr. E.B.T.
> Was no small twig of this family tree;
> A man among men, as county squire,
> He stood for right regardless of hire.
> A Yankee he was, born in New "Yawk,"
> In eighteen eleven, of Puritan stock.
> He lived there only a year or so,

Then came with his parents to Ohio.
After fourteen years in the Buckeye state,
He moved on West through the Hoosier gate
To the county of Warren in 'twenty-five,
While yet his parents remained alive.

'Twas here he proposed to start life right,
And took as his wife, Mary Cronkhite,
After which his family grew in scope
Till at last he came to live in Hope.
Twelve children were born to Mr. T.
And of the twelve, he lost but three,
The rest all thrived and ate good ham
On the farm he bought from Uncle Sam.

Van Doren's grandfather, Jeremiah Butz, had been born in another Hope—in New Jersey—and, like his father-in-law, settled down to farming. Writing about his family origins in the midst of the Great Depression, Van Doren described his grandfather almost as a type, "like most men of his generation in that older America. He looked upon the future as a perpetual adventure and never doubted that it was an endless source of benefits to come. Men had only to work and wait for them. He had seen the wild prairie blossom under his hands. His contemporaries at Hope... held his general opinions. They were solid, civil squires who had prospered, whose land by 1890 was worth forty times what it had been when they had claimed it from the Government." With their six children, Jeremiah Butz and Becky Tillotson settled in to a life of country farming. The couple's third child, Eudora Ann "Dora," married Charles Lucius Van Doren, country doctor and farmer, in 1883. Dora had been a school-teacher at the age of fifteen and thereafter served stoically as a farmer's wife, mother, and home-maker. Of their five sons, Carl Clinton Van Doren was the eldest, born in 1885, followed by Guy (1887), Frank (1892), Mark (1894), and Paul (1899).[14]

Carl grew up "as happy as an animal" in the provincial com-munity of Hope. His childhood, not unlike that of rural children across America, consisted primarily of school, farming, and fam-ily gatherings. And reading. Always reading. Van Doren could not remember a life before books. The young Carl, along with his brothers, read Hawthorne, Plutarch, Dickens, Thackeray, Twain, *Ben-Hur*, and of course, Gibbon, "in whom I dipped." He read Shakespeare, Fenimore Cooper, and Irving. But no Poe, no Whitman, no Tennyson or Browning, these perhaps too modern for the Middle Western sensibility. Still in his youth but grow-ing more and more strapping by the year, Van Doren discovered a mail-order business in Chicago and thereafter ordered books for himself as well as books to gift to family members, which he could then borrow and read. Books and more books: always books. Van Doren recalled, "We all read. We read greedily and uncritically.

A book was a book, and it was interesting or not." Books allowed Van Doren's mind to travel without leaving home, to experience the wider world beyond Hope, before the world beyond Hope opened up for good. Through books, "we traveled without leaving Hope. When later we did leave, life was not so strange as we expected. Books had enlarged the village."[15]

In 1900 when Carl was fifteen, his parents decided to leave the farm for town living. With his father's income as a doctor, Carl's parents had enjoyed financial success beyond that of the typical farmer. It took his parents only ten years, compared to his grandparents' forty, to reach retirement. Van Doren saw his parents' move away from the farm as part of a larger cultural shift reshaping the country. In twenty years, and for the first time in history, more Americans would live in urban areas than rural. Thomas Jefferson's ideal of the self-sufficient American farmer was giving way to the lure of the industrial city and the jobs, opportunities, and urban anonymity to be found there. One could invent, or re-invent, oneself in the city. "All of us, whether aware of it or not, were in the drift of an impulse which in 1900 was common in Illinois and throughout the Middle West. Farming had become old-fashioned... The value of land, at least the price, had risen so fast in a generation that the owners had turned from working farmers into landlords... It was a powerful instinctive migration which was to transform a large part of America."[16]

Van Doren's father, along with many men of that generation, felt the pull of progress and believed whole-heartedly in an optimistic future. American exceptionalism, Manifest Destiny, and the promise of orderly and rational growth propelled a generation into the turn of the twentieth century. "My great-grandfather had been a pioneer, my grandfather a squire. My father was ready to be a landlord and a capitalist." And so in 1900 Charles and Dora Van Doren left the farm and moved their five growing sons to town. In Urbana, religious teachings became less important and less relevant to Carl and his brothers. No longer was the family's Hope Christian Church the epicenter of community life; life in town had intellectual and spiritual centers beyond the church and its congregation. Much to their mother's despair, Carl announced that he and his brothers were all "cheerful unbelievers by sixteen or seventeen, with brief worry and no regret." Leaving the rooted foundation of a religious community freed this younger generation to become more mobile, more detached, more modern. More *American*:

> The shift in our attitude toward church must have been the same as thousands of American families were then going through. With us it was the first step in a larger process...Uprooted from a community in which we had been absorbed, my brothers and I never took root, but lived detached, like Americans.[17]

A thirsty reader since childhood, in high school Carl started writing short book reviews for himself when he was not playing on the school's football team. Unaware that the formal book review as a genre even existed, he knew by his teen years that he wanted to pursue a career in the world of books and writing. While these bookish interests caused Van Doren to feel somewhat detached from his less dreamy-minded classmates, he did not truly mind the intellectual divide, and writing kept him focused on his future. The young scholar meant to make a career in the literary arts. After graduating high school in 1903, he took his entrance exams and was admitted to the University of Illinois, where his intense curiosity into the lives of the men and women he read about in history books and novels fed a passionate desire *to know.* At the university, Van Doren's curiosity led him from book to book to book, reading became a "passionate experience" and when it was not, he put the book aside. Time was not to be wasted on books that bored him. If the books young Carl read in his childhood had expanded his ideas about the greater world beyond Hope, the literature he discovered at university was pure nectar feeding his voracious curiosity about *life.* "I was a skeptic in religion but in nothing else." Van Doren read so that he might understand the human condition in all of its permutations.

As for as his own ambitions as a writer, Van Doren was most keen on poetry. This bent, admittedly, stemmed from a desire to belong to the company of the world's great poets, much in the same way the fictional D'Artangnan had yearned to belong to the Musketeers. The undergrad discovered "the glory of great verse" through the poet Marlowe, whose writings changed Van Doren's world "as if mountains had sprung out of the prairie." In his earliest days at the university, Van Doren wrote poems, stories, and essays, published in the collegiate literary magazine. He was named assistant editor and then full managing editor by his senior year, elected Class Poet for his 1907 commencement for which he composed the annual Class Poem. This early poem overflows with youthful vigor; its author has all the time in the world to generate inspiration and incite noble reflection from its captive audience. At the same time, the poem is infused with "the black melancholy of young men," that pang which stems from a young man's desire to do more than he, with his still limited resources and experience, is presently able.

I

Wide are the prairies of the West,
The unfenced playground of the wind and sun,
Where they in lusty joy can leap and run
As a free fancy tells them it is best.
Deep are the prairies, for the mold
Of countless centuries has made sacrifice
To the new glory that shall rise,
A harvest from the sowing of the old,

And bid the eager harvesters be bold
To reap—yet not forget, yet not forget
The sowers and the seed-time that have set
Their ever-during mark for time to hold.

II

O powerful, powerful western lands,
With us co-heirs of an increasing heritage,
    Make us well mindful of the hands
    That toiled from youth to age
To build our portion large of liberty!
O make us pay with reverent memory
Poor daily tithings of the debt we owe
Of gratitude, that still must fall below
Half their deserts, who, given to foresee
What the strong future of the West would be,
    Made Illinois American!

III

Grave on our hearts the letter of his name,
The soldier with his ragged company
Who won our level fields for us,
And let us not forget his fame,
Who, when our land was vext internally,
Made us before the nation glorious;

But O, whatever come to grieve the heart,
Or raid the golden treasury of the brain,
One monument be ever set apart
From any danger of oblivion-stain,
To stand a Mecca that grows every day
More potent to draw pilgrims from afar
In search of relics that will heal dismay
And bid them still be bravely what they are,

Trusting the Fate that can not lie
So long as man's heart does not die!

IV

One name the West has added to the scroll
Of life eternal on the earth,
One who will never shame the roll
Of heroes, tho himself of birth
As lowly as the Christ he trusted in.
Nothing so well adorns the West as he,
Save that with true spirit of democracy
They recognized him to be kin
Of conquerors and saviors, with the might
To lead them from the horrors of their night,
And overthrow the foes that stood around
On their own native ground.
He bore the burdens on him laid,

Invincible and undismayed,
Wise in peril and in need,
Wise in thought and wise in deed,
Wise physician of his land,
Surgeon with the gentle hand,
Father bowed unselfishly
To the yoke, that he might see
His children one day wholly free,
And ever in his love as true
To the foe in gray as the friend in blue.
And then when half his work was done,
When half his victory was won,
When he saw the sun of hope arise
Over a night of tragedies,
And turned his tired face to the east,
Hoping he would be released
From half the agony he had known—
Wo—O wo! the deed was done!
And we sadly laid him down
In a sad but honored grave,
Close to those who died to save,
Crying in our hearts: He gave
A kingly life for a martyr's crown.

V

Not all the tears that have been shed,

Not all the words that men have said,

Can bring us back our Lincoln, dead

That Freedom might not be a creature to despise.

Grief boots us nothing here,

Yet there doth still appear

One balsam for our wounded memories.

From the grave where he lies

Will endlessly arise

Courage and strength and hope,

That in our lives we may more bravely cope

With enmity and enemies.

He is not dead, but sleeps

In the calm tomb that keeps

The best beloved of the world.

The banner of his fame will be unfurled

That nations far and wide may see

How gladly and exultantly

We hail in our fraternal joy

The elder brother of tall Illinois,

While they give him the title he has won,

Our century's transcendent son.

VI

But what are words or tears
For him or for the pioneers
Who won a land for him to save?
Words are no wreath to lay upon the grave
Of sturdy men who never wrought with words.
They could not deem it brave
To see spring daisies hung about their rusty swords,
Or their long muskets now the idle toys
In playtime of neglectful boys.
The best memorials are deeds
Done to the memory of those who died,
And if we wish them glorified
By aught that we can do, so we must needs
Be boys no longer, but brave men.
Not war—God shield that war should come again—
But peace has victories to gain,
And guerdons that strife may attain.
To do right boldly what the hand may find,
Ever to humble quietness resigned,
Can never shame the stronger souls who fought
Great battles, and with their own life-blood bought
For us their children what they could not have.
In these days do we see no more the slave
The public traffic of the market-place,

But other bonds that are still disgrace—
And shame it is unto his friends that see—
The mighty thews of slow democracy.

VII

Only few there are can give
To a race its liberty,
Who is there who can not live
From self-welded fetters free?
Earnestness a pearl dissolved
In the wine of ridicule;
Truth the limitless involved
In a labyrinth of rule;
Superstition's ghostly clutch
On the heart of ignorance;
Dogma's old and rotting crutch
Hindering the soul's advance;
These are fetters to be broken
By the hand of Everyman,
And the past is but a token
If he wills it that he can.

VIII

Today our hearts are filled with young strong pride
And courage for the things we hope to do
Upon the tourney-field whereto we ride,
Wearing the colors of our lady true,
The alma mater who has cared for us
As truly as our fathers dared for us,
And now all smilingly behold us sent
Away with kind words of encouragement.
Many there are to smile, with half a sneer,
And say we boast because we can not hear
The mighty breakers of the world without
The sheltered bay we have been anchored in,
But when we hear the fulness of that din
    Our courage will not be so stout.
Tomorrow, true, will wear the self-same face
As yesterday, and all the world will run
    As calmly on its race
    As it has ever done,
Yet in the heart of each one who has yearned,
    Forever is an image burned
Of his ideal, that, thru a hundred years
    Of gladness or of tears,
    Of idleness or haste,
    Can never be erased.

IX

And O, strong Fate, that can not lie
So long as man's heart does not die,
Watch over us with justice in your hand,
    As here in eagerness we stand,
In eagerness to do what may not shame our land,
      Forgive if we seek dreams too high
      For our poor purse of strength to buy,
      Lend us your pity if we choose
      To love a hope that we must lose,
      If we are beaten in our strife
      Instruct us in a lowly life,
And keep our hearts forever young to see,
In all that has been and is yet to be,
      That hope defeated is half gain,
      And no one can aspire in vain.

Van Doren's verse would never be published beyond the pages of his alma mater's literary productions. The critic in Van Doren judged the poet harshly and he had to be honest with himself: desire alone did not make a poet. Assessing the body of his poetic efforts to date, he wondered if the poetic juice did not flow with a necessary vitality; the passion, if it existed at all, seemed to fall flat. Twenty years later, Van Doren's friend Sinclair Lewis pulled no punches when he offered his critique of Carl's first published novel, counselling his friend that a novelist "had to feel strong attraction or antipathy at sight for people or he could not represent them with necessary force." It didn't take Van Doren much introspection to admit that he had too much "Dutch indifference" to feel the necessary passion or aversion for people required to create fully formed fictional characters. The poet's heart might be there, but Van Doren regretted that he probably lacked the poetic gift.[18]

After earning his bachelor's degree in 1907, Van Doren stayed on for a fifth year at the University of Illinois as a graduate student and instructor. Already harboring a critical yet courteous view of academia—Van Doren was nothing if not respectful, measured, contemplative—he admitted that "like half the college professors in the United States, I was a teacher by inertia." And so the thwarted poet fell easily into the life of a graduate student and instructor. During this first year of graduate study, Van Doren made his first real *connection* when he formed a personal and literary relationship that would guide the next phase of his career and his entrée into the New York literary world. Stuart P. Sherman was a bit of a young celebrity, as much as one can be a celebrity in the world of the academic humanities. Earning his Ph.D. at Harvard under the veritable and much esteemed Irving Babbitt, the man credited with founding the New Humanism school of literary criticism, Sherman arrived at the University of Illinois after teaching briefly at Northwestern University in nearby Chicago.

The *buzz* surrounding Sherman's doctoral work under the legendary Babbitt preceded his arrival on campus; his appointment was a boon to Illinois' public land grant university.

Van Doren was not, as a rule, impressed by mere academic credentials. The graduate student/instructor had no real academic ambitions himself and was admittedly only staying on at the University due to the scientific law of inertia. Walking to campus from his apartment one day, Van Doren ran into Sherman and the two men struck up a genuine conversation. Suddenly, this Sherman fellow was *interesting*. To the curiosity-driven Van Doren, being *interesting* was everything. He recalled, "I remember the uprush of my spirit in that moment when it seemed to me that an electric charge of understanding passed between us." Van Doren found a kindred spirit in the slightly older Sherman. He felt liberated and transported by their frequent conversations. The pair talked about books they had read, exchanged ideas on authors and their works; Van Doren shared his poetry with Sherman and asked for critical feedback. Could he make it as a poet? Van Doren knew the answer to his question even before he finished his recitation. Sherman patted his friend on the shoulder and asked, "Well, Bard, what are you going to do to make a living?"[19]

And so to Columbia University he went, to work on his doctorate. Van Doren needed a paying profession, and he shrugged that teaching was no worse than any other. For a Middle Western farmer's son who had grown up near the old Tillotson homestead, surrounded by an extended family of great-aunts and uncles, cousins and second-cousins, the move to New York was an adventure. Mobility and detachment: the modern American migration was an urban migration, and the center of the urban scene was unquestionably New York City. New York's glorious architectural wonder Pennsylvania Station was not yet complete in September of 1908, and so Van Doren departed the train in Hoboken, New Jersey before crossing the Hudson River by ferry. The myth of New York held strong in Van Doren's mind: New York City was more of an *idea* than physical locale. "New York was still less a city of men and women than a symbol," he would later recall.[ii] New York was the literary capital of the nation and Van Doren had a conscious desire to live where writers wrote and publishing houses printed the books the western world would read. Perhaps most urgent, however, was Van Doren's desire to live in a world considerably larger and freer than that of his conservative upbringing on the Illinois prairie.[20]

The "excited fog" that clouded Van Doren's mind throughout his eastward journey grew as he boarded the ferry. Before him

....

ii   Van Doren was on to something: by the turn of the twentieth century, New York came to dominate the public's conception of what a modern American city looked like. More than any other city, New York embodied the diversity, complexity, and modern reality of urban life. New York was *The City*, but in the first years of the twentieth century it was also becoming the ideal and preeminent symbol of modern, urban living.

rose New York, that city of cities, where Van Doren's arrival was as natural to him as if he had been born there. He smelled the salt water of the Hudson River, heard the cries of seagulls overhead and the whistles and hoots of various and sundry river traffic beside him. Manhattan stood before him like solid rock. The city was alive and waiting, and Van Doren took advantage of the few days before the fall session began to explore by foot and by bus the city that would become his adopted hometown. He was ready for adventure. As a graduate student at the prestigious Columbia, Van Doren vowed to do what was required of him, naturally, but knew the bulk of his energies would be directed toward his own intellectual inclinations. That is, he was just arrogant enough to, what degree he could, master his own ship.

Youthful arrogance aside, occasional anxieties as to the practicality of his literary ambitions—that black melancholy of young men—haunted the twenty-four year old. Could one reasonably make a living as a writer, or was he kidding himself in thinking that writing could ever be more than a thing of passion or leisure? Was he wasting his time studying the "dusty lumber" of writers long dead, when other graduate students, those who were studying the law or medicine, were clearly involved in great industry, on their way to prosperous careers? In one particularly melancholy mood, Van Doren penned a letter home to his mother:

My lovely Mother, I have caught a miserable cold in some way and have been sitting about my room all morning and a part of the afternoon studying and half seduced from attention by the warm day outside. My indisposition is nothing, just enough to put me in a melancholic mood—of the kind that will come now and then, no matter how little there is really to bring it on, or how hard I fight against its coming. It seems to me that I have wasted and still waste so much time and get so little done. They tell me here my learning is perhaps the largest among the graduate students in English (altho that is by no means sure) and yet I am the youngest of them all. Next year too I am to have the fellowship. I have the best parents in the world and everything that their kindness can get me. Is it not strange then that I should have sat all these past few hours kicking my heels in sullenness? I can see the folly, well enough, but I cannot forget how much of a dissipation of energy is obligatory upon me. My roommate is wholly bent upon the study of the law. He has a good head and great industry, and what he is doing is a preparation for the thing he most wants. He can grudge every minute stolen from his work, while I am divided. My whole ambitions are for original work, but here I must plod dully on in scholarly pursuits, filling my head with a vast deal of dusty lumber that seems very far from a prospect of ever being useful, and letting my imagination rust in its sheath. I wonder whether it is fair that professors of literature should be obliged in the corrupted currents of this world to do something outside of literature to earn their bread and butter and give only the fagged out hours of their leisure to the only thing they live for. Some days I grow a despicable coward, and am nearly tempted to turn my back upon all the bright ideal to which I have been true now for nearly a third of my life, and drop my energies to a slighter task where there is a chance of wealth and ease after a time. I know I could be rich—but I don't care to be—and I suppose I could attain some kind of worldly prefer-ment. What is the good of all this feverish distracted effort, and all this silent sacrifice? I ask myself, and then I grow ashamed and vow that I will use the wretched talents that have been given me, and tho I may curse with all my hate the cruelty that gave me a giant's ambition and a child's powers, I will not be downed, but hold my head erect, tho it reach no further than the waist of most of my companions.

On such a day I wish I could be in Urbana again, to greet all my beloved ones, and to walk about the kind, quiet old streets until a little calm could find its way into my angry peevish heart. But for your sake it is just as well I am here.

I send you all as much love as you can hold and all I have. There is no one in this world so dear to me.

Your loving son, Carl (April 1, 1909)

These moments of discouragement were fleeting; a com-passionate mother, after all, is the perfect recipient for a young man's flashes of doubt. A keen interest in the works of Dante and Chaucer, Elizabethan drama and Romantic poetry, fueled Van Doren's study of literary history and righted his course when he momentarily floundered. When it came time to declare his dissertation subject, Van Doren looked to the early nineteenth-century English poet and novelist Thomas Love Peacock, whose books had "amused" him in Urbana. Owing to his keen sense of personal curiosity, and having no particular interest in current trends in academic scholarship, Van Doren chose to study the life of the obscure Peacock (no biography had yet been written) in order to discover how another writer had done what he himself wanted to do. As to the dissertation process, Van Doren's committee, on the whole, *left him alone*. He was left to his own devices in choosing his topic, conducting his research, and writing his dissertation. Glory, Glory and Halleluiah! A doctoral student cannot ask for anything better than to be left alone to do his or her work. In the summer of 1910, Van Doren and Stuart Sherman journeyed to Europe where Van Doren would complete his research in the archives of the British Museum.

Van Doren's first trip abroad was an exquisite journey. He and Sherman visited Ireland's purple hills, the tombs of Scottish kings and poets, and the old city of Inverness, high in the Scottish highlands and as far removed from the prairies of Illinois as Van Doren could imagine. He admired ancient churches and bridges that had survived the centuries of conquest marking the history of the British Isles. In Edinburgh the pair visited museums and libraries, where "the monuments were alive, not the men and women who walked the streets." In the Dutch city The Hague, Van Doren waited outside the gates of the royal palace, as any tourist might, to catch a glimpse of the royal family and the infant Princess Juliana, after which he quickly jotted off a postcard to his grandmother back in Illinois. Van Doren noted a distinct quaintness in the old cities of Europe, a feeling that uncomfortably bordered on sentimentality. Marked by a self-described and healthy dose of "Dutch indifference," Van Doren noted in his travel diary that he was "still thinking about the quaintness, I'm afraid" as he travelled on to Nuremberg and the ancestral city of the great Albrecht Dürer. The man of practical disposition and stoic temperament did not cotton to sentimentality or cultural nostalgia, and was momentarily taken aback at finding himself touched by the charm and quaintness of old Europe.

The thrill of the European Tour quickly faded once Van Doren settled into the real task of completing his dissertation research. Carl wrote near daily to brother Mark, who followed Carl's lead and had recently matriculated at the University of Illinois. From the reading room of the British Museum, Carl described the increasingly stale routine of a research scholar in the archives: the slow-going, solitary, and often tedious digging and cross-checking of facts long forgotten in their quiet hiding place. In addition to this ponderous unearthing of Peacock's life, Van Doren

read page upon page of the writer's poetry and novels, both published and unpublished. The scholar in Van Doren, or perhaps the
emerging critic, judged several examples of Peacock's early works
as juvenile and overcome with a "pestilent gloom," while other
poems bordered on excellent. "The Cypress Shade" was, according to Van Doren, one of Peacock's best.

> I dug, beneath the cypress shade,
>   What well might seem an elfin's grave;
> And every pledge in earth I laid,
>   That erst thy false affection gave.
>
> I pressed them down the sod beneath;
>   I placed one mossy stone above;
> And twined the rose's fading wreath
>   Around the sepulcher of love.
>
> Frail as thy love, the flowers were dead
>   Ere yet the evening sun was set:
> But years shall see the cypress spread;
>   Immutable as my regret. (1807/8)

Before leaving London, Van Doren called on several publishing houses in the hopes of finding a printer for his manuscript,
well before he submitted the final analysis to his dissertation

committee. Upon securing a book deal with J. M. Dent & Sons,[iii] Van Doren returned to Columbia with the completed manuscript in hand, prudently keeping all mention of the book deal under wraps. As for his dissertation committee, which would likely have at least one round of revisions to hand back to its student, Van Doren was hardly concerned. "Any corrections they made I disregarded, certain that if they ever looked into the printed book they would by that time have forgotten the manuscript." Van Doren was satisfied with his work, his publisher was satisfied, and that was all that mattered. While he graciously thanked his professors A.H. Thorndike, Brander Matthews, and W.P. Trent in the published work, the time for academic advisement was over.[21]

....

iii   The terms of Van Doren's first book deal with J.M. Dent & Sons gave 10% royalties to Van Doren if/only Dent sold enough copies to cover its production costs. Van Doren's concerns over the financial profitability of a career in writing were not unfounded.

CHAPTER 2

→ · ←

A MAN OF IDEAS

How, exactly, does one become the Man Who Knew Everybody, literarily-speaking? A Ph.D. in English from Columbia might seem the sure ticket, but in 1911, the year Van Doren received his doctorate, there was already a concerted and growing divide between university professors—that is, academics—and those who wrote essays and short stories in magazines like *Scribner's, The Nation, Century,* and the *Atlantic Monthly* for a general, albeit educated, reading public. Quick: name ten academics today who prolifically write essays or books for a general public readership. Name five. I can think of a few. Steven Pinker and Jill Lepore, both at Harvard, immediately come to mind. But the fact that we must rack our brains for a more extensive list is indicative of the great crevasse that exists today between academic writers, who tend to write jargon-filled articles for each other in peer-reviewed journals or university-press textbooks, and writers who write for a public readership.

In fact, the prejudice against university professors writing for a general audience was already blooming in the first decades of the twentieth century. In 1910, one could not easily straddle the world of academia *and* the world of criticism. And so it wasn't enough that Carl Van Doren had earned his Ph.D. from Columbia. He required entrée into New York's literary circle, which in 1911 fueled the nation's literary interest.

Much farther along in our story, in 1946, Elizabeth Marion was looking for a mentor, or at least some guidance as she struggled with her own writing projects. One might assume, having three published novels under her belt, she would feel secure or at least comfortable about a fourth book deal with her publisher, Thomas Crowell. Maybe she suffered from the dreaded writer's block, but that seems unlikely. She appeared to be constantly writing. Maybe she had so many things to write about, she couldn't hone in on any one particular project. The opus eluded her. Maybe she was simply over-thinking it.

In the spring of 1947, Elizabeth Marion wrote to Van Doren about her recent and extended trip to the desert country of southern California, east of Los Angeles and south of Palm Springs.

Introverted by nature, her desire for solitude so that she might be free to sit and think and write is evident in these early letters. Van Doren's response that he wished to join her in this desert hermitage indicated his deepening fascination with her mind, her talent, and her wit. Through their letters, the two writers created an emotional intimacy we don't see in any of Van Doren's other personal correspondence. Elizabeth wrote of the California desert:

> I should like to go again, my own way, with time enough and sufficient solitude to sit and think about it and look...the only fault I had to find with it is that it's too damned full of people.

> I mean to go back for another look one day, either alone or with a deaf-mute if there's no way of going with someone whose mind and prejudices coincide with mine!...a fool and his conversation are soon exhausted, that's sure; likewise his audience, come to think of it...[iv] (May 19, 1947)[22]

To which Van Doren responded:

....

iv   The ellipses (...) are EM's. Her writing style in all of her letters to CVD contain frequent ellipses between her thoughts. She rarely used capitalization: a habit she picked up, possibly, from an earlier pen-pal relationship she had with writer Hendrik William Van Loon, about whom we will learn shortly...

Dear Elizabeth: If you pitch that hermit tent or dig that hermit cave, how about letting me pitch or dig somewhere in the neighborhood? Some 18th-century poet or other, Cowper as I remember, said it was best in solitude to have a friend to whom you could now and then say that solitude is sweet. The hermitages have got to be, any way for a time, in the desert. Then, if you let me stay within gunshot or smoke signal range, I might now and then drop over to your tent or you to my cave. At sunset, don't you think?... You sit by the fire and mutter to me, if you feel like it, in the language you use for letters—so swift and sure and beguiling: like this in your latest letter: 'little pine trees blown there by the chancy winds from some anonymous parent tree.' That's what I mean when I say the gal can write! Affectionately, Carl (Aug 25, 1947) [23]

Elizabeth shared with Van Doren the joy she found in the written word. Writing even ten sentences a day was a day well spent. She admitted that brevity was not her forte, and proudly described the fun she had putting pen to paper. Elizabeth Marion, like grateful writers everywhere, reveled in the muse's touch:

...sometimes I've the odd notion that what I do, what little there is of it, isn't mine at all but sort of leaks out through me from some other source altogether...as if the muse is a sort of Thorne

Smith ghost doing the dictating over my right shoulder!...
(Aug. 31, 1947)[24]

The fun she had with words and sentences was balanced by
the frustration she felt with false-starts, trudging through the
weeds before one finds the sentences worth keeping. If you wonder what it means, exactly, to have "fun with sentences," consider this excerpt from Elizabeth Marion's novel, *The Keys to the
House*. Published two years before she and Van Doren met, the
passage proves a wonderful example of the joy she took in writing sentences that get longer and longer under the joyful watch
of her pen:

> It was the empty silence of the house, the immobile silence of
> the barnyard, that enhanced her imaginary fears. She herself
> seemed to move wraith-like about the house and yards, sur-
> rounded by an ominous oblivion she could not combat when
> he was gone. He was a very quiet person: he walked quietly, he
> talked calmly and without temper, he amused himself placidly
> with books and magazines and radio, even when he cursed over
> a stubborn total in his book-keeping his profanity was mild and
> without explosiveness...
>
> The convenient commonplace of good pavement and ser-
> vice stations and legible road signs has almost erased, not the
> wonder of any country, but the human ability and desire to see

the wonder. When a man travels fast toward a distant goal, he seldom sees the thing at hand. It hides behind a transparent haze of speed, and vanishes backward before he can look.[25]

The descriptive quality we find in her fictional writing is the same verve Elizabeth Marion summoned in her letters to Van Doren. She wrote enthusiastically and at length, her letters running four, five, six or more typed pages and arriving in Van Doren's mailbox twice weekly at least. She rarely paused for a paragraph break and capitalization was an unnecessary extravagance. Elizabeth Marion wrote of the weather, usually snowing or raining or otherwise not for the faint-of-heart, in her rugged corner of the Northwest. She wrote of the books she was reading or would like to read but could not find at either the library or the local bookstore because the library and the bookstore did not carry the titles she was looking for. (She preferred volumes of letters, she loved them in fact. Letters, she felt, told so much about a person's character and mentality and *whatnot*. She wished such volumes weren't so few and far between.) She wrote of the cats who shared her room, and the crowded and usually cold office nook she carved out of the small room behind the family's kitchen, which could use a good cleaning. She wrote of cowbells, of how much she fancied them and figured she would probably begin a collection. She wrote of using patterned stationery versus plain paper, and wondered if using patterned stationery made writers write better. She wrote of the new calf in the barn, the sounds of the local birds (chinooks), the precise shade of brown she saw in the turbulent river rushing through town after a rainy spell. She addressed her letters, "Dear Mr. Van Doren." Elizabeth Marion had a lot to say, and she was very happy to write all of it to Van Doren, who was enchanted and beguiled by her elaborate correspondence. For his part, Van Doren asked how her writing was going, requesting that she send him whatever she had written, and advised her not to over-think any of it. Just write.

What Elizabeth really needed, she admitted, was *a room of her own*, a quiet place to get her writing done, undisturbed. Living at home at the age of thirty with her mother and father and three younger siblings whom she called "the kids" (two brothers were away with the Army); a newlywed sister and her young husband; visiting aunts who had been known to stay for such an excruciatingly long time as to warrant An Emergency; the chores required of farm life; the secretarial position she took when the state's Congress was in session; and her many beloved cats all added up to *distraction*. Elizabeth Marion preferred to write in the middle of the night, with plenty of coffee to fuel her busy writer's mind (her love of coffee would not have helped her frequent insomnia...). She found the midnight hour the best time for thinking about books and politics and *whatnot*, and the only time of day where she could work undisturbed. And yet she fretted:

...it's one reason why I do without sleep—the middle of the night is the one time of day when it seems most likely that nothing will change very much or turn out surprisingly different, when nobody is apt to drop in to be fed or talked to...some nights I just sit here and don't write more than twenty words maybe, and it seems like a fearful waste of time I suppose when about all I accomplish is getting my mind calmed down before another day comes round and knocks it galleywest and end ways...and about once a day I get so furious with people I could kill 'em with my bare hands—such wanton thieves, of time... (Sept 1, 1948)[26]

When Elizabeth admitted to Van Doren that she was struggling with fits-and-starts, could neither attend to her "opus" properly nor seem to finish the "watchman story" she was working on, Van Doren donned his mentor cap and advised, "You must somehow stop thinking so much and do more acting. A book is an action, not a thought." He had seen this before: a writer plodding through his or her work, struggling to write five pages a day, clicking out the sentences only to strike out the superfluous words that got in the way of clarity and concision.[27]

A book is an action, not a thought. Van Doren had, by that point, approximately forty years as a writer under his belt. When he graduated from Columbia, he knew he wanted to write, but he also knew his inclination to write poetry was not going to pay the bills. While completing his studies at Columbia, Van Doren had met Irita Bradford, also at the university and pursing her graduate degree in English. Irita, by every account a sweet Southern girl from Birmingham, grew up in Tallahassee with her mother and three younger siblings (her father was murdered by a disgruntled former employee when Irita was a child). After graduating from Florida State College for Woman, Irita enrolled at Columbia, where she met Van Doren as he was completing his dissertation on Peacock. Although she did not, in the end, finish her own doctorate, Irita began work on her thesis, entitled "How Shakespeare Got Dead Bodies Off the Stage."

Graduating with his doctorate in 1911, Van Doren accepted an Instructor of English post at Columbia; he figured that teaching, for now, was as good a way as any to make a living. It was May, and that meant most of the students would be returning home for the summer break. Rotten timing, as Carl and Irita were just beginning to discover what each might, potentially, mean to the other. With Irita in Tallahassee for the next three months, Carl began to write a few tentative letters to the clever young woman who was more and more on his mind. His first letters to Irita that summer nurtured the early stages of a relationship that began with a shared sense of intellectual curiosity.

He wrote to her of the novel he had just started writing, remarking how pleased he was with the pace of his work to date, which he felt was moving along much more easily than had the biography on Peacock. Perhaps too easily; he didn't trust it, didn't trust that the writing was any good when the novel was seemingly writing itself. "I suppose it must be bad, but it really seems tolerable, tho slow." His writer's anxieties would not be abated, but he was hopeful that a dream very dear to him—*to become a writer!*—might actually come to fruition. He resolved not to spend endless days and nights worrying over the work, he knew these self-inflicted regrets did him no good. Alas, he resolved to stop beating himself up over the work and to simply write ("a book is an action, not a thought" : advice he would give several decades later to Elizabeth Marion as she too was struggling with her craft).

Van Doren wrote to Irita throughout the summer of 1911, from both New York and Urbana when he made his own visit back home. He was delighted to secure an invitation to stop over in Tallahassee on his travels back east, and shared his train schedule with Irita once those accommodations were secure. He would depart from Urbana, travelling south to Oklahoma City before heading east to Tallahassee. After spending a few days with Irita's family, he would continue north to New York City in time for the fall semester, and his teaching schedule, to begin.

That trip, and the couple's growing affections for one another across the following months, sealed the deal. By December, Carl and Irita were engaged, and the bridegroom-to-be was over the moon in love. Writing from his dormitory room in Livingston

Hall, Van Doren addressed a love letter to his "Best and dearest girl, who never had a love letter, this first one, full of love and devotion: Dear heart, dear spirit, beloved Bride-to-Be, who has wrapped your sweet self about my heart and thoughts until I do not see how I can ever get away—and I do not want to!" Now an officially engaged couple, the pair no longer had to hide their affections for one another around campus. Now she was *his girl*, and he could pour out his heart and his soul to her with a joy that was bursting at the seams.[28]

When Irita had some early anxieties about the engagement, about the practical effects marriage would have on certain ideals and dreams she had planned for herself, Van Doren assured his *Dearest Heart* that they would talk everything through, make their plans together, and her heart would surely become light again. He loved her and he was going to marry her. He loved her, in fact, to such an extent which no general description of love could possibly capture. Their love was unique, intense, earth-shattering. Van Doren wrote to Irita, "There is no general truth to love; all is particular to each who loves." His best girl, his woman, was uniquely divine; Van Doren felt sorry for all of her other suitors who had let her slip away.[29]

He felt sorry for the ex-suitors who had blown their chances with the most desirable woman in the world, but he was also sick with jealousy at the thought that other men might have been in love with *his girl*. In fact, he had terrible dreams about it. He dreamt that Irita was wearing a ring that a former suitor had given her, which had stricken and horrified his dream-self. And then her dream-self had become angry with his over-reaction, had scolded him until he thought his heart would break. He had awoken in a frightful sweat. *Ahhhhh!* he rebuked himself in a letter the next morning to his betrothed, "I am such a jealous brute!" He wanted her all to himself, even in his dreams. She couldn't possibly understand the extent of his jealousy because he was mostly able to keep it under wraps. But he would never, *ever* forgive a man who encroached upon his love for this woman. He acknowledged he would be "absolutely ruthless" with any man who came between them. Furthermore, he couldn't imagine that any man who had once loved her could, or would, ever forget her, even if that man married someone else. It made him sick just thinking about it. He knew he was being foolish, he admitted these jealousies likely cast him in a bad light, but he was so deeply and passionately in love with Irita, his *Woman my own Dearest.* The wedding could not come fast enough.[30]

Carl and Irita's wedding was planned for August, 1912 in Tallahassee, which meant another summer the lovers would be apart. With Irita home in Florida for yet another summer break, Van Doren busied himself with his novel, which he had titled *The Devil's Lane*, and searching for an apartment. The newlyweds would live in Morningside Heights, near the Columbia campus, but the particulars still had to be decided. Van Doren checked out several apartments in the Upper West Side neighborhood before finding one that seemed exactly right. The six-room flat on the second floor of a building not far from campus rented for $55 a month. The natural light coming through the generously sized windows made this apartment better than any he had yet seen. In addition to the living room, dining room, and kitchen, the apartment had two bedrooms, one that let in noticeably more sunlight than the other. He suggested they take the darker room for their own bedroom and keep the lighter room for their books: what did she think about that? His only wish was to serve her.

Heart's Truest, Sometimes I ask myself whether love is not after all the weakness I used to think it. What else can be the nature of this strange blindly, mysteriously working force which has compelled my soul to the service of yours? And then I remember that out of my love has come my greatest strength, and out of my love the profoundest knowledge and truth and passion of my whole life. —Love you always, Carl

(May 30, 1912)

Van Doren could not get his beloved out of his head. He wasn't sleeping well. He laid awake at night, wishing his wife were with him instead of in Tallahassee, where she was making plans for the wedding and honeymoon. While trying to sleep in a lower berth of the sleeper car from New York to Chicago, all he could think about was a similar journey the newlyweds would certainly make the following year, when they could share the lower berth he was presently occupying alone. He needed her constantly, and felt absurd and foolish without her.

Van Doren was not the only one suffering from sleepless nights. Irita wrote that she, too, missed her beloved, missed her man. She suffered from "wicked days" and longed for him, feverishly. She wrote that her entire body ached for him; she imagined his cool hands, gentle and strong, slipping over her body in the impossible Florida heat. In her "sweet and loving" letters, Van Doren felt the palpable rush of emotion she was able to transfer from her heart to her pen. The countdown to the wedding and the honeymoon was on both of their minds. In late June, Van Doren gushed with anticipation: it was barely two months until she would be his wife. He wished he was there, right at that moment, to hold her <u>very</u> close in his arms and whisper in her ear how very much he loved her and would like to love her. He didn't care, quite frankly, where they honeymooned. His only wish was to be have her alone as much as possible. The details and routes of the honeymoon voyage were of little importance. He wrote her, "Darling, dearest woman... everything makes me think of you."[31]

The separation was brutal, but Van Doren was trying to spend the months productively, diligently working on his novel. *The Devil's Lane* was proceeding apace, and by June he had written

17,000 words. By July, the novel was half finished. The novel itself was dominated by page after page after page of dialogue. There was not much in the way of character development or those narrative passages which speak to the individuality or humanity of characters that Van Doren would, as a literary critic, look for in the works of other writers over the coming years. There was no indication in this novel from a fledgling writer of the soaring and graceful talent he was to become and for which he would win the Pulitzer. This was the work of an overwrought, maudlin young romantic. And yet, pleased to announce to Irita that he had just completed the sixth chapter, he was cautiously optimistic that the novel might, after all, be acceptable.

CHAPTER VI

Although Dr. Thank moved tempestuously when he was aroused, he seldom proceeded far before he felt his mood cooling, if the predicament were really grave. The present case he knew he must handle with delicacy. In another than his wife, the vicarious conscience which he was sure would make her take upon herself some burden of the responsibility for David's prank, would have vexed him, but his knowledge of her was so intimate that he accepted her almost inevitable anxiety without mental comment, certain no means of lessening her distress could have slighter effect than the attempt to prove to her the unreasonableness of her position...[32]

With September approaching, the intolerable wait was nearly over. As his train rolled in to the Tallahassee station, Van Doren's anxieties about Irita's former beaus, and the sleepless nights he spent waiting to hold his wife in his arms had, mercifully, come to an end. Carl Van Doren and Irita Bradford were married in the bride's hometown on August 23, 1912. The couple made a glowing impression on all who knew them. Alfred Kazin, writer and critic of twentieth century American culture who studied under Carl Van Doren at Columbia, later described the young Carl and Irita Van Doren as "tremendously good looking...They had an air about them...[they had] that look of being sexually superior to other people." The match was a good one, both intellectually and otherwise.[33]

During the first few years of marriage, Van Doren settled into his role as Instructor of English at Columbia. Teaching would do for the time being, and the steady paycheck appealed to Van Doren's new role of husband and provider. He was not, however, had never been, and never would be enchanted by the ivory tower or its inwardly-directed gaze. Writing his autobiography many years later, Van Doren bristled that most of the university's public influence "was indirect or hard to trace" and that, on campus, "time seemed to stand still."

Some of the teachers grew into deans or chairmen of departments, and buzzed and managed as if this were any practical enterprise. Some of the others slumped into increasing idleness, sometimes elegant, more often colorless... What mattered was that the facts they found had not been found before, not that they were worth knowing. Some other specialist might sooner or later make use of them. The specialists in all the universities wrote for one another, for mysterious ends.[34]

Van Doren's dissatisfaction with the whole of academia mirrored a criticism shared by a growing cadre of men of letters who wrote essays and literary and cultural criticism not for fellow scholars, but for a public readership. History can trace a fundamental shift in academic interests to the year 1862, with the passage of the federal Land Grant, or Morrill, Act. Before that time, higher education in the United States meant small liberal arts colleges which provided a classical education for well-to-do young gentlemen. Primarily, these men went on to practice law or medicine, went into business, or joined the clergy. With the passage of the Morrill Act, a land-grant university (like Van Doren's alma mater) was established in every state, with an educational focus not on the liberal arts, but on science and agriculture. These universities created specialized departments in the sciences and social sciences, which demanded objective modes of study and an empirical approach. By the turn of the century, the application of scientific process and reason to *all* fields of study, including the humanities, was making serious encroachments on the man of letters and his generalist leanings. By 1910, during Van Doren's days as a graduate student, a traditional classical curriculum in the liberal arts had ceded intellectual territory to philology, linguistics, and literary history, each demanding "objectivity" and "method" in practice.[35]

Not everyone was on board with the ideological shift that reorganized humanities departments across the country, and in fact many of the leading men of letters spoke out in opposition. Van Doren's friend Stuart Sherman, who had received his Ph.D. at Harvard and was teaching at the University of Illinois, wrote about the regrettable new direction. A frequent contributor to *The Nation*, Sherman argued these "pseudo-scientific specialists" were ruining humanities education and were forcing out liberal arts students who had "real taste and literary power." John Erskine, who received his Ph.D. from Columbia, advised universities to drop the new philological-historical approach to literature and halt the new cultivation of "specialists" in English departments. Erskine called instead for a program of *Great books*, later adopted at St. John's College in Annapolis, designed to resurrect a classical curriculum. Henry S. Canby of Yale described the decades between 1880 and 1910 as "the triumph of applied science" and "the defeat of the classics," lamenting,

> Now the scientific approach became fashionable. Scholars in literature who called themselves scientific began to dominate

the graduate schools and extend their influence into the sacred precincts of the undergraduate college... Accuracy in little things was the new virtue, and we were encouraged to believe that the world was more in need of correct texts, exact dates, and knowledge of sources, than of estimates, appreciations, and opinions which, however just, were not scientific because they could not be proved.[36]

Even a young graduate student like Carl Van Doren from Urbana railed against the philological method that had recently come to dominate humanities education, its "pseudo-scientific" method intent on garnering the same respect paid to departments of math and science. In a letter to the editor of *The Nation* in its July 9, 1908 issue, the student Van Doren had aligned himself with his mentor Dr. Sherman, arguing, "The truth of the matter is that the whole position of the champions of so-called 'accurate scholarship' is founded upon a fallacy." Terms like *accurate* and *scientific* did not adequately or properly describe the work of literary scholarship, and until graduate schools learned to support the creative genius as well as those students who merely saw professional writing as a trade like any other, universities would continue to lose their more creative students and instructors. The present course was serving no one, save the specialists themselves.[37]

Here, Van Doren was alluding to the exodus of *generalists* from the nation's universities. One was now required to be a specialist of his own, however obscure, niche. Those men of letters who were not on board with philology, method, or a scientific approach to literature began to move out of the universities—where the intellectual climate had become indifferent if not openly hostile to the generalist tradition—and into the public sphere. They became editors of literary magazines, appeared on bookish radio-shows, headed up book-of-the-month clubs, and used their erudition and Ivy League training to write readable essays for a public audience. Sherman left the University of Illinois and became editor of the *New York Herald-Tribune Review of Books*. Canby left Yale to become editor of the *Saturday Review* and was a prolific literary critic, book reviewer, biographer, essayist, and lecturer. The divide between academic scholars and public intellectuals became a growing crevasse (and has only continued to widen). One might move back and forth between the two worlds, but universities were becoming increasingly interested only in the specialist, which a man of letters, by definition, was not.

Jacques Barzun, one of the twentieth century's most brilliant literary critics, later wrote that a scholar who concentrated on literary criticism for popular readership would have no chance for advancement in academia even as early as the 1910s and '20s. In fact, a *scholar* was defined as someone whose writing would not *ever* be accepted by a critical journal for general readership. Barzun argued that beginning in the early decades of the twentieth century and ramping up as the century progressed, the scholar was distinguished from the critic by his inability and unwillingness "to interest anybody but his alter ego at another university... The critic, on the contrary, was a man with ideas..."[38]

Not surprisingly, the best writing came not out of university English departments, but from essayists and novelists who published in a variety of literary magazines proliferating at the turn of the century. Compulsory education laws in the post-Civil War era meant that by the final decades of the 1800s, literacy rates had jumped to 89% for native-born and foreign-born white Americans, although literacy rates for black Americans struggled to reach the 40% mark. In addition, technological advancements and more efficient modes of production in the publishing industry meant more newspapers and magazines were being printed, and expanding distribution channels ensured speedy delivery of these timely reviews.

Between 1890 and 1905, magazine publication in the United States tripled. A mass culture of readers had been born, and essays and articles written by the nation's top composers of poetry and prose regularly filled the pages of *Ladies Home Journal, Saturday Evening Post, Scribner's, Century, The Nation, Atlantic Monthly,* and *Harper's,* soon joined by an expanding field of literary journals like the *Bookman* and the *Critic.*

The new breed of essayists who wrote for this increasing literary market was more socially relevant, often leaning towards the satirical, and more accessible than the conservative and genteel tradition which had characterized the previous century. Modern writers like Edmund Wilson, Gertrude Stein, F. Scott Fitzgerald, Langston Hughes, and Dorothy Parker continued to write about books, art, and culture but did so with an intent to relate these works to the issues of modern life. Their essays were witty, urban, sophisticated. A good essay had to be personable and accessible to the general reader; no jargon-filled mumbo jumbo. On the art of writing, Van Doren explained,

> There are as few good writers among the many who want to write as there are good lovers among the many who fall in love. Writing is like love in this: a writer falls in love with his subject. He may calculate in advance to his mind's content about the subject it would be wise or prudent to choose, as a man may calculate about a woman. But for the writer, as for the man, calculation alone is of little use. More than his mind is needed...Only love could carry him through the labor that goes into a book.[39]

Although he had found steady employment at Columbia, Van Doren had no real passion for teaching. Nor was he doing much in the way of profitable writing. His completed manuscript, *The Devil's Lane*, sat quietly in a drawer: abandoned. Dedicated "To My Wife, subtle, soaring, radiant," the novel was either not good enough to pass Van Doren's personal muster, or lacked a certain literary or marketable quality any potential publisher would demand (or: both). And so in 1916 when Brearley, the elite girls' preparatory school on New York's Upper East Side, offered him the position of Headmaster, he had no trouble accepting the post. Van Doren admitted that no one knew or cared less than he about the "secondary education of fashionable girls," but since he felt no real calling as a teacher, he was intrigued by the opportunity to lead an entire school. He did, however, retain one course at Columbia, a graduate seminar in American literature, which he continued to hold on Friday afternoons for the next fourteen years. It quickly became clear to Carl that the position at Brearley was not a good match (a conversation with one mother who implored Headmaster Van Doren to persuade her daughter to wear a corset was perhaps too much for the scholar to bear). The work was entirely uncongenial, and Van Doren quite simply found Park Avenue *dull*, remarking, "Money and smartness do not clearly distinguish one society from another. It takes intellect to do that." Dullness was a destroyer of interested living, it was the antithesis of curiosity. Van Doren had signed a three-year contract and so was bound to the post at least for the time being. But neither the position nor the school nor the Upper East Side held any appeal to Van Doren's intellectual pursuits. Brearley would be a stop-over, and not much more.[40]

These unsatisfying years at Brearley were compounded by the personal and national effects of the Great War. Is any generation prepared to face the shock of war? To grapple with the realization that the beliefs or convictions one was raised upon were quite possibly naïve, that mankind is not necessarily marching ever-forward in the inevitable pull of progress? That man is not basically good? The war was a turning point for an entire generation; it signaled "the end of an illusion by which my contemporaries had lived. This was not a world of humane and reasonable order finally arrived at. This was a world in which anything still might happen." When the United States instituted the first draft registration in 1917, all men between the ages of twenty-one and thirty-one were required to register. Carl Van Doren, at thirty-two, had missed that age requirement by one year. His younger brothers Mark and Paul, however, would each serve.[41]

Although he had an instinctual aversion to the war and felt the powers that be had no clearer understandings, no keener insight, no better answers than men in general, Carl felt wretchedly guilty about not serving. Could a human being decently *do nothing?* He did not want to kill or be killed, "did not want to be involved in any madness that must always see black or white." All the same, those left safely at home began "to feel guilty because they [were] safe, and to despise themselves." He wrote letters every day to Mark, drafted into the Army, and to Paul, who enlisted in the Marine Corps so that he *wouldn't* be drafted into the Army. Close to all of his siblings, Mark was the first of Carl's brothers whom he had really understood as a man. He found this brother the most gifted, the most charming of all. The intellectual, philosophical, and in many ways, spiritual bond between the two would connect Carl and Mark for a lifetime.[42]

Carl and Mark wrote to each another at length of the cultural shifts that inevitably occur during wartime. Carl asked Mark if he had noticed much religion among the recruits, to which Mark responded that he has observed none at all, admitting his own unit had remained in Iowa and Arkansas, far from the battle lines of war where one might feel more obliged to "get religion." Mark pondered the effects that military training might have on the whole citizenry; although he loathed the idea of universal conscription, he felt that physical training "undeniably does straighten a man out, and drain numerous contemptible weaknesses out of him."[43]

Carl's brother Paul opted to enlist in the Marine Corps rather than take his chances with the Army. In the summer of 1918, while Mark was stationed with his unit at Camp Pike, Arkansas, Paul went through basic training at Parris Island and was then sent on to Quantico, Virginia. In September, Paul shipped out to France with the 3rd Battalion, 13th Regiment, U.S. Marine Corps. Near Bordeaux, his battalion was attached to a larger Army unit and responsible for guarding German prisoners of war. In his own letters back to Carl, Paul described the interminable rain and mud that had created a verifiable quagmire of the base. The road in front of camp was crowded day and night with troops on the move, although Paul was stuck on base with his own unit, far from the front lines.

The Armistice of November 1918 made clear to the lads that the war was winding down, and Paul was sorry he never got the chance to make it to the front lines. His Marine Corps unit had been "sidetracked [with the Army] until it was too late." Still, at least he had actually made it overseas, chiding that brother Mark was stuck with his Army unit back in Little Rock. Paul boasted: Mark should have been a Marine. With a tone of inter-branch rivalry any serviceman or woman will recognize, Paul added, "You should see the difference between a Marine outfit and any Army outfit you can pick out. I'll convince you altogether when we meet."[44]

On the issue of politics, Carl was guardedly hopeful about the 1920 presidential election. While Carl and Mark, both humanists and liberal thinkers, had broken rank with family tradition and were clearly aligned with the Democrats, their brothers Paul and Guy, along with their father Charles, were staunch Republicans. Political rivalry was fair game for discussion. But with President Woodrow Wilson in failing health and nearing the end of his two terms (the Constitutional amendment limiting the president to two terms was still twenty-seven years in the future, and so another bid for re-election was technically possible), the race between Republican Warren Harding and Democrat James Cox was not much of a race at all. In 1920, lingering anti-war sentiment following the Great War made for an unlikely possibility of any win for the Democrats, the party of Wilson. Paul did not hesitate to taunt his brother, in advance, over an impending Republican victory, cheering "Long live the Republicans!"

In the summer of 1919, just as Paul was returning home from France, Van Doren completed his three-year contract with Brearley and immediately resigned the position that had been a mismatch almost from day one. Professionally unsatisfying, yes, but these had not been not years ill-spent. In addition to his post at Brearley, Van Doren had been named managing editor of *The Cambridge History of American Literature*, a massive undertaking. Along with John Erskine, his old friend Stuart Sherman, and William Trent, who had been his professor at Columbia, Van Doren co-edited the comprehensive literary anthology, which stretched to four volumes. He also began writing essays for *The Nation*, and in 1919 he became the magazine's literary editor.

The Nation exemplified a journalistic shift taking place in the early 1900s from the "genteel tradition" of the nineteenth century literary magazine towards a more sophisticated, socially relevant approach. Originally a conservative literary supplement of the *Evening Post* and predominantly a reviewer of books as opposed to a commentary on public affairs, *The Nation* made a concerted effort during and after the war years to report on violations against civil liberties, racial discrimination, and abuses of authority. Van Doren described the weekly publication as "the newspaper of a passionate minority clamoring for justice." New voices, those of H. L. Mencken, Theodore Dreiser, Willa Cather, and Lewis Lewisohn, appeared regularly in the magazine's pages, a situation that would have been impossible in the more conservative magazine only a few years before.

In addition to his position as literary editor, Van Doren was also a literary critic at *The Nation* and wrote regularly through his "Roving Critic" column. Recalling the personal and intellectual curiosity that had fueled his childhood reading, Van Doren recognized that as a critic,

> I would sometimes read to find out how men had thought and felt long ago, or how different writers had dealt with the same habits of life, or how bare facts had been molded to poetic shapes, or how new ideas or idioms had been welcomed or rejected: to find out these and many things that specialists in literature hunt for...But... I had not read with my mind fully awake and emotions generously engaged: I had not read as a whole man.[45]

The work of the *literary critic* is perhaps not as apparent to the twenty-first century reader as it was in Van Doren's day. This is primarily because present-day magazines and newspaper book supplements contain only the *book review* format. Van Doren once gave an astute description of the difference between a *book review* and *literary criticism,* in which he said a book review is written for someone who has not yet read the book and, for the most part, is simply a *reporting* on that book. (A book review is, primarily, meant to sell books). Literary criticism, on the other hand, is written by the critic for those who have already read the book, and includes the critic's literary and historical analysis, informed by his erudition and larger understandings of the literary canon. The best literary criticism is written in the form of an essay, and therefore says as much about the critic and the present cultural climate as it does about the book itself.

The zeitgeist of the Roaring Twenties and the proliferation of new literature from the Younger Generation provided plenty of fodder for literary critics, book reviewers, and the magazines and supplements for which they wrote. With Van Doren's experience editing the *Cambridge History of American Literature,* as well as his own book of literary criticism *The American Novel,* published in 1921 and providing "a record of the national imagination as exhibited in the progress of native fiction," he knew the canon of American literature better than perhaps anyone.

He was certain this new generation of writers, the Younger Generation, was unique.[v] Covering the likes of the burly-voiced and caustic Mencken; Sinclair Lewis, with his controversial depiction of American Life in *Main Street* and *Babbitt*; F. Scott Fitzgerald and his fashionable flappers and party-boys, Van Doren's literary criticism for *The Nation* covered the new, modern literature that was "catching up with life." The Younger Generation captured and depicted a changing American Scene which the elder generation barely recognized. Contemptuous and outspoken, it rejected the wisdom of its elders who had been unable to avoid the calamity of the Great War. Tradition, familiarity, indeed the *sentimentality* of small-town American life could neither satisfy nor contain the ambitions of the Younger Generation's demands for experience beyond the village confines. Traditions no longer held uniformly. Van Doren dubbed this changing cultural and literary landscape, "The Revolt from the Village."

Van Doren's critical essay "The Revolt from the Village" first appeared in the October 12, 1921 issue of *The Nation*. Here, the literary critic pointed to Edgar Lee Masters' 1915 *Spoon River*

....

v   Van Doren purposefully eschewed the more popular phrase, *The Lost Generation* (coined by Gertrude Stein in the 1920s), when describing this cohort which was born roughly between 1883-1900 and came of age during WWI. CVD himself was a part of this Younger Generation, and did not feel "Lost" was the most appropriate descriptive. Van Doren took a more generous view of youth in general and of his generation in particular. When writing about youth, he insisted "All wisdom is incommunicable" and that the future belonged to the youth, who "detach themselves and move toward the front while their parents gradually slip toward the rear and are left behind. What other course, after all, is there to take?"

Anthology (a collection of fictitious post-mortem epitaphs written about 244 deceased citizens of the fictitious Spoon River, Illinois) as the reigning influence over "the newest style in American fiction." Whereas before the publication of *Spoon River*, village life had been wholly sentimentalized in American literature, a change was now coming about.

> For nearly half a century native literature had been faithful to *the cult of the village,* celebrating its delicate merits with sentimental affection and with unwearied interest digging into odd corners of the country for persons and incidents illustrative of the essential goodness and heroism which, so the doctrine ran, lie beneath unexciting surfaces.[46]

In his essay, Van Doren recounted the history of American literature's predominant depiction of village life, wherein, on the whole, "the village seemed too cosy a microcosm to be disturbed." While individual authors might have registered a discontent or ambivalence with rural life, might have harbored a preference for the excitement and complexity of urban over farm living, they generally "hesitated to touch the village, sacred since Goldsmith in spite of Crabbe, sacred since Harriet Beecher Stowe in spite of E.W. Howe." The iconic images of the American village, from the white church steeple to the sober schoolhouse, from the tradesmen at work to the merry children playing in the schoolyard, from the fragrant summers to the cool winters... these were not easily discarded, even in the midst of an industrial revolution that was erecting unsightly factories along the banks of the village's sacred streams and attracting droves of immigrants who neither spoke the local dialect nor understood its traditions.

There had been some American authors brave or cynical enough to call out the stagnant and spiteful underpinnings of village life, but those works of prose had not been widely embraced by the American reading public. *Spoon River* was different, and with it, Masters had done something entirely new:

An admirable scheme occurred to him: he would imagine a graveyard such as every American village has and would equip it with epitaphs of a ruthless veracity such as no village ever saw put into words. The effect was as if all the few honest epitaphs in the world had suddenly come together in one place and sent up a shout of revelation. Conventional readers had the thrill of being shocked and of finding an opportunity to defend the customary reticences; ironical readers had the delight of coming upon a host of witnesses to the contrast which irony perpetually observes between appearance and reality; readers militant for the 'truth' discovered an occasion to demand that pious fictions should be done away with and the naked facts exposed to the sanative glare of noon. And all these readers, most of them unconsciously no doubt, shared the fearful joy of sitting down at an almost incomparably abundant feast of scandal. The roofs and walls of Spoon River were gone and the passerby saw into every bedroom; the closets were open and all the skeletons rattled undenied; brains and beasts had unlocked themselves and set their most private treasures out for the most public gaze.[47]

It was the *scandal* of *Spoon River*, the airing of, however fictitious, dirty laundry, and the bright white light exposing long-held local secrets and deceptions that made the book such a popular success. The thrill of voyeurism: Masters exposed the filth behind the gleaming façade of church and steeple, he portrayed the demoralization of ordinary citizens, the unchaste sex that takes place far and away from the silent Victorian bedroom. There was greed, hypocrisy, apathy. The town "clings to a pitiless decorum which veils its faults and almost makes it overlook them, so great has the breach come to be between its practices and its professions."[48]

In "Revolt," Van Doren's confident, measured prose assured its reader the newest style in American fiction sprang directly from Masters' vision in *Spoon River*. Confident in his knowledge of the American literary canon, exceedingly well-read on the growing body of contemporary writers and their works, Van Doren attached recent books by Sherwood Anderson, E.W. Howe, and Sinclair Lewis to a string of *Spoon River*-inspired works.

Of Lewis's novel *Main Street*, originally published in 1920, Van Doren wrote,

> Mr. Lewis, like Mr. Masters, clearly has revenges to take upon the narrow community in which he grew up, nourished, no doubt, on the complacency native to such neighborhoods and yet increasingly resentful...No other American small town has been drawn with such exactness of detail in any other American novel. Various elements of scandal crop out here and there, but the principal accusation which Mr. Lewis brings against his village—and indeed against all villages—is that of being *dull*.

> Mr. Lewis hates such dulness [*sic*]—the village virus—as the saints hate sin. Indeed, it is with a sort of new Puritanism that he and his contemporaries wage against the dull a war something like that which certain of their elders once waged against the bad...Mr. Lewis must be thought of as sitting in the seat of the scornful, with the satirists rather than with the poets; must be seen to have understood the earlier, vexed, sardonic 'Spoon River' better than the later, calmer, loftier.

> Before 'Main Street' Mr. Lewis had belonged to the smarter set among American novelists, writing much bright, colloquial, amusing chatter to be read by those who travel through books at the brisk pace of vaudeville. If it seems a notable achievement

for a temper like Mr. Masters's to have drawn such a character into its serious wake, it seems yet more notable to have drawn in that of Zona Gale, who for something like a decade before 'Spoon River Anthology' had had a comfortable standing among the sweeter set...[49]

The thing is, when you write about the work of living writers, living writers tend to write back. Mr. Sinclair Lewis agreed with approximately none of Van Doren's assessment. Immediately after Van Doren's essay appeared in the pages of *The Nation,* Lewis responded to Mr. Carl Van Doren in a lengthy defense. The fiery writer, called "Red" by his friends, was indignant. Or, if not indignant *per se*, then profoundly concerned that Van Doren's essay, should it later be published in book-form, had rather missed the mark. Lewis wrote to correct Van Doren's misinterpretation of *Main Street*, indeed his misinterpretation of the entire body of Lewis' work to date, before the essay made its way to a larger publication.

Lewis began his letter by stating that he had in no way been influenced by *Spoon River*. He began planning *Main Street* in 1905 when he was a sophomore at Yale, years before *Spoon River* was published. What's more, he told Van Doren, he hadn't even read *Spoon River*. Lewis questioned whether Van Doren could fairly claim that Zona Gale or Sherwood Anderson had also been influenced by Masters. He insisted a more accurate explanation for any commonalities between the authors' works was the fact that Masters, Gale, Anderson, Lewis himself, as well as a hundred other writers, had all been "influenced in various ways by the same spirit of the times," something, he argued, that is commonplace in literary history.

Lewis' next complaint: he wondered if Van Doren realized, exactly, how shabbily he represented Lewis as merely a freakish best-seller, as if *Main Street* simply emerged from an abyss. Lewis resented this misrepresentation even more than the first, since he had spent the last eighteen arduous years honing his craft as a working (*i.e. paid*) writer. Lewis further resented Van Doren's characterization of his work as "amusing chatter." Like Edith Wharton and H.G. Wells, Lewis defended his use of colloquial language as a "serious presentation of human affairs." The strength in his characters' dialogue lay in its realism. This, Lewis argued, is how people speak.

Lewis took great exception to Van Doren's claim that his previous work had been much "smarter" than what he produced in *Main Street*. In fact, Lewis acknowledged that three of his previous novels were quite bad. Lewis challenged the critic, "Have you ever read any of them? I doubt it." Lewis instructed Van Doren to go back and read some of his earlier works, admonishing the critic, "And then I want you to think with considerable care about each word you wrote regarding me." What Lewis didn't argue was whether or not his work was any good. It was not for him to judge whether *Main Street* or any of his other novels, essays, or short stories was bad, very bad, or badly conceived. But what he could not allow to stand was Van Doren's analysis that Lewis had simply been a Smart Chatterer who was miraculously converted into a *Spoon River*-imitator by the influential Mr. Masters. Nor did he hate all *dull* people. On these points, he insisted on setting the record straight.

Lest the critic Van Doren chalk all of this up to a temperamental writer who couldn't stomach a little criticism, Lewis added that he had, until that day, written only six letters to critics or journalists concerning reviews of his work, out of the hundreds of reviews he had read. Four were notes of thanks; only two contained words of protest. However, owing to the prestige of *The Nation* as an important literary magazine and to Carl Van Doren's esteemed reputation as a literary editor, Lewis had to write to set the record straight, because this particular review mattered. He closed the letter, written from his current home-away-from-home in Pallanza, Italy, "Sincerely yours, Sinclair Lewis." (Oct. 25, 1921)[50]

We don't know Van Doren's immediate response to the Sinclair Lewis defense. However, the literary critic made subtle yet significant edits to his essay before it was published in his 1922 book, *Contemporary American Novelists, 1900-1920*. The original essay read:

Before 'Main Street' Mr. Lewis had belonged to the smarter set among American novelists, writing much bright, colloquial, amusing chatter to be read by those who travel through books at the brisk pace of vaudeville. If it seems a notable achievement for a temper like Mr. Masters's to have drawn such a character into its serious wake...

The edited version for the book was more nuanced. The critic considered the author's rebuke, and retreated from any definitive link he made regarding *Spoon River's* influence on *Main Street*:

Before *Main Street* Sinclair Lewis, though the author of such promising novels as *Our Mr. Wrenn* and *The Job*, had been forced by the neglect of his more serious work to earn a living with the smarter set among American novelists, writing bright, colloquial, amusing chatter for popular magazines. If it seems a notable achievement for a temper like Mr. Masters's *to have helped pave the way to popularity* for Mr. Lewis...[51]

Subtle changes? Yes. Carl Van Doren was not an unreasonable man, but neither would he be cowed. His revised essay made allowances for Lewis' earlier works, the novels and short stories, without simply dismissing these as frivolous. Instead of pronouncing *Spoon River's* definitive influence on *Main Street*, Van Doren altered his criticism to say simply the *popularity of Spoon River* had helped pave the way for *Main Street's* commercial success. In this instance, the critic was subtly, yet significantly, swayed.

Of his work as a literary critic, Van Doren wrote that his central query, when reviewing any piece of literature, was always, *Is it alive?* "The measure of the creator [writer] is the amount of life he puts into his work. The measure of the critic is the amount of life he finds there." Sinclair Lewis had enlivened *Main Street,* and the body of his earlier work, through his defense of his craft. Van Doren, wanting to get it right, found new life where he originally found only contempt for dullness.[52]

With that first letter, written on the embossed stationery of Pallanza's Hotel Eden, a friendship began between the two writers that would last the rest of Carl Van Doren's lifetime. Whatever was contained in Van Doren's response to Lewis's first letter—most certainly Van Doren was gracious and polite in his reply—the correspondence immediately turned friendly. Lewis next informed the critic that his ensuing project, which would become the novel *Babbitt,* owed much to Carl Van Doren himself. Lewis described this next novel, brought on by Van Doren's own interest, as of the "same general sort as *Main Street,*" in which the protagonist was an Average Business Man, a Tired Business Man, trudging through the daily grind in a "commercial oligarchy" of a city, population three or four hundred thousand. Lewis wrote, "I hope to make that man live!" He eagerly wanted to talk to Van Doren about this project specifically and about novel-writing in general. Soon, Red was regularly inviting Carl up to his summer home at Twin Farms in Barnard, Vermont. When many months had gone by without a visit, Red lamented, "We have been missing you all summer...Come on!"[53]

After Lewis became the first American to win the Nobel Prize for Literature in 1930, Van Doren was determined to write a biography on the man he called "the first satirist of this American age." *Sinclair Lewis; A Biographical Sketch* was published in 1933. How, exactly, does one write a biographical sketch of a living writer? It helps if the biographer has the cooperation of the biographied, which Van Doren certainly had. The men were, by this time, very good friends, and Van Doren asked Lewis to send him a family history, a chronology of his life to-date. Every writer knows that in order to grab his reader's attention, he has got to open with a *hook*. And so Van Doren began the biography by describing Sinclair Lewis's acceptance speech in Stockholm:

> Sinclair Lewis stood up like a restless, determined, tall flame. He was at Stockholm in December, 1930, and, having just been given the Nobel Prize in Literature, he was the most conspicuous American man of letters living. For weeks his name had had its daily place in the headlines of two continents and more. His countrymen, pleased that the honor had at last fallen to the first American, were touchily uncertain that this American deserved it. A satirist, as they called him, he had killed sacred cows,

washed native linen before the eyes of the world, fouled his own nest, discredited a fatherland. Provincials shivered. Patriots thought up loud irrelevances. Only in Stockholm, innocent center of the storm, was there enough quiet to let the winner of the prize be heard. Even in the grave presence of the Swedish Academy he had to raise his voice, he felt, above the mutterings beyond the Atlantic.[54]

After Lewis gave that speech, he was angered to see the American press had thoroughly botched it. Even the respected *New York Times* had printed a highly edited, and therefore inaccurate according to Lewis, account of the speech. Lewis contacted those press outlets and demanded a proper re-print. Van Doren got it right in his biography on Lewis, in which he described the seemingly cantankerous celebrity—because Sinclair Lewis was very much a celebrity; the press loved him, or, rather, loved to report on the writer and his doings; his fiery nature made for good copy—calling out the American Academy for being "a divorce in America of intellectual life from all authentic standards of importance and reality." Lewis called out the American universities, whose humanities departments were "far from reality and living creation." He called out university professors for ignoring the very good work of so many contemporary American writers, chiding, "Our American professors like their literature clear and cold and pure and very dead." The first American to be awarded the Nobel

Prize for Literature had mocked the Academy, the universities, and the New Humanists who had overrun English departments everywhere. This was, of course, music to Van Doren's ears: the writers were on the same page. While Van Doren, in his own critical assessment of academia, was always diplomatically polite, Lewis held nothing back. In Stockholm, he had "turned his hornets loose again."

Van Doren's earlier disclosure of an innate personal inquisitiveness, in which he read histories and novels with a powerful curiosity that fueled his desire *to know* about the lives of the men and women contained therein, is evident across the body of his own writing. For it wasn't enough for this critic to recount what the celebrity novelist said or did at the ceremony in Stockholm. Van Doren was curious about the man behind the prize. Why did Lewis use this platform to attack the whole of American academia? Van Doren wrote that Lewis was not, contrary to popular opinion, simply a cantankerous publicity-seeker using the world stage to amuse himself. No, said Van Doren, there was much more going on here. Sinclair Lewis was an artist, a *creator*, and that meant a great many things.

> He had, by nature and by instinct, always burningly demanded that human life be beautiful and splendid; always been disappointed that he could not everywhere find what his passion looked for; always offset his anger at stupidity by his delight

in comedy; always spoken without muffling his words. His address before the Swedish Academy was as characteristic as any of his novels. The man who had, somehow, expected that the American Academy and the universities and the New Humanists could be sensitive, powerful friends to creative literature, and had felt compelled to own that they were not, was the man who had expected that prairie villages could be aspiring, minor businessmen profound, bull-necked evangelists just and lowly, and had been driven to the truth about them. His speech had been, no matter what anybody said, almost amusingly American. Though he had condemned many of the low houses which his country's literature had built, he had done it in the interest of skyscrapers now building, and in the face of all his arguments he had predicted other skyscrapers which would some day cast their shadows to both oceans. The satirist had actually been patriotic and grandiose.[55]

Writing about the man behind the artist, Van Doren described Lewis as a man easily rattled by the irritations and hub-bub of everyday life. He was easily worn out. Lewis required the quiet repose of his New England farmhouse as a necessary antidote to the chaos of New York City, a place that "disintegrated" him. But he required the quiet on his own terms, as Red was known to invite friends, and groups of friends, to visit him often, whether in Barnard, Vermont, Stockbridge or Williamstown, Massachusetts.

Lewis's hospitality was limitless, even if a houseful of guests meant that he would need to abruptly excuse himself from the dinner table and spend the rest of the evening alone. Society, and the conviviality of friends, must take place on the artist's own terms, and Red would often get up and walk out of his own party when the collective energy no longer served him. The creative mind lived furiously, dashing from one moment to the next.

Where Van Doren's first critical essay on Lewis's work, "The Revolt from the Village," had characterized Lewis's early novels as simply "amusing chatter," the intervening decade had altered the critic's perspective. In *Biographical Sketch*, Van Doren wrote,

> If his early novels, characteristic as they are, were not as full-bodied as the later ones, it was only because he was himself not yet filled, to a lavish overflowing, with the wide and microscopic erudition in common life which his appetite demanded. When he was filled he wrote *Main Street*.[56]

The literary critic was decidedly more generous in this later analysis. Literary criticism, like anything else, does not exist in a vacuum. Every writer writes from the very particular circumstances of the present, and Van Doren's accumulated understanding of Sinclair Lewis, the man *and* the artist, had adjusted his perspective. Where Van Doren had, in 1921, attributed *Main Street*'s success to its likeness to *Spoon River*, in 1933 he shows an appreciation for the deeper societal discontent erupting in the early years of the twentieth century and Lewis's keen perception thereof. Sinclair Lewis was one of countless Americans who found village life *dull* in comparison to the exciting and wondrous world daily reported on in newspapers and magazines, dramatized in motion pictures and radio shows. Sinclair Lewis was not simply an artist or creator or storyteller; he was a *prophet.*

For his part, Sinclair Lewis described Carl Van Doren as one of his most valued friends. Most summers, Van Doren took Red up on his offers to visit him in the country, responding to his friend's repeated entreats to come and visit for a day, a week, a year. Red wrote, "When are you coming? The place needs you!" when too much time had passed. One particularly festive year, Lewis wrote a note of Happy New Year to Van Doren from a rented villa in Semmering, Austria, in the hills above Vienna. He wrote from Bermuda, wishing Van Doren could see the pink sands and crystal blue oceans of St. George. Red invited his friend to join him in England in the spring, and if that was not possible, then Carl must certainly come to Twin Farms in the summer. When Lewis, a known alcoholic, was feeling particularly blue over beginning work on a new novel and went on a drinking binge that lasted for days, Van Doren tended to his friend who was "almost [at] the edge of delirium." After a particularly difficult year for Van Doren, Red wrote, "I've seen so little of you, the past couple of years. Let's not lose each other, Ever. *Red*" [57]

$\rightarrow\!\!-\cdot\!\!-\!\!\leftarrow$

Across the 1920s, Van Doren made his living writing literary criticism and editing *The Nation* and *Century*. He had become a writer. And while he didn't exactly know *everybody*, Van Doren's circle of friends and colleagues would have impressed anyone who cared about books. In New York, Carl and Irita lived on 114th Street near the Columbia campus with their three young daughters. They spent their summers in West Cornwall, Connecticut, a picturesque New England hamlet in the northwest corner of the state. Rumor has it that Carl and Mark headed north from the city one day in search of a summer retreat, driving as far as they imagined anyone would possibly commute, and then drove fifty miles further. Thereupon arriving at Cornwall, not quite one hundred miles from the city, Van Doren found a "cool green wilderness," where most of the farmland was owned by families who could trace their Cornwall lineages back two hundred years. In 1915, Carl and Irita settled into Threeways, the old parsonage located at the intersection of three roads and across from the North Cornwall Congregational Church. The house was a rustic dwelling with no heat save for the fireplace and no plumbing except for a pump in the kitchen.

Eight years later, the Van Dorens purchased a larger farmhouse up the hill on Cream Hill, called Wickwire after its former owners, which boasted several acres of fertile soil and a red cottage that Carl used as his study. The house was about a mile from Cream Hill Lake, where the couple enjoyed a daily swim and were delighted by the chirping frogs and abundant dragonflies. The agrarian landscape of Cornwall reminded Van Doren of his youth on the farm in Hope (although the surplus of trees was new to the boy from the prairie), and the athletic build that had served Carl well on his high school football team was equally suited to the physical demands of country living. Maintaining Wickwire, which was built in 1800, provided a healthy balance to Van Doren's more intellectual pursuits. He built walls and fences, planted and harvested an annual vegetable garden, pruned trees or cut them down for firewood, dug ditches, cultivated hedges, and served as the home's mason, carpenter, plasterer, and plumber.

By 1920, a slew of literary critics and editors had followed the Van Dorens to Cornwall and turned the quiet New England enclave into a literary retreat. In addition to Carl and Irita's home on Cream Hill, Mark and Dorothy Van Doren had a farm at Cornwall Hollow, Lewis Gannett of the *New York Herald Tribune* was just up the road from Van Doren on Cream Hill, Joseph Krutch of *The Nation* was in Cornwall Center, and Henry S. Canby of the *Saturday Review* was nearby on Yelping Hill. Canby declared that during these years, Cornwall "touched the literary taste of all America."[58]

When the Van Dorens moved downtown to Greenwich Village, this literary circle literally encompassed his own backyard. With

Carl and Irita on Charlton Street and then 11th, the Mark Van Dorens on Bleeker, Sinclair Lewis on 10th Street, Elinor Wylie and William Rose Benet on 9th, and the Joseph Wood Krutches on 12th Street, Van Doren rarely dropped into one of his favorite cafés, such as the Breevort, without bumping into friends. He described the 1920s as a golden time for writers, with Greenwich Village, a neighborhood that had been the center of bohemian America only a decade before, the hub of the nation's literary scene. Greenwich Village in the 1920s was the place to be if one wanted to live in the company of other writers.

By 1922, the year Van Doren moved his family downtown from their Morningside Heights apartment, Greenwich Village sat very comfortably in its reputation as a bohemian, artistic, and intellectual enclave. Dominated by twisted streets in an otherwise orderly grid-like city, low houses, repurposed stables, hidden alleyways, and several delightful mewes scattered across a neighborhood that reached from Tenth Street south to Houston and stretched from the Hudson River east to Fifth Avenue, the Village developed a very unique personality in the first decades of the twentieth century. Historian Christine Stansell has written that "Nowhere did the instinct for the *new* flourish more extravagantly than in New York City, where a group of writers who collected in Greenwich Village between 1890 and 1920 transformed an unexceptional shabby neighborhood into a place glowing with a sense of the contemporary."[59]

The *moderns* who moved into Greenwich Village around the turn of the century included novelists, journalists, painters, political activists, reformers hell-bent on reforming social and political issues, theater people, poets, feminists, revolutionary zealots, and assorted hangers-on. The aim of this cultural fusion was to "fashion modern possibilities" across all social, political, literary, and artistic spheres, a purposeful rejection of all things bourgeois and dull. The new, the untried, and the untested trumped the familiar and ordinary at every turn: this was the modern ideal. During the 1910s, the Village was the city's hotbed for the discussion and cultivation of free speech politics, sexual freedom, radical and liberal ideals, and labor reform. The epicenter of American modernism, it was where radical reformers, bohemians, and intellectuals converged to reject The Establishment, the academy, and the genteel critics who had one foot, if not two, firmly planted in the nineteenth century and its boring bourgeois sensibilities.

The Masses, the famous monthly radical/socialist magazine headed by Max Eastman from 1911-1917, was headquartered in the Village and attracted many leftist writers to the neighborhood. Emma Goldman, anarchist-feminist extraordinaire, lived on 13th Street and earned her reputation as one of the Progressive Era's most vocal and radical champions for free love, homosexuality, and labor reform through her work among political agitators on the Lower East Side and later through her connections with the Village's growing intellectual base. The Liberal Club, a gathering place on MacDougal Street which counted as its members both older progressives and younger bohemian radicals, advertised itself as "A Meeting Place for Those Interested in New Ideas." One member described the Club as "the most energetically wicked freeloving den in Greenwich Village." Which, in a neighborhood known for its roarin' good times, was saying something. Drinking and conversation were in abundance, especially where men and women inter-mingled, and came to be seen as the very essence of the modern ideal.[60]

Heiress and socialite Mabel Dodge, the beneficiary of great wealth amassed by her financier father Charles Ganson, organized a weekly salon from her apartment near Washington Square. Mrs. Dodge recently spent several years living in Florence and had inherited a vast fortune. The purpose of her salons, which Dodge held across the reform-minded 1910s, was to exchange exhilarating *Views and Opinions*. Conversation was the key. Dodge invited a mixed bag of guests to ensure lively conversation, which, on any given evening, might include socialists, trade unionists, anarchists, suffragists, poets, lawyers, newspapermen, New Women, educated bohemians, and an assortment of revolutionary characters. One could not be vulgar or crude in Dodge's salon, although differences of opinion and even outright antagonisms were encouraged. Where the décor of the Liberal Club was decidedly shabby, Mabel Dodge's apartment was certifiably elegant. Decorated in silks and Victorian brocades, the apartment was at once a hotbed of free speech and reform-era conversation, while at the same time illustrative of the very class and economic disparities the reformers challenged. This curious juxtaposition seems only to have emboldened the salon's participants in voracious conversation.

Of course, not every resident of the Village was of the bohemian, radical, or literary set. Most residents of the twisted streets and low houses were working men and women and modest professionals. Pockets of Italians, Irish, black Americans, and artists dotted the neighborhood. But it was the artistic and literary set which gave its identity to the neighborhood and solidified the *imagined community* of bohemians and intellectuals who converged upon the neighborhood in the 1910s and '20s. New York in the early decades of the twentieth century was a *writer's city*, and downtown had become the epicenter of artistic and literary talent, creating what Stansell has described as "a distinctly American modern culture of letters—an assemblage of writers, publishers, and readers quite different from what had come before." Many of these writers and publishers, if not fully espousing the modernist ideal themselves, made their careers speaking for or against the new tradition in literature and art. These were the critics.

It was *this* Greenwich Village that Van Doren discovered when he took visitors to Washington Square by bus, or when he passed by the low houses during his commute on the Elevated from his uptown apartment to *The Nation's* offices at Vesey

Street. Van Doren admired the "small, weathered houses excitingly unlike the piled-up tiers of flats on Morningside." In 1922, Van Doren purchased a small house on Charlton Street which the Henry Canbys had recently occupied. After selling that home for a small profit five years later, the Van Dorens moved nearby to 11th Street. In the Village, Van Doren found all the comforts of a small town, but "without the bondage." One could have one's privacy and everyone did not necessarily know everyone else's business. One could keep one's friends in separate circles, if one preferred. And yet one could drop in to one's favorite café or theater and be almost certain of seeing someone one knew.[61]

After the Great War, leftist reformers and anarchists across the country were quieted (or deported, jailed, or executed), and so the overtly radical climate that had occupied the Village was quelled by the time the Van Dorens moved to Charlton Street. Still, the neighborhood was the workplace and living space of many writers, artists, editors, and publishers, a literary and intellectual sphere that held fast to the modern ideals that had propelled the country into the twentieth century. The moderns' focus was still on "the shining now as opposed to the discredited then." As a critic of this cultural and literary scene, Van Doren embraced the modern sensibility, and was committed to modernism's precept that the meaning of art is in the eye of the beholder: works of art do not have any *single* meaning, but mean various—and often contradictory—things to various minds."[62]

In 1922, Van Doren left *The Nation* as its literary editor, although he continued to publish literary criticism there, and moved over to *Century*. Although *The Nation* had made a concerted swing to the left during Van Doren's tenure, *Century* gave the editor more power to publish what he liked and to write about authors who had still not made the pages of *The Nation*'s literary reviews. As literary editor of *Century*, Van Doren published works by new writers Sherwood Anderson, Theodore Dreiser, Edna St. Vincent Millay, Elinor Wylie, Robert Frost, George Santayana, and his brother Mark Van Doren. Carl wanted to do more than just write literary criticism of individual works; his deeper ambition was to study the new writers in the totality of their works, not simply book-by-book. "Criticism was not enough," and Van Doren was intent on expanding the canon of American literature to include the newest and the boldest writers.

The changing tone of poetry and prose, with its modern bent and shifting form, held up a mirror to the changing American scene and Van Doren meant to study the new literature as it reflected, or imagined, a changing society. He wrote,

Writers need not be prophetic but they may be seismographic, recording tremors of opinion while they are still sensations to most people, finding the earliest clear words for roiled emotions.[63]

Call it the writing on the wall, canary in a coalmine, or art imitating life. Van Doren understood that *good* writers are not simply social commentators or reporters on the cultural scene. Those writers who succeed best are storytellers of individual truth. As Van Doren would write to Elizabeth Marion years later, *a book is an action, not a thought.* The writer "must *strike*, must put himself behind the blow, without too much weighing of the consequences." As one of the nation's foremost literary critics, it was Van Doren's job to determine how well, exactly, a given writer had done just that. Van Doren asked of each body of work he critiqued, *Is it alive?* [64]

CHAPTER 3

→ ·· ←

THE MAN WHO KNEW EVERYBODY

At *The Nation* and *Century*, Van Doren was *not* publishing book reviews. He was, rather, publishing historical context, literary history, analysis of themes and form and influence, which all speak to the purpose of literary criticism: to form an educated reader through the critic's erudition and unique insights. Literary criticism during this golden era—and most certainly this stemmed from the larger ideals of the Progressive Era, with its dreams of creating better citizens and ennobling the human spirit—meant to create a larger cultural and literary consciousness, not simply to sell books. The literary editor was not a stooge for the publishing houses; his work was more akin to English instructor than sunny book salesman. Equally important, Van Doren specifically intended to expand the existing canon of American literature through his critical essays and those he published by other critics as the magazine's editor.

By 1920, that canon still consisted of a core group of eighteenth and nineteenth century writers, the very writers Van Doren himself grew up reading. In his 1921 book *The American Novel*, Van Doren covered the works of this group, which included James Fenimore Cooper, Herman Melville, Nathaniel Hawthorne, Mark Twain, and Henry James. Van Doren described *The American Novel* as "a record of the national imagination as exhibited in the progress of native fiction." But any closed group is a dying group; life insists upon fresh blood and new imaginations (Sinclair Lewis chided the American Academy for refusing to accept this most basic fact of nature). Van Doren felt he had to "do something" about American literature and the older writers' continued stranglehold on the canon. And so, across the 1920s, he and other literary critics like Stuart Sherman, H. L. Mencken, Edmund Wilson, and Henry S. Canby wrote and published essays on the new voices that would enliven the body of work known as American Literature.

After publishing *The American Novel* in 1921, Van Doren set to work on his next book, *Contemporary American Novelists, 1900-1920*, compiled from essays he had written at *The Nation*. Inspired by the stream of new books that were crossing his desk daily, Van Doren surged with fresh vitality. Whereas one once read the classics from a distance, detached from eras whence they came, Van Doren now read "close to books." Searching for a common denominator he could use to understand the new writing, he came up with a diagnostic query: *Is it alive?* Curiosity drove Van Doren's desire to read, and it drove the manner in which he wrote about authors and their books. If Van Doren had the habit of strolling through the city streets, observing the daily goings-on of people and the lives they lived and writing those stories down in books or essays, then we might dub him a *flaneur* à la Walter Benjamin. Instead of strolling the city streets, he observed people and communities through literature: a literary anthropologist.

I was not the most effective kind of critic. More and Babbitt, Sherman and Mencken, Lewisohn and Van Wyck Brooks, all demanded that literature take more certain courses toward more certain ends than I felt any need for. They took part in controversies. I never did. Though I had favorites among contemporary writers, they were those I understood best rather than those I sympathized with most. Edmund Wilson called me amiable. I was not. Instead, I was so arrogant that I did not particularly care how anybody besides me chose to write. As an anthropologist I took nature as I found it, pleased with variety and leaving to the moralists to say which varieties must be kept, which discarded.[65]

Published in 1922, *Contemporary American Novelists* covered the works of the new writers Sinclair Lewis, Theodore Dreiser, Edith Wharton, Willa Cather, and Mary Austin. When writing about *living* writers, Van Doren remarked that the critic was working with "shifting materials" and allowed that his were not necessarily the final words on the authors and books in question. Judiciously, Van Doren admitted the best a critic can do when working with a living author is to seize upon the specific moment in time and make his most accurate assessment possible. There was room for revision as time went on because, "While criticism pauses to take stock, creation steadily goes on."[66]

As a reader and a literary critic, Van Doren admired authors who were civilized, intelligent, skeptical, and lucid. He looked for a *rational mind* in any writer. That mind might be disciplined, impetuous, speculative, or empirical. However, the mind must, in whatever leaning, be on the side of reason as opposed to superstition, sentimentality, or tradition. This was the modern ideal. When Van Doren came upon a book that he felt was lacking in reason, or was simply undistinguished, or trifling, he tended to remain silent. Some books were simply not worth explaining. A literary critic, however, prided himself on relaying his insights, whether positive or negative, to his reading public. Sometimes the truth hurts. In describing the lamentable task of reviewing the banal or the sentimental, or those books which, for critical reasons unknown, became popular successes despite their egregious shortcomings, Van Doren was sometimes baffled. He wrote that Gertrude Atherton "somehow fails to transmute her materials to any lasting metal and leaves the impression of a vexed aristocrat scolding the age without either convincing it or convicting it of very serious deficiencies" ; while Rupert Hughes suffered from a "fatal lack of true distinction" ; and Irving S. Cobb was simply "capable of better things."[67]

Just as Sinclair Lewis had done, these living writers were not about to let Van Doren's criticism of their work go unanswered. Gertrude Atherton wrote an impassioned reply to the critic, marking her letter *Confidential*. She wondered if something in her personality was particularly antagonizing to male critics. She also insinuated that Van Doren had not actually read her book.

> I began antagonizing the critics with my very first book and I have gone on antagonizing them ever since. It may be something in my personality that men in particular resent, possibly it is merely because I am not orthodox and have never allied myself with any school. If critics do not like my work, that is their privilege. But I have a healthy human objection to having my books adversely criticized unless they have been read first. I imagine the public, if it knew, would feel much the same way, for a critic without justice is without value.
>
> (June 26, 1922)[68]

Rupert Hughes wrote to Van Doren sporting his own bone of contention. The dismissed writer blasted the self-assured critic, demanding to know what, exactly, had qualified this critic to judge so harshly. Hughes challenged,

> Will you please tell me just what you mean by 'true distinction,' how it differs from plain or untrue distinction, and how you came to be sure of just what is 'lasting'? ... The history of criticism is paved with bad guesses as to what is lasting. If I were a critic by trade, I would avoid prophecy as a major symptom of dementia.
>
> Of course, I don't know what posterity will think of me, if anything, but I wonder if you are really posterity's advance agent, and who signed your credentials and guarantees your decisions. My training and my toil and my ideals have been founded in much deeper and longer scholarship and artistic experience than your own or those of most of the authors you are dusting off for posterity. Why have you and they 'true distinction' and I only a 'fatal lack'? ... I marvel at your pretense of knowledge and your audacity in pinning immortal medals on chests of your own choice. (1922)[69]

Rupert Hughes could not have known, nor could Carl Van Doren for that matter, that the subsequent decades would erase his name from literary memory. As it turned out, posterity doesn't think of Rupert Hughes at all. This fact may or may not have any bearing on how we feel about Van Doren's critical view of Hughes' work or of Hughes' clear indignation. Living writers tend to write back to those who evaluate their work for a public audience, and not merely when that evaluation is negative. Willa Cather was especially pleased with Van Doren's essay on her short stories *The Sculptor's Funeral* and *A Gold Slipper,* in which the critic praised her for "enlisting in the crusade against dulness [sic] which has recently succeeded the hereditary crusade of American literature against wickedness." Cather was, admittedly, most interested in his essay on *her* work, beaming "I think you have done well and generously by me." Thomas Wolfe sent words of grateful thanks following Van Doren's "magnificent review" of his first book, *Look Homeward Angel.* Theodore Dreiser wrote to Van Doren with an open invitation to drop by his studio for a salon-style open house,[vi] which was sure to include "a wide range of personalities likely to interest you."[70]

Dreiser, the author of *Sister Carrie* and *An American Tragedy,* appealed to the critic to intervene on his behalf over a deal with Paramount Motion Pictures. Dreiser had sold reproduction rights to Paramount for a film version of his book *An American Tragedy,*

....

vi   After one such evening at Dreiser's salon, CVD recalled a rather mopey Elinor Wylie, who felt herself egregiously neglected. CVD remembered of his beloved friend, "She could not bear being less than first in any company."

but he felt the screenplay had moved so far away from his original text that his professional reputation was at stake. Dreiser charged the screenplay was in no way representative of the core of his book, and fretted the film would offer a distorted and belittling interpretation of his work. The distressed author asked Van Doren to serve on a committee to review the film and give his professional opinion as to whether or not the film conformed to the author's "ideology." Van Doren was happy to oblige Dreiser's request, and after viewing the film went on record with his professional and learned opinion that it "almost completely" misrepresented Dreiser's book.[71]

Sometimes writers sent letters to Van Doren after reading his essays on the work of other writers. Robert Frost wrote to Van Doren after reading "The Revolt from the Village." Although Van Doren had much to say about small town life in America in that essay, Frost suspected that Van Doren would actually have more to say in a private conversation. He wrote, "I'm afraid you hold with Lewis and some others that a little European charm would do America good. You like to dream that small town life over there is perhaps more authentic than with us." Thorton Wilder sent Van Doren a note of admiration from The Quandrangle Club in Chicago, having just read the critic's latest essay on the poet and novelist, Elinor Wylie.[72]

Van Doren personally adored Elinor Wylie, as did most of New York's literary world. Wylie, one of the group of new modern voices Van Doren found so crucial to enlivening the literary canon across the 1920s, wrote four novels and four volumes of poetry during her lifetime. From the moment her first collection, *Nets to Catch the Wind*, was released in 1921, her poetry and novels received almost universal critical acclaim. Van Doren met Elinor Wylie in the winter of 1922 and was immediately enchanted by the beautiful poet who would become an icon of the 1920s literary scene. In his autobiography, Van Doren wrote, "She was a legend before she was a fact, and the legend came to New York ahead of her."[73]

As the legend went, Elinor Wylie was from Philadelphia and brought with her to New York some vague sense of scandal. In actuality, she was born to Henry Hoyt and Anne McMichael in the small town of Somerville, New Jersey on September 7, 1885 (three days before Van Doren's own birth) and had moved to a suburb of Philadelphia with her family when she was a small child. Both the McMichaels and the Hoyts were prominent families in Philadelphia high society: her great-grandfather Morton McMichael had been mayor of Philadelphia and her grandfather Henry Martin Hoyt had been governor of the state. The Hoyt family, which soon included Elinor's four younger siblings, moved to Washington D.C. in 1897 when Henry Hoyt was appointed assistant attorney general in the McKinley administration. Mr. Hoyt served under three presidential administrations, including those of Theodore Roosevelt and William Howard Taft, in addition to

McKinley's. Raised in affluence and social prominence in the nation's capital during the turn of the century, Elinor studied art at the Corcoran Museum of Art in Washington D.C. before travelling to Paris and London at the age of eighteen.

Amid the glitter and charm of young Elinor's personal gilded age, various manifestations of mental instability plagued the family. Elinor's father suffered more than one breakdown during his tenure in Washington, serious enough to require a leave from his official duties. A brother, a sister, and her first husband all committed suicide. Elinor Hoyt married this first husband, Philip Hichborn, Jr., in 1906 at the age of twenty, although she was never quite factual about the year of her birth and claimed to be younger. Hichborn also came from a prominent family and the match was considered a win on both sides. Teddy Roosevelt, then-President of the United States, attended the society wedding. The groom had attended Harvard and was a member of its prestigious Hasty Pudding Club, although his behavior was generally described as mildly erratic and would become more unbalanced as time went on. Elinor and Phillip had a son, Phillip Hichborn III, the year following their marriage.

Elinor later confided to Van Doren that this first marriage felt like a prison. She felt stifled, suffocated. There was no room for her mind and she had to get out. Bored and frightened with a husband who increasingly threatened suicide, Elinor began seeing Horace Wylie, a lawyer fifteen years her senior and also a member of Washington high society. After two years of flirtations and secret meetings, including frequent rendezvous in Rock Creek Park, the pair determined to leave Washington together. They left notes for their families, Elinor's husband and Horace's wife Katherine, and ran away to England in 1910. Elinor later admitted to Van Doren that leaving behind her small son was the one thing she had ever done in her life that she felt was "utterly bad." While the couple retreated to England to "live quietly," Elinor's mother appealed to President Taft to help reclaim her wayward daughter. For his part, Taft wrote that he would do what he could, and if he could locate Horace Wylie, he might engage the diplomatic corps to try and talk some sense in to him. This was much too small an affair for actual intervention by heads of state, and the steadfast couple remained in England.

Two years later, Philip Hichborn filed for divorce and headed west to start a new life. Having threatened suicide on numerous occasions while married to Elinor, Hichborn succeeded in killing himself at the home of his sister. His suicide note said that he had lost his mind. Elinor and Philip's young child, Philip III, was thereafter raised by his father's family and saw his mother only rarely during his lifetime. He too died young, after a drunken fall at the age of twenty-eight.[74]

Seeking refuge from a scandal that was fueled by whatever bits of information the press could dig up as to the elopement and self-imposed exile of Elinor Hoyt Hichborn and Horace Wylie, the couple lived under the assumed name of Waring near New Forest in the south of England. The pseudonym came from the poet Browning, whose verse included the line, "What's become of Waring, since he gave us all the slip?" Elinor's literary hero, the English Romantic poet Shelley, had also lived in the south of England and was friends with Browning, and so the name's subtle connection to Shelley, however roundabout, pleased her. While in England, Elinor actually met Shelley's grandson, a turn of events that delighted her. They had tea, that most proper of British rituals. An ocean away from the public drama that would not die down, "The Warings" remained in England, and Elinor, surrounded by the ghost of Shelley, met with literary people and began to write her own poetry. Horace studied Napoleonic history, and there were always books to be read. Dangerously high blood pressure and severe headaches frequently confined Elinor to the house, and her doctor advised she temper her diet and consumption of alcohol. The soaring blood pressure and headaches, however, would plague Elinor until her death.

Elinor and Horace returned to the U.S. by way of Boston, legally marrying in August 1916 after his divorce from Katherine was finalized. The developing scandal continued to follow Elinor and Horace from Boston to Philadelphia and back to Washington, where Horace accepted "a minor post," according to Van Doren, with the Interstate Commerce Commission. The couple moved into a run-down house owned by Elinor's mother on Florida

Avenue, near Dupont Circle. Though Elinor was still very much shunned by Washington society, Sinclair and Gracie Lewis were among the few friends who remained supportive of her and frequently invited the newlyweds to dinners and theater parties. Lewis had gone to Yale with Elinor's brother Henry Hoyt and was currently working on his novel *Main Street* from his home in Washington.[75]

While Horace's responsibilities at the ICC required frequent travel away from home, Elinor continued to write poetry and began sending pieces of her work to literary magazines. In 1920, the Chicago-based magazine *Poetry* published her poems "Atavism," "Silver Filigree," and "Fire and Sleet and Candlelight." In New York, "August" was published in the *New Republic* and "The Fairy Godsmith" found its way into the *Century*. William Benet, a good friend of Henry Hoyt and Sinclair Lewis, admired Elinor's poetry immediately. A writer and poet himself, who was well liked in New York's literary circles, Bill Benet was also a literary critic at the *Century* and editor at the *Saturday Review*. After the recent death of his wife in the influenza epidemic of 1919, Bill shared an apartment with Elinor's brother Henry. Henry, afflicted with the Hoyt family's tendency toward mental instability, had been suffering from suicidal thoughts; Bill returned to the apartment one day to find that he had asphyxiated himself. His friend's death, coming soon after the death of his wife, gave Benet a shock from which he would never completely recover.[76]

Following the glowing reception of her first published poems in the literary magazines, Elinor Wylie was invited to speak in New York at the Poetry Society's formal dinner in early 1921. She arrived on the scene cloaked in an aura of myth. Van Doren recalled, "Almost nobody knew quite what her story was, but everybody knew she had a story and thought of her as some kind of heroine." During the rest of the year, she travelled back and forth between Washington and New York and began spending more and more time with Bill Benet, who was still haunted by Henry's recent death. When Yale University Press rejected Elinor's first collection of poetry, Sinclair Lewis suggested she try Harcourt, who agreed to publish her *Nets to Catch the Wind*. The book was released in 1921 to wide critical acclaim and Elinor quickly became a literary icon of the Jazz Age. The 1920s were an especially friendly time for female writers, with a sizable coterie of female editors in the ascendency and influencing the types of poetry that were being published in the literary magazines. In addition to their male cohort, Harriet Monroe at *Poetry*, Lola Ridge at *Others*, Winifred Welles at *Measure*, and Margaret Anderson at the *Little Review* ensured that Elinor Wylie would have no trouble finding editors desirous of her poems. In this decade of high spirits, sophistication, and self-consciousness, in which "understatement, irony, and ambiguity were appreciated," both the literary critics and the reading public loved Wylie's style of poetry.[77]

Yet underneath the roaring good-times, speakeasies, and incessant parties lurked a collective awareness that traditional norms had broken down in the postwar era. A profound sense of alienation and dissolution also characterized the Younger Generation and the Roaring Twenties. Elinor's poetry spoke to all of it.

> We are so tired, and perhaps to-morrow
>> Will never come. Be fugitive awhile
> From tears, and let the dancing drink the sorrow,
>> As it has drunk the color of your smile.
>
> Your face is like a mournful pearl, my darling;
>> Go, set a rose of rouge upon its white,
> And stop your ears against the tiger-snarling
>> Where lightning stripes the thunder of the night.
>
> Now falling, falling, feather after feather,
>> The music spreads a softness on the ground;
> Now for an instant we are held together,
>> Hidden within a swinging mist of sound.
>
> Put by these frustrate and unhappy lovers;
>> Forget that he is sad and she is pale,
> Come, let us dream the little death that hovers
>> Pensive as heaven in a cloudy veil.

"Viennese Waltz" (1923)

In 1922 she left Washington, and Horace, for good, and soon filed for divorce. Her twelve-year love story with Horace Wylie had run its course and their love, which had epitomized the classical ideal of romantic love, passed away like any other less dramatic encounter. And so Elinor decided to move to New York permanently, where the scandal of her past did not mean so very much among the city's bohemian and literary crowds. Living separately in New York until her divorce from Horace went through, Elinor Wylie and Bill Benet were married in the fall of 1923. While she had quickly become the more esteemed of the two poets, his status as one of the most well-liked writers of New York's literary scene had expanded Elinor's professional and social circles instantly. Finding new friends, and admirers, in writers like John Dos Passos, Edmund Wilson, Carl Van Vechten, Dorothy Parker, and Edna St. Vincent Millay, Elinor's fortunes improved immediately; she would never again be at a loss for camaraderie or flattery.[78]

Carl Van Doren first met the poet-heroine Elinor Wylie in 1922. Literary critic Mary Colum, who wrote for a variety of magazines including *Scribner's*, *The Nation*, *The New Republic*, and the *New York Times Review of Books;* and Jean Wright Gorman, who had written a handful of book reviews for the *New York Times*, arranged a poetry reading at New York City's MacDowell Club early that winter. Colum asked Van Doren to chair the event and introduce the poets. Van Doren later recalled of Elinor, dressed in a white crepe de chine dress, "She looked like the white queen of a white country. White-faced in white satin, she had no color but in her lustrous eyes and her bronze hair. She seemed restless and remote. I said her poems were like bronze bells. This delighted her."

Indeed, this was music to Elinor's ears, a woman who needed always to be the most beautiful woman and the most talented writer in a room, and if anyone should dare utter anything to the contrary, Elinor was known to burst into tears or leave a party abruptly. It was simply impossible to flatter her too much. After one particular argument with Benet, she wrote a letter apologizing not for any misbehavior, but instead serving as an explanation: "To make up for being vain, you must know I am inordinately scared and sensitive and think everyone hates me." She couldn't stand the idea of anyone being angry with her. After one of several weekend visits to Cornwall, in which she arrived at the train station at an obscure hour, or perhaps on a train later than she had indicated, Elinor entreated Van Doren to please not be cross with her. For his part, Van Doren admitted that he could never be angry with the graceful beauty. He adored her in spite of her "vain tantrums," which "might have been unendurable if she had not so freely admitted it and laughed about it."[79]

Van Doren and Elinor Wylie shared an inside joke in which she would insist that she loved him and he would bat the flirtation aside with an air of humble modesty. After a weekend visit with Carl and Irita, Elinor wrote, "If I told you how much I love you—you admit you would never believe it!" She insisted that Van Doren's skepticism of her adoration was charming. Van Doren felt that Elinor Wylie could never love any man—any *living* man—as she loved her hero Shelley, and he was not the only writer-critic who had become enchanted with the *white queen*. Sinclair Lewis, John Dos Passos, and Carl Van Vechten equally admired her. Edmund Wilson wrote that at one point he became "quite addicted to her." Wilson published many of her poems in *Vanity Fair* and the *New Republic* while he was editor there, enjoyed a lively personal correspondence with the enchanting poetess, and enjoyed escorting her to the theater.[80]

Wilson was no fan of Elinor's marriage to Bill and he very directly told her so, although he later admitted the marriage had done her some good, had somewhat tamed her tendency toward emotional volatility. Wilson shared Wylie's deep interest in mysticism and witchcraft, a fascination that would appear again and again in her poems and novels. She had a supernatural belief that she would die early, and was rather resigned to it. Whether stemming from her manic-depressive tendencies, family history of suicide, dangerously high blood pressure—her doctors had warned her of the very real possibility of a paralytic stroke—or her belief in mysticism, Wylie sensed she would depart this world early. In 1927 she wrote to her ex-husband Horace, saying that she would remain with Bill for the rest of her days, "But you & I know now that remainder is not long."[81]

While editor at the *Century*, Van Doren published as much of Elinor's poetry as she would send him. At the suggestion of those who better understood the publishing industry, the poet agreed to turn novelist as a sure source of income, although she found that novel-writing took more time and energy than she liked; poems, she wrote down fully composed. Money, however, was always a problem. Wylie's income consisted of royalty earnings from her scattered reviews and articles, and occasional money from her mother to help fund her lifestyle. Even writers with family money were more often than not in financial straits. In 1925 Elinor wrote her second novel, *The Venetian Glass Nephew*, specifically for serialization in Van Doren's *Century*, sending chapters to him as soon as she wrote them. Flirting with disaster, Elinor Wylie composed her stories directly at her typewriter and did not use carbon paper in which to make a copy. The manuscripts she sent through the mail to Van Doren, therefore, were the only versions that existed. Van Doren was more than a bit frantic that a chapter might get lost in the mail before it reached him safely in the *Century* offices, although he felt that Elinor herself enjoyed taking the risk.

Well before she had completed the story, Elinor wrote to Van Doren asking for an advance on the work. Perennially short on funds, she had quickly realized the charming old house she and Bill purchased in Connecticut not only had pesky mortgage payments due, but interest on top of the principal as well. Sordid details like a monthly mortgage payment, and variable or fixed interest rates, existed beyond the ken of the artist.[vii] Without informing the publishers that the book was only partially written, Van Doren arranged for accounting "to pay her at once for the whole."[82]

Van Doren had high words of praise for *The Venetian Glass Nephew,* a strange and fanciful tale of a boy, Virginio, magicked from Murano glass at the behest of Cardinal Peter Innocent, who laments the lack of any nephew on whom to dote; and a philosophical girl, Rosalba, who determines to change herself into porcelain so that she and her love Virginio might live happily ever after. Van Doren was delighted with the bizarre tale; he immediately squirreled himself away from a gathering of friends to read the first chapter which Elinor hand-delivered to him. While Van Doren laughed aloud at something he'd read, Elinor cried with delight from the other side of the closed door. As far as Van Doren was concerned, the novel rightly belonged "among the small timeless masterpieces of satiric fantasy." He described the story as a moral

....

vii   A list of writers who have requested an advance from their publishers, or a loan from friends
       or family, would be exhaustive. Of the YG's cast of characters whom we have met so far:
       Elinor Wylie, F. Scott Fitzgerald, Ernest Hemingway, Edna Millay, Ludwig Lewisohn, CVD, etc
       etc etc, occasionally or routinely (depending on one's manner of living) found a discrepancy
       between one's living expenses and one's income as a writer. When Carl wrote to brother
       Mark, "My boy, stick to your professorship. Living by writing is not too satisfactory," he was
       speaking for writers everywhere.

fairy tale, "simple in its essence as it was rich with lovely and witty decorations."[83]

Elinor Wylie's other literary admirer, Edmund Wilson, did not care for the novel, no matter his personal adoration for its author. In a review for the *New Republic*, Wilson wrote that the novel had "mingled the fictitious with the real in a manner hardly allowable..." The story itself was absurd; its allegorical intentions: licentious. Perhaps for Wilson, the author's poetic passion did not justify her novel's fantastical presentation. However, Wylie's fantastical presentation and her creation of these unique characters was exactly what Van Doren found so delightful. It was the subtle depiction of character and humanity in a story that truly interested him. He later wrote of himself-as-critic, "Criticism has never been with him a major aim. What really interests him is human character, whether met in books or out of them, and it is always human character which he studies."[84]

In 1926, Elinor Wylie was elected to the board of editors at the Literary Guild, a monthly mail-order book club. Publisher Harold Guzinburg has personally asked Van Doren to chair the editorial board of this new book club venture, with the stipulation that Van Doren could then select whomever he wished to serve as his associates. He chose Joseph Wood Krutch, whom Van Doren knew from his days at *The Nation*, and Elinor Wylie. The editorial board at the Book-of-the-Month Club, which included several of Elinor's friends, chose her next novel, *The Orphan Angel*, as its December 1926 selection. A boost in sales by 50,000 units and a $8,000 paycheck was a windfall for the financially-strapped Wylie, who naturally used some of the earnings not to pay down the mortgage, but to purchase a trove of Shelley's letters that had just come on the market. Of her lifelong infatuation with the poet, Van Doren wrote, "She loved Shelley. He would have loved her if he had known her. They loved each other."[viii]

In June of 1928, Van Doren travelled to England and France to spend the summer "among the expatriates." Immediately upon his arrival in London, Van Doren visited Elinor at her tiny rental house in Chelsea, where the friends met for Sunday dinner. Unaware that he had been expected *to dress* for the occasion, Van Doren arrived in a brown tweed jacket. Elinor Wylie was moderately horrified. Certainly he had brought proper evening clothes with him? She had planned a dinner party for later in the week, and was looking forward to introducing Van Doren to *everybody*. She insisted her guest of honor be properly attired for the event. "Please don't wear the brown coat to my party," she beseeched.

....

viii   A Man of Letters could not be expected to know *every* literary person of record, but Carl Van Doren was well acquainted with the work of Elinor Wylie's literary love, Percy Bysshe Shelley. Shelley was a contemporary and close friend of Thomas Love Peacock, the subject of Van Doren's dissertation. Van Doren had read many linear feet of correspondence between Peacock and Shelley during his time at the British Museum in 1911. He was, therefore, in a good position to gauge the love that Elinor Wylie and Shelley might have had for each other if only the two writers had lived during the same age.

Van Doren got the message, and dutifully arrived at the dinner party in proper evening wear.

At the end of a lively evening, and after the rest of the party guests had departed, Van Doren stayed behind while Elinor read to him some of her latest sonnets. As she read, "her words rushed and tumbled, and her eyes were wild. She was as pale as a priestess at the mercy of her oracle, flaming through her." The white queen did not disappoint, the poetic flame burned magnificently. Perhaps, in hindsight, befitting: this was the last time Van Doren would see his friend Elinor alive.[85]

A few weeks later, Elinor fell down a flight of stairs in what turned out to be the first of three strokes she would suffer over the next five months. Assuring Bill, who was still in New York, that it was nothing more than a simple fall, Elinor suffered in terrible pain and was laid up in bed for a month of recovery. In November, a second stroke left her face paralyzed on one side. The woman who usually tended towards emotional excitability downplayed her condition once again, and sailed alone back to New York on December 1st. While at home in her apartment with Bill, Elinor suffered a third and fatal stroke on December 16, 1928. She was correct when she had written to Horace that her life would not be a long one, and while she had long suffered from nervousness and incapacitating headaches, most of her friends were unaware of the two recent strokes.

The death of Elinor Wylie at the age of forty-three came with the shock of suddenness to all who knew her. When family and friends gathered at the Benets' apartment on West 9th Street for a private memorial service, Van Doren was noticeably overcome by the loss of his white queen. Elinor's anguished friend and admirer wept openly and had to be escorted home by Irita, her arm wrapped protectively in his. With some years and distance separating himself from the rawness of grief, Van Doren later described that Elinor's death came "as swiftly as the curtain falls after a tragedy." He had found an unequaled grace and luminescence in his heroine poet, the light she threw off dimmed not a bit in the years after her death. In his autobiography, Van Doren wrote, "She both wrote and spoke with a lovely, amused formality which baffled the downright. But life had two or three times got out of hand with her, and had been tragic. She could never forget that. It kept alive the perpetual contradictions of her nature. She was a woman who had beauty and genius."[86]

After her death, Van Doren established the Elinor Wylie Poetry Fellowship in association with the American Academy of Poets. A campaign to raise $100,000 to fund the fellowship's endowment failed to progress, however, and the plan was eventually dissolved. Fellowship or no, the woman had been a legend in her own time. Van Doren recalled, "There were of course many Elinor Wylies. I can claim to know only one of them...No poet of her time would be longer remembered, and no woman."[87]

CHAPTER 4

SHIFTING MATERIALS

No author, man or woman, told Van Doren more about herself than Mary Hunter Austin. Born in 1868 in Carlinville, Illinois, Mary Hunter Austin was slightly older than Carl Van Doren, but both had been born and raised in small towns on the Illinois prairie during the last decades of the nineteenth century. Mary recalled that even as a young girl, she liked to sit perfectly quiet and still on her father's desk while he worked, happily looking at books. Even before she could read, books presented an unavoidable allure. As a growing child, Mary told her father that she wanted to write books of her own, all kinds of books. When she repeated this ambition to others, the adults barely contained their laughter. Writing of herself in the third person, Mary recalled her life as a young girl, those carefree but fleeting days before she had "heard the popular superstition that you can only do one kind of thing, and that to suppose yourself capable of doing more is to get yourself suspected of conceit."

Conceit, pride, an unwillingness to be liked: these were considered personality defects for a woman in the 1880s, a time when "the prevailing notion that the most desirable feminine trait was to 'draw people to you,' which was second only to the other mannerly obligation that you must not 'antagonize' other people." Mary admitted that she was fairly immune to these expectations for the fairer sex. She was not a go-along-to-get-along kind of gal. Artists rarely are. Nor would she apologize for it. Not that this made life simple for Mary, she would be the first to admit.[88]

After high school, Mary Hunter attended Carlinville's Blackburn College, where she studied science. She, like Carl Van Doren, was elected Class Poet, and graduated from Blackburn in 1888. In her autobiography *Earth Horizons,* she quite intentionally spares the reader any verse from her college days; the curious reader is left to his own imagination as to the aesthetic or stylistic form her poetry might take. The child who loved to sit on her father's desk and look at books was now a young woman who knew the surge of her own intellectual curiosity. Mary Hunter did not simply want *to know,* she was "plagued with an anxiety to know."

Her older brother had not long before relocated to California and so, after Mary's graduation, the family followed suit and headed west. Folks from the Middle West were leaving the prairies and wooded hills of family homesteads for the roar of Eastern cities or the echoing call of the West. By rail and by stagecoach, the Hunter family headed to the harsh clime of Owens Valley, California. From the window of her train car, Mary's first sight of the long stretch of desert between Salt Lake and Sacramento "grew upon her mind." She was enthralled with the desert, so different from the wooded hills and twisting creeks of Illinois. Here, she saw something "brooding and aloof, charged with a dire indifference."[89]

Arriving at their western destination, and, one hoped, closer to their own personal destinies, the Hunters promptly settled in the tiny town of Lone Pine in Owens Valley, "a long narrow trough of the earthquake drop that makes the great Sierra Fault, through which a river burrows to a bitter lake, cupped round with desertness." A hard landscape by any standards, but one with a fresh and steady water supply. To the west and north sprang the Sierra Nevada mountains; to the east and south lay Death Valley. Soon after, in 1891 at the age of twenty-three, Mary Hunter married Stafford Wallace Austin. Mr. Austin was hired to manage the construction of an irrigation canal in nearby Inyo, to which the newlyweds promptly relocated. Mary would write about the landscape surrounding Inyo in her first and well-received book, *The Land of Little Rain*. The Austins' new community was peopled with miners, at least one professional gambler, and a hodgepodge crew of men working on the irrigation project. The cadre of local clientele expanded when the Sierra Club, founded by the naturalist and conservationist John Muir, soon discovered the wilds of Inyo, followed by assorted mountain climbers and adventures, botanists, and connoisseurs collecting Native American art and artifacts. An undiscovered, pristine landscape—however rugged—remains undiscovered and pristine for only so long.[90]

For the sake of practicality, Mary Hunter Austin accepted a local teaching appointment, yet, still determined to be a writer, met with "writing people" in San Francisco and Oakland. How to get her stories published? To whom might she send her manuscripts? These are the questions of any writer, and Van Doren's admonition to "curse all publishers!" is a sentiment known to many who attempt to navigate the process. This, too, was Mary's frustration, this too was her path. When the Inyo irrigation scheme soon collapsed, Mary's husband lost his employment and drifted into another local endeavor. Much to her growing and gnawing regret, Mary had to face the fact that she found her husband aimless in all things, he was, to her curiosity-driven mind, a man entirely without ambition. No intellectual curiosity. For a woman plagued with *an anxiety to know*, the situation was untenable.

Added to the stress was the couple's newborn daughter, Ruth. The child was born with an unspecified congenital abnormality for which, in the absence of a clear medical diagnosis, Mary felt personally responsible. Needing some stability, some direction, some solid foundation for herself and her daughter, Mary admitted that she might have bent to her husband's direction, if only there was a direction in which to bend. The situation became increasingly unbearable primarily because Mary's future with her husband was so unknowable. Mary and Wallace were not of like minds. It wasn't simply that husband and wife were not on the same page; Mary had no indication that Wallace had any page at all.

Mary sold her manuscript, *The Land of Little Rain,* to the *Atlantic Monthly,* which serialized the story in 1903. The immediate critical and commercial success was such that Mary began to meet "writing people" who were becoming increasingly aware of her work. She started on her next book, *The Basket Maker,* and in the summer of 1903 journeyed to the coast, to Monterey and Carmel-by-the-Sea. Here, she happily fell in with a literary circle that very much enjoyed the wild beaches at Carmel, walking the dunes and hiking among the cedars. She became good friends with the poet and playwright George Sterling, the environmentalist John Muir, the writer Jack London. Of Jack London, Mary recalled that women quite literally "flung themselves" in his masculine direction. She was not, however, impressed with writer Ambrose Bierce, whom she found somewhat of a *poseur.* The circle of writers fell into a daily routine at Carmel, which included steady work throughout the morning, followed by leisurely strolls down the piney trails and along the sandy dunes by early afternoon. Following the success of *The Land of Little Rain,* Mary sold her next piece, *Isidro,* to the *Atlantic Monthly.* She began work on a play.

In 1903, the National Reclamation Bureau arrived in Inyo in search of a water supply for the expanding city of Los Angeles. In 1870 the population of the City of Los Angles was a sparse 5,728 souls. By 1890 that number had grown to over 50,000. Ten years later, at the turn of the century, Los Angeles was home to 102,500 persons and required a steady and clean water supply to grow further still. Enter the National Reclamation Bureau and the conception of the Owens Valley Project. Buoyed by the 1902 Reclamation Act, the Los Angeles Water Commission quickly approved plans to build an aqueduct from Owens Valley to the City of Los Angeles. In less than ten years, the completed aqueduct would carry 300,000 acre-feet of water per year from Owens Valley into L.A. by diverting water from sixty-two miles of the Owens River. The success of the scheme ensured that by 1924 Owens Lake would become a dry lake bed.

Of course, Mary Hunter Austin did not foresee the exact timetable of the project, but she knew the majestic solitude of Inyo would be desolated, destroyed. She and Wallace, along with many local and increasingly irate farmers and ranchers who knew their livelihoods hung in the balance, fought the Reclamation Bureau in what became known as the California Water Wars.

But to no avail; progress marches ever forward. The City of Los Angeles demanded its water supply. Mary could not stay to watch the inevitable decline of the landscape that had so capti-vated her imagination, although Wallace chose to stay behind while she sold the house in Inyo. She knew what future awaited Owens Valley, and she wished never to return. The matter of young Ruth's care had to be determined, however, as the child required more care than Mary could provide. And so the mother, weary from marital disintegration, the lost fight of the Water Wars, and suffering from an undisclosed medical ailment her-self, put her daughter in a private institution in San Francisco and returned to Carmel. Her daughter would remain in the institution for the rest of her short life.

With a group of writer friends, Mary decided to go to Italy. Feeling unwell and suffering from generalized and near constant pain, she thought Rome would be a good place in which to die, if that were her fate. She counted her money and determined that she had enough to get her to Italy where she could live out her days, which, she was certain, were not many. In Rome, the con-firmed renouncer of the Christian faith met Cardinal del Val and Mother Veronica of the Order of the Blue Nuns. She took lessons from Mother Veronica on how to escape her pain through prayer. Mary noted in her autobiography that by the time she reached Siena, her pain had lessened remarkably. By Venice, it had left her.

She travelled on to Paris and London, where she met H.G. Wells and G.K. Chesterton. She became friendly with Mr. and Mrs. Herbert Hoover, years before Hoover would become the 31st

President of the United States. Mary Austin spent a good deal of time with the Hoovers, whom she described as amiable hosts, recalling, "Their house was always open to these stray visitors and there was an immense amount of interesting and informative talk going on about their table, thoroughly American talk, and a great deal also that was rather boring." With Hoover she toured Stonehenge, Bath, and the local cathedrals. She met Joseph Conrad, who was by then ailing and rather low in spirits. She met the playwright Bernard Shaw and the poet William Butler Yeats. Always curious, always anxious to know, Mary's impression of the English people she met was a sense that "they seemed uninterested; at least they were not interested and curious about me as I was about them." Curious, always curious. Mary Austin had to experience life and talk about those experiences so that she could, finally, write what she had lived.[91]

After the Great War, Mary Austin reconnected with Herbert Hoover back in the U.S. She travelled to D.C. to hear him speak, recalling that he "was trying then to get into something over here." In Mary's opinion, Hoover had big ideas, many of them quite grand, but no inkling as to how to bring them to fruition. These impressions were perhaps swayed by her friendship with a true political dynamo, the larger-than-life Theodore Roosevelt. Mary Austin had first met Roosevelt, after his presidency, when persuading him to use his influence to quash the Indian Bureau's attempts to remove Indian music from the schools; she was by that time one of the leading voices in American Indian folklore and culture and was often consulted by persons seeking her expertise. She assessed that, unlike Hoover, Teddy Roosevelt "had a solid and plangent relation to the public mind; he knew what was going on in it."[92]

Following her return from Europe, Mary lived, without Wallace, in New York across the 1910s and early 1920s, although she was not especially fond of that city. Hub of the nation's literary world or no, New York in Mary Austin's mind "lacked freshness, air, and light. More than anything else it lacked pattern, and I had a pattern-hungry mind." She met many women involved in the Suffragist movement, including Emma Goldman, Alice Paul, Margaret Sanger, and Mabel Dodge, at whose Greenwich Village salon Mary often lectured. Every woman in this New York circle, she insisted, was a suffragette. Renting an apartment at 10 Barrow Street in the Village, she lived at the epicenter of the Suffragist movement in America, and while she had no interest in getting pulled into the party line, so to speak, the influence of feminist thought had a profound effect on her and her writing.[93]

Still, the New York crowd was not particularly interested in the sorts of things that truly interested her. Mysticism. Landscape. Pre-Columbian cultures of the Americas. The best conversation Mary found in New York came by way of Sinclair Lewis. The literary critic, historian, and writer Hendrik Willem Van Loon lived two floors above Mary Austin at Barrow Street, and Sinclair

Lewis often came by to visit. "The talk was very good. It came nearer being folk talk than anything else I found in New York; it had substance and plasticity." While Mary Austin did not find camaraderie in New York to the extent she had found it among the writing people in Carmel, her curiosity for interesting people and conversations was satisfied in bits and pieces.[94]

During these New York years, Mary realized a divorce from Wallace, who had remained back in California, was the only reasonable thing to do. Although they had been estranged for many years, she had kept alive some hope of reconciliation. They had tried to remain friendly, but that too was strained. The mismatched pair had completely different instincts as to how to live, how to live in relation to a spouse. In all things during the course of her marriage, Mary felt that she had had to take care of herself, had to secure her own present situation and future possibilities. She regretted that she had never really experienced the traditional, however bourgeois, ideal of marriage, of union. She wrote in 1931, "I have never been taken care of, and considering what that has meant to women in general, I feel a loss in the quality of charm and graciousness which I am unable to rationalize." The suffragette acknowledged and regretted that she held these feelings of loss over something so *traditional*. She should *know* better. She had other things *to do* besides play the role of protected wife. These feelings were irrational. And yet the loss wounded her in some way.

In addition to her upstairs neighbor Hendrik Willem Van Loon, Mary Austin met all of the usual suspects in the New York editorial world, the reigning men of letters. She met Brander Matthews, preeminent scholar and writer at Columbia, and president of both the National Institute of Arts and Letters and the Modern Language Association; William Dean Howells, editor of the *Atlantic Monthly;* leading editors at *The Nation, Century,* and *The New Republic.*

And she met Carl Van Doren. In 1919, Van Doren approached Austin about writing a chapter on "Aboriginal American" literature for his upcoming book *An Anthology of World Prose.* Mary Hunter Austin was *the* expert in American Indian lore. She congratulated Van Doren on being the first editor to present material of this kind to the American public and was pleased to be included in the broad undertaking.

Mary Hunter Austin had, admittedly, "more than a little trouble with editors and publishers." Reviewers and editors seemed to miss the point of her work entirely, as far as Austin was concerned. And there was always too much direction from above: male editors and publishers determining what they felt female writers should write about. Mary Austin recounted an experience in which she shared with an editor her idea for a series of articles about a female writer's "amorous experiences." Some time later she received a phone call from said editor's assistant, who was working on the very series of articles that Austin had proposed.

When the assistant described the articles, they in no way resembled Mary's proposed work, although her name was attached as author. The writer protested. The editor fired back, insistent upon having his way. Mary Austin promptly took her articles to a friend at the *Evening Telegram*, who agreed to print the series in its original form. Copyrighted, published; done. The series was later picked up by *Harper's Weekly*. And so now the pushy editor found there was nothing *he* could do about it. He had been beaten to the punch.[95]

In 1922 Van Doren wrote an essay for *The Nation* on Mary Austin's recent work, which he titled "The American Rhythm." The critic praised Austin's writing for revealing the subtleties of particular individuals as well as the larger American Indian community. He applauded her intelligence and genius, but wrote that she had not quite managed to combine the two. "Much of her significance," he wrote, "lies in her promise." Van Doren described Mary Austin as a prophet, an oracle, a mystic. After these many years in the California desert among its native peoples, the landscape took hold of her spirit and left its mark. "All that Mrs. Austin wrote is interwoven...The whole stream of her experience and reflection has passed through her and, no matter what the theme at the moment, has taken the color of her spirit... She speaks as if she had just come back from the desert with fresh truth." Van Doren called Mary Austin a *seer* who anticipated the direction of social change.[96]

As he had of Sinclair Lewis, Van Doren wrote that Austin had her finger on the pulse of the times. She was a seismographer, sensing and recording the tremors of change. She was a thinker, contemplating and speculating, remarking where social habits were being formed and where the patterns of human behavior were breaking apart. Van Doren wrote, "Her interpretations of various movements of opinion and sentiment about religion, the status of women, the forms of society, have been delivered in instance after instance so early as to have, apparently, and element of prophecy in them."[97]

However, the critic found flaws in "the occasional looseness of her technical knowledge and the bold hand with which she uses it to draw bold conclusions." Her "long view" of existence and life came into conflict with the "brasher intellectuals" who would not share these views. This last point may have been of no personal consequence to Van Doren, who was no fan of the *brasher intellectuals,* per se. For Van Doren, it was more important to be interesting than academic. Still, the critic's job was to elucidate and to evaluate a literary work based on its aesthetic, cultural, and technical merits. Van Doren wrote this author lacked the ability to focus her interests into "a necessary narrow field. The far-sighted sometimes fumble when they try to do neat tasks at hand."[98]

It is curious that Van Doren, a generalist himself and no fan of the intellectuals' demand for specialization, criticized Mary Hunter Austin for this same tendency. His suggestion that she focus her work on either poetry or novel writing or anthropology does not jibe with his own generalist leanings. After reading Van Doren's essay in *The Nation,* Mary Austin wrote to the critic and asked to speak with him about his comments, primarily his belief that she should pull her gifts together and focus. She quite frankly disagreed and had reached the opposite conclusion. She challenged Van Doren, asking why a writer must do one sort of thing or the other; why must a writer choose a standard form or an archetype at the expense of his or her other gifts? This pigeon-holing was not expected in the other arts. One never, for example, heard criticism of Michelangelo for working in both paint and marble. Austin defended her right to use of *all* of her gifts, which included her intellectual penetration, creative imagination, and poetic drama. The problem of the age, she concluded, was this demand on the modern (female?) writer to choose one path over another.[99]

With Van Doren unable, or perhaps not especially interested, to accept Mary Austin's invitation to dinner before she headed west, the writer continued her personal revelations while onboard a train bound for Santa Fe in the summer of 1923. This form of communication might even have been preferable to Austin, since conversing by letter left Van Doren unable to fire back immediately. Mary Hunter Austin meant to say her piece. It was important for her to reach a clear understanding with the esteemed critic so that he might truly understand the value of her work. This was especially important now, as she felt she was entering the final phase of her work, and Van Doren's literary criticism could very well play a role in her legacy.

Austin had four days of travel via the Southern Pacific Railroad Company to reach Santa Fe, plenty of time to gather her thoughts and tell Van Doren what she thought of his critique. She felt his essay had not done her proper justice and questioned his charge that she failed to combine all of her gifts into "one characteristic piece of work." Instead of needing to focus and specialize, Austin felt that every creative genius in America was currently trending toward variability, not specialization. Austin asked, "Isn't it the approaching ideal that we should become more plastic to the thought stream of our time?" The modern ideal was against static tradition, against conformity with the old ways of doing things. On this point Van Doren would most certainly have to agree. Variability was the mark of creative genius, not conformity or uniformity.

Mary Austin wrote page after page of her life story to Van Doren. She described her small-town upbringing and the "utter isolation" she felt from any literary people until she was thirty-eight years old, the year she moved to Carmel. She wrote about the secret sorrow that pervaded her personal life, her daughter who had to be institutionalized and then died in early adulthood. As Sinclair Lewis had done, Austin wrote that if her work was simply bad art, then so be it. But she sensed that Van Doren had not entirely read the body of work he criticized, and wished that he had read her work as thoroughly as she felt he had read Upton Sinclair.

> Several times I have had the experience of having my work treated as a total failure only to discover years later that it was simply ahead of its time... I often fail with our Intellectuals by my deliberate avoidance of the patter of professional scholarship.
>
> *(July 14, 1923)*[100]

Here, Mary Austin was speaking Van Doren's language. Van Doren, a scholar and a writer working outside the walls of academia, was no fan of that institution where time seemed to stand still and professional scholars fell into teaching through a process of inertia (Van Doren had been offered a Professor of English position at Amherst College in 1920; he declined the offer, preferring the freedom and autonomy he had as a writer and editor). He was no fan of intellectual jargon. The man wrote simply and elegantly. When Mary Austin wrote, "If you have found out any way in which an American writer can be really learned and still get printed, I wish you would pass it on to me, for I can't find it," she identified the gulf between learned yet creative writers, and professional/academic writers. She resented the forces to box her into a niche.

Of the editors of the "intellectual publications" like *The Nation* and *The New Republic* (she didn't name names...), Mary Austin "found them lashed to their publications, able to talk of what was written, or what was going on under their noses, and not able to talk of what might be going on elsewhere, not willing to accept the idea that there might be anything else going on. I was bothered by the rage for success; the idea that an immediate success was the sign of capacity." They didn't get it, didn't get her work. If Mary Austin was a seer and a prophet, she scanned constantly the *earth horizon* for subtleties and imagery and stories beyond the ken of the obvious here-and-now. Maybe this is what the reviewers, the editors, and the publishers missed. Whatever it was, Mary Austin wrote always "a little in advance of the current notion of it... I wrote what I lived, what I had observed and understood. Then I stopped."[101]

During her years in New York, Mary Austin made frequent trips to the West. She became immersed in the Spanish culture of California and soon discovered Albuquerque and Santa Fe. Meeting with Mexican revolutionaries, she wrote a series of articles for *The Nation* about these agents of the Mexican revolution. The writer of books of American Indian folklore and poetry was now drawn to the hand-craft and folklore tradition currently experiencing a rebirth in Mexico. She felt something similar might germinate in New Mexico. When the Carnegie Foundation hired her to survey the Spanish population of Taos County, Mary

Austin decided to settle permanently in Santa Fe, where she "would write the closing years of my life into the history" of that landscape.

Building a home at the foot of Cinco Pintores Hill, she turned her attention to establishing an arts and folklore community in Santa Fe. She helped create the Indian Art Fund and the establishment of a living museum, which was supported by John D. Rockefeller after the industrialist and preservationist came through town and was intrigued by the project. She travelled to Cuernavaca in Mexico and met the muralist Diego Rivera, whom she called a great painter and a great man. Always she wrote what she experienced. She wrote what she lived. And by the time of her death in 1934,

> I realize that practically all my books...come out of the arc of the Earth Horizon from which, for me, 'all its people and its thoughts' come to me. That is why my books have no sequence other than the continuity of the search for the norm of moral and spiritual adjustments which I have tried herein to describe. They take their rise in the deep blue ring of the encompassing horizon.[102]

In 1950 a reprint of Austin's first book *The Land of Little Rain* was published; this edition included photographs taken by the landscape photographer Ansel Adams, who had worked with

Austin in Santa Fe, and an introduction by Carl Van Doren, who wrote there was a greatness in her. By 1950 the critic's opinions on the writer and her craft had shifted since his first critical essay on Austin's work. When working with living writers, after all, Van Doren had stressed that one was dealing with "shifting materials." Criticism is not static. Where he had once described her work as lacking in a "surer science," he later found that Austin "invested the land with magic, and yet looked at it with level eyes, relying upon history and science in her descriptions of her desert and celebrating its human nature with an eloquence which was also analytical." Van Doren wrote an homage to the writer who was both poet and prophet.

> Readers who now, wherever they live, discover or rediscover her, will find in this selection from her work the records of a woman who in our age left the rough temporary frontier which was a large part of America, went into the venerable desert, put her heart to the ground, heard men walking and gods breathing, mastered herself by generous surrender to the earth and sky, and came back to the world of muddy tumult with clear eyes. [103]

Through her poetry and prose, Mary Hunter Austin created an imagery of the American Southwest which helped to stir a national imagination of that desert landscape. When Elizabeth Marion visited the California desert in the spring of 1947 and wrote of her longing to go back and pitch a hermit tent, Van Doren replied that he was "homesick for that desert, with the neighboring hogans and smoke signals between them." Van Doren never spent any real time in the American Southwest, and yet that place lived for him. *Is it alive?* Yes, Mary Austin's prose had made it so. In *The Land of Little Rain*, she wrote:

> East away from the Sierra, south from Panamint and Amargosa, east and south many an uncounted mile, is the Country of Lost Borders...There are hills, rounded, blunt, burned, squeezed up out of chaos, chrome and vermilion painted, aspiring to the snow-line. Between the hills lie high level-looking plains full of intolerable sun glare, or narrow valleys drowned in blue haze. The hill surface is streaked with ash drift and black, unweathered lava flows. After rains water accumulates in the hollows of small closed valleys, and, evaporating, leaves hard dry levels of pure desertness that get the local name of dry lakes. Where the mountains are steep and the rains heavy, the pool is never quite dry, but dark and bitter, rimmed about with the efflorescence of alkaline deposits. A thin crust of it lies along the marsh over the vegetating area, which has neither beauty nor freshness. In the broad wastes open to the wind the sand drifts in hummocks about the stubby shrubs, and between them the soil shows saline traces.[104]

CHAPTER 5

THE ROVING CRITIC

Van Doren wrote prolifically across the 1920s, when he not only published essays in *The Nation* and *Century* as literary editor, but also wrote for publications like *Atlantic Monthly*, the *Literary Review*, the *Texas Review*, and *Bookman*. His book *The Roving Critic* was published in 1923, comprised of essays he had written over the year, followed by *Many Minds; Critical Essays on American Writers* in 1924. In his essay "The Revenge of the Bards," Van Doren pondered who, exactly, gets remembered throughout history. His conclusion: primarily the kings and the politicians. We remember those who are spoken of and written about in their day. But every profession, over time, forgets those who once shone so brightly among the guilds, everyone, that is, except for men of letters. Van Doren wrote, "Only of the men of letters—bards and biographers—is it the trade as well as the delight to keep the old reputations burning."[105]

In his essay "Creative Reading" the critic wrote the process of creative reading was essentially the same as the process of creative writing. One must strive to be an active reader, engaged with the book before him. Just as the "man of action" associates with other active people, so to the "man of contemplation" must associate with others who enjoy the printed word. Book people unite! The creative reader was not passive, instead he "challenges, disputes, denies, fights his way through his book and he emerges to some extent always another person." *So go ahead, Reader,* mark up the book with your pen or pencil, write yourself notes in the margins, talk back to the text as you read it. Van Doren entreated the creative reader to rejoice in "shaping his own designs and make his own conclusions." Van Doren advised his readers not simply to read what the critic—he, or any other—said you should read. Engage with the new and find your own message there.[106]

In "The Silver Age of Our Literature," Van Doren wrote the current state of literature had most certainly devolved from the Silver Age, which he dated to the years 1870-1910. Perhaps not surprisingly, those years marked Van Doren's childhood and formative years; this was the stuff on which he was raised. Since 1910, the rise in "proletarian vulgarity," the vagaries of public taste, a preference for more "violent stimulants" as well as a "sharper critical temper" were joining forces to overthrow the reigning canon of literature that had filled the nation's literary magazines for decades. Whatever the exact cause, Van Doren noted his distress at having witnessed the end of an epoch. For him, the masters were Whitman, Twain, Emerson, Thoreau, James, and Santayana, men who wrote during an age in which "scholarship grew to Alexandrian proportions." Pondering public perceptions of *the past*, Van Doren believed that most Americans tended toward vague images of the past when they thought of it at all, surmising "the vaguest images will do for most people." And yet, the writer argued, we very much need to understand the past. As modern humans, we rely less on instinct and mostly on memories and reason and, therefore, "a knowledge of history and literature is indispensable in affairs."[107]

In *Many Minds*, Van Doren amused himself with—and hoped he would intrigue his readers by—a critical essay on his own work as a writer. In "The Friendly Enemy," Van Doren wrote about himself in the third person, studying his work in much the same manner that he studied the work of other writers. Describing "Mr. Van Doren" as less a critic than historian, he wrote, "Without being clever or notably astute, Carl Van Doren has always been lucky." He wrote that Carl Van Doren was not interested in the academics of literary criticism, he was a historian not interested in "method" or quasi-scientific ideas about literature, but in *human character.*

Being so occupied with history, that is, with things already done, Mr. Van Doren has almost no interest in the metaphysics of criticism...He undertakes only plain jobs with definite materials. He sets forth the patterns which he believes he has found...Criticism has never been with him a major aim. What really interests him is human character, whether met in books or out of them, and it is always human character he studies. He insists that his usefulness, if he has any, must be based upon the opportunity which he affords for unprofessional readers, with his professional help, to make up their own minds about the authors whom he interprets. [108]

Here, Van Doren admitted that he was writing for a lay audience. An educated audience, to be sure, but he was not writing for "professional readers" or academics. When Van Doren was elected to the National Institute of Arts and Letters in 1924, the same year that *Many Minds* came out, the historian/biographer was unmoved. He didn't feel the Institute had any weight to it and did not especially care whether he was a part of that society or not. In classic Van Doren style, he graciously declined the offer. He would rather be on the outside, with the outspoken Mencken or the controversial Dreiser, than on the inside, suffocating under the weight of dead tradition. Van Doren recalled, "I knew I had no business in any academy which ranked professors above poets." He had earned his Ph.D. at Columbia and continued to teach a graduate seminar there, yet the scholar was not interested in belonging to any learned societies or academies. Of academic writers, he lamented, "thousands of dull men have written millions of true things which no one but their proof-readers, wives, or pupils ever read." The good writer, Van Doren insisted, must be scrupulous and he must be honest.[109]

> His truth must have a tone, his speech must have a rhythm which are his and solely his. His knowledge or opinions must have lain long enough inside him to have taken root there; and when they come away they must bring some of the soil clinging to them.[110]

He loved the tradition of the old masters and determined the height of American literature to already be several decades passed. Yet he made his living writing about the new moderns, and was adamant about publishing the works of those writers who were relegated to the outside by more conservative magazines. He was unapologetically antireligious, and in an essay entitled "Why I am an Unbeliever" explained that by "unbeliever," he meant that he was not simply no Mormon, Methodist, Christian or Buddhist, but that fundamentally he did not believe in any god or any doctrine yet devised, revealed, or expounded upon. And yet he titled one of his essays "On Reading for Delight as the Lord Intended," in which he said that he liked to read books, and write about those books, but did not like people who liked to read books simply because they thought they ought to like them. These apparent dualities do not have to be easily reconciled, and to attempt to do so, in any sort of quasi-scientific analysis, would surely do an injustice to any man. We are more complicated than that.

In the summer of 1923, Van Doren wrote an essay on the work of his friend and fellow literary critic Stuart Sherman. For most of his career, Sherman had been a strong supporter of conservative standards in English and American literature. He was no fan of the more radical voices of H.L. Mencken or Theodore Dreiser, for example, and publicly maligned the two writers as *pro-German* during the Great War. In an essay for the *Century,* "The Great and Good Tradition; Stuart P. Sherman: Scourge of Sophomores," Van Doren wrote that Sherman was the one man who successfully bridged the lamentable gap between creative writers and academics. While scholars spent their time engaged in "antiquarian research," rarely acknowledging the good writing being done in the present moment, creative writers generally did not know or care about those kinds of learning which added weight and historical context to the work of great literature. Van Doren conceded, "Doubtless there is no cure for this division."

Happily, Stuart Sherman was the one academic who did not fit the typical model. A professor of literature who was not dull, a critic who understood the contemporary issues of the day, Sherman was a poet and a wit. Van Doren wrote, "If he has slain Theodore

Dreiser with a violent right hand, he has with a gentler left given the accolade to Sinclair Lewis...Even H.L. Mencken, his principal antagonist, pays Mr. Sherman frequent tributes for his style and for his power." No worthy criticism can be entirely amiable, however, and Van Doren swiftly switched gears to charge Sherman with sometimes being an outright *nag*. He wrote that Sherman was too harsh a critic of the new generation. He alluded to a streak of nativism in Sherman's leanings, suggesting the scholar/writer was too conservative in his sentiments. Van Doren insinuated that Sherman had flip-flopped his views on major issues, such as democracy, war, and "the problems of economic life." He wrote that only a few years before, Sherman "distrusted democracy with his favorite teacher, Paul Elmer More; now he upholds that mode of government at all hours." Van Doren insisted that "certain of his former readers have given up hope... certain of his more loyal readers, despite the snubs they have suffered from him, still hold to the belief that he will some day integrate his instinct and his reason and will become the voice and guide which his capacities could make him."[111]

In addition to this essay in the *Century*, Van Doren penned another Sherman-focused criticism earlier that spring as the anonymous critic for the literary journal *Bookman*. Sherman had been unaware that Van Doren was in fact the anonymous critic for *Bookman* until several weeks after he first read the piece. Once he had discovered the critic's identity, the writer immediately composed a response to what he felt were wholly unjust critiques, addressing his response not to the editor of the *Century*, but to his good friend Carl Van Doren. He was not at all pleased, and found the main substance of Van Doren's article to be "fairly unsound," something he might expect from the critic Burton Rascoe, but not from Van Doren's usual sure touch (In a later series of articles for *The Nation* entitled "Our Critics," the famously shrewd writer Mary McCarthy named Burton Rascoe as the "pace-setter" of the amiable, anti-intellectual set which wrote only ebullient and undisciplined—never critical—reviews. As such, this was not company Carl Van Doren would care to be placed alongside).

Sherman charged the essay was "seriously misrepresentative" of his actual sentiments and opinions. He stated emphatically that he had never followed More "in his raids on the democratic spirit," had never uttered a word in print on the problems of economic life. He wanted to know who, exactly, he was accused of snubbing, and scoffed, "And what you can have in mind by that last paragraph beats me." Sherman closed the letter by saying that he was not writing this to the editor of the *Century*, as he couldn't care less what this or any other editor may think of him or his work. He was, however, writing to his old friend Carl Van Doren, and wondered if the friend could possibly believe what the editor had written. He signed off, "Yours as ever, Stuart."

This professional disagreement did not end the writers' friendship. (If the Enlightenment and Age of Reason taught us anything, it taught us to trust in reasoned discussion and believe that reasonable people could understand each other even if they did not agree). The next year, when Sherman moved his family from Illinois to New York City to head up the newly formed *New York Herald-Tribune Sunday Review of Books*, he stayed with Carl and Irita for several weeks while his apartment was being readied. Sherman had accepted the position under the explicit condition that he be allowed an assistant, and the assistant he insisted upon was Irita Van Doren.

Irita had been brought on board *The Nation* in 1920 as literary editor and occasionally wrote book reviews for the magazine, and Sherman admired her sharp editorial instincts. From *Books'* debut in 1924, Sherman manned the helm as editor, with Irita Van Doren a close second-in-command as editorial assistant. Sherman's biographers Zeitlin and Woodbridge later wrote that "there was something more than cordial harmony" between Sherman and Irita. It is clear that Sherman held great admiration for Irita's editorial competence, her southern charm, and her critical judgment. Listening to the soft rain falling on the green mountains of Vermont during a summer vacation in 1925, Sherman wrote to Irita of his immense gratitude for her companionship in getting *Books* off the ground. He found her "in all respects so superior: so wise, so generous, so sympathetic, so independent, so invariably and unfailingly equal to every occasion, so unerringly right.. so swift, tenacious, and firm, so full of courage, and hope, and kindness, and joy..." With Irita by his side, Sherman looked forward to another successful year of *Books*, certain that they could do more good work. Why couldn't they go even further? "Growing in grace and favor with gods and men. Let's!" Sherman told Irita that *she* didn't need any encouragement or inspiration, she *was* it.[112]

Writers can be effusive. After all, the writer works in the domain of the written word; these are his daily tools, his familiar companions, his joy. Sometimes there is much to be found between the lines, but not necessarily. Carl Van Doren once wrote, "Talking and writing are such different matters that I have often thought they should not both have to use words and so appear to be the same thing." It is a distinction worth pondering. The following summer, while Sherman was in Colorado Springs for a summer teaching assignment, he wrote near constantly to Irita, who was holding down the fort at *Books* before taking off for her own summer holiday at Cornwall. Sherman wrote playfully to his second-in-command, "Medusa! Write me a line!...Two weeks elapse to-day since we left, and not a word." He worried that Irita may have already left for the country, that his letters might sit un-opened and un-read while she soaked up the summer sun in Cornwall.

Are you in Cornwall by now? Have the rough edges of your throat worn smooth? Have you put on five pounds, like a properly recuperating 'little whale'? ... Are you beginning to regain that look of the wild rose which you brought back from weekends in the fall of 1924?—There is a nice little row of questions to which I know not the answer. The only point of which I am sure is that <u>you are not wasting any of your vacation in</u> writing letters to the person who undoubtedly would more fully appreciate one than any one else of your acquaintances.

Be a good girl and write at least once, as you promised. If it is any inducement, I will even promise <u>not</u> to write in reply.—xx ...But you had better send a line just the same. It would be a nice thing to do. Love to you all, Stuart [113]

Irita's two brief notes—bringing an end to the silence from New York—brought no end of joy to the editor upon his mountaintop. From the slopes of Pike's Peak, Sherman picked some forget-me-nots and enclosed the pressed flowers in his next letter. He wrote that he was thinking of Irita on the mountainside, wishing she were there to see the snow-capped peaks, the floating white clouds, and the purple mountains of the Continental Divide. Following the teaching stint in Colorado, Sherman and his wife made a brief visit to the wooded shores of Lake Michigan. Amid a flurry of shop-talk regarding the next issue of *Books*, Stuart wrote to Irita that he planned to be back in New York by the 24th of August. He had hoped to return sooner, but his "manager"—that is, his wife—had decided upon the later return date. He assured

Irita that he would try to make it up to her—his delay, that is—in some other way.[114]

Stuart Sherman, one of the leading generalists in the field of literary criticism, died just a few days later. The forty-four year old went swimming in Lake Michigan and suffered a fatal heart attack; a shocking end to a summer of daydreams and a lifetime of literary study. With Sherman's sudden passing, Irita Van Doren was promoted from her rank as assistant editor to managing editor of *Books*, and held that coveted and highly influential position until she retired in 1963.

CHAPTER 6

BIOGRAPHER ON THE TRAIL

The close of the 1920s brought with it an economic depression unlike anything the nation had ever seen. It was also a time of a troubling, personal depression for Carl Van Doren. Six months before the stock market crash of October 1929, Van Doren entered his own private depression. Of the reasons for this downturn in spirits, Van Doren alluded to several factors, all of them vague. He indicated in his autobiography that "private passions and treasons wounded me." He did not elaborate on this, did not indicate *whose* private passions or treasons wounded him. It had to be something very close, something emotionally devastating to crash through that Middle Western brand of stoicism. In addition to those private betrayals, Van Doren had become weary of the constant parties, the drinkers and their speakeasies, the "counterfeit high spirits." He saw "noisy sterility" on all sides. And then one day, when his general irritation became something more oppressive, he "found a penthouse and turned hermit."

Sometime in 1929, Carl and Irita separated. Irita and the couple's three young daughters, Anne (born in 1915), Margaret (born in 1917), and Barbara (born in 1920), were still living at the family's home on West 11th Street, while Carl relocated to a small apartment in a larger building not far away on West 13th Street. Whatever the reasons for his depression, his irritation, his need for solitude, Van Doren needed "to understand myself and my life. I felt nothing clearly but a strong instinct to rid myself of tangible bondages." He gave up his graduate seminar at Columbia after fourteen years, he sold many of his books from his personal library, he stopped visiting the family home at Cornwall. Adrift, "the hours of the day ceased to matter."[115]

In 1925 Van Doren had left the *Century* in order *to write*. As an editor and literary critic, yes, he was certainly and by all accounts a professional writer. But in 1925 the critic resolved to leave editing and begin work on his own, original material. That year he published *Other Provinces*, a compilation of original sketches and short stories; the following year his novel, *The Ninth Wave*, was published. While the books received some critical acclaim, neither was a commercial success by any measure. He had known, many years back, that he did not have what it took to be a poet. Van Doren now fretted that he didn't have what it took to be a writer in his own right. When he was offered editorship of The Literary Guild of America, a monthly mail-order book club, he accepted. However, he was admittedly disappointed to "still be a critic."[116]

The fact of the matter was there: writers do not get paid to write books that don't sell, and the boom years of the 1920s, with a constant stream of new books emanating from the Younger Generation, ensured a busy workload at The Literary Guild and a steady paycheck. The pace was hectic. Long days at the office were followed by evenings at one of the many Village speakeasies for dinner or cocktails. While Van Doren was never much of a drinker—in fact he found drinkers quite simply *boring*—speak-easies were the "essences and centers of those hectic times" and where life happened after the work day was through.[117]

Monthly mail-order book clubs like The Literary Guild of America amounted to big business. The Literary Guild was founded in 1921, with the Book-of-the-Month Club soon following in 1926. Harry Scherman, a New York City advertising exec-utive, founded BOTM with his good friend Charles Boni. (Boni, incidentally, had married Irita Van Doren's sister, Margaret). One of the Boni brothers' early ventures was the Little Leather Library Corporation, a merchandising scheme in which a tiny leather-bound book was included in every box of Whitman's chocolate samplers. By 1920 the Little Leather Library Corp. had sold over twenty-five million tiny books, primarily through mail order. The Scherman-Boni team leveraged this marketing know-how into a new bookselling strategy.

While books had been available via mail order before, the Book-of-the-Month Club was an entirely new endeavor. Customers now became *subscribers,* who agreed to purchase one book every month for the length of the subscription. The books were selected by a panel of *experts,* literary critics and editors, who chose *the best books* for an eager audience. The book clubs were heavily advertised in newspapers and magazines. Ads for Book-of-the-Month Club and the Literary Guild, for example, featured photographs of their expert judges and listed their credentials. BOTM Club's panel of experts included Henry S. Canby, Dorothy Canfield Fisher, Christopher Morley, Heywood Broun, and William Allen White. The Literary Guild's experts were Carl Van Doren, Hendrik Willem Van Loon, Burton Rascoe, Zona Gale, and Joseph Wood Krutch. The Readers Club, which would come in 1941, boasted Carl Van Doren, Sinclair Lewis, Alexander Woolcott, and Clifton Fadiman as its editors and expert critics of "the best already-published books." The Literary Guild's advertisements boasted that American readers *preferred* the sorts of books its experts selected, enticing would-be subscribers, "You want to read and own *the best.*"

The mounting assemblage of monthly book clubs attracted a good deal of pushback and criticism from the publishing community. In 1929 the American Booksellers Association denounced the BOTM Club and the Literary Guild, arguing it was impossible to label any one book "the best book of the month." How exactly did one, even if one was an expert, make such a definitive designation? And what were the bases for choosing *the best* books? What exactly was the scoring mechanism?

Much of the criticism from the publishing houses and booksellers appears to have been financially motivated. Book sales were certainly skewed by the book clubs' selections and the widespread promotion of these selections; the not-chosen books perhaps suffered in greater obscurity than if there had been a level playing field. The book clubs heavily advertised and marketed their selections, and for new or struggling authors who never achieved the coveted distinction, a deficit in marketing and publicity could be deadly. Publisher Frederick A. Stokes denounced the book clubs by arguing a few chosen authors were helped, but the rest found it increasingly difficult to find any audience whatsoever. Instead of the book clubs' expert panels of judges, Stokes argued that librarians, local booksellers, and literary journals would provide better reading advice. Indeed, Stokes demanded, "Why should there be book clubs at all?"[118]

The criticism, however, was not merely financially based. The more highbrow criticism came from those in the literary community who attacked the book clubs as encouraging a standardization and homogenization of culture. Dr. Edward Stevens, head of the Pratt Institute Free Library, wailed that these mail-order clubs amounted to the "emasculation" of the human mind. Stevens was appalled by the certain "disastrous" effects these book clubs would have on individual choice and deterministic thinking. Instead, one should enjoy the power to choose one's own books. The Secretary of the American Library Institute went even further, admonishing the mental laziness and intellectual confusion which resulted from the public's increasing reliance on "best" lists. This was a travesty, a stunting of the public's intellectual curiosity.

> From this date forward we shall offer none of our publications to the Book-of-the-Month Club, The Literary Guild, and all other similar organizations, except when our authors insist upon it.—Publisher Frederick Stokes (1929)

One writer who was a vocal opponent to any and all monthly book clubs was Edmund Wilson. Wilson was a prolific writer and critic. He was an editor at *Vanity Fair*, wrote for *The New Republic* and the *New Yorker*, and was the author of novels, short stories, and several volumes of literary criticism. He was married four times, most famously to the writer Mary McCarthy. Wilson, the writer *and* the man, was ubiquitous. He was no fan of the monthly book clubs nor of many of his fellow editors and critics. He was also no fan of Carl Van Doren's specifically nor of the Van Doren literary dynasty generally, which by now, in addition to Carl, included Carl's wife Irita, who edited the *New York Herald-Tribune Review of Books*; Mark Van Doren, professor at Columbia, poet, and *The Nation's* poetry critic; and Mark's wife Dorothy Graffe Van Doren, author of many books of fiction, book reviews, and personal recollections which often appeared in *The Nation*. In a review disguised as a letter to Elinor Wylie about her own work, Wilson wrote that Mr. Van Doren, "like the sun of tropical latitudes, which sheds its warmth all the year around, diffuses his mild benignance upon the excellent and the unworthy alike, till, by its uniformity, it causes us to long for the asperities of more inclement climates."[119]

Wilson lampooned both Carl and Mark Van Doren, in addition to other well-known literary critics, in a satirical piece he wrote for *The New Republic* entitled "The Fable of the Three Limperary Cripples." The 1930 piece poked fun at a group of not-so-fictional literary editors of the "Book-of-the-Lunch Club," whom Wilson alternately dubbed Carl van Doorman, Carl van Gorham, and Cardboard S. Boreman. Wilson's fictitious book club selected from titles such as *Black Majesty*, by Dark van Moron; *The Life of Joseph Wood Peacock*, by Doc van Doren; and *A Farewell to Farms*, by Mark van Dorman. Later, in his 1942 book *Memoirs of Hecate County*, Wilson devoted an entire chapter to "The Milhollands and Their Damned Soul." The piece was a snarky commentary on the world of book clubs and the fictitious Millholland brothers, who had sold their souls to the devil in exchange for publishing success. According to Wilson's biographer Lewis Dabney, The Milhollands grew out of Wilson's annoyance and overall criticism of the Van Doren family, and what he perceived to be "sunny salesmanship" in lieu of true literary standards.[ix]

Whatever his personal motivations and deepest feelings about the Van Dorens, Edmund Wilson was of that vocal faction which heartily derided the monthly book clubs. Whether these detractors cited financial or ideological opposition to the expanding literary marketplace, the pushback was real. We who live in the age of Amazon and Powell's and myriad online booksellers might easily scoff at this book club-based hysteria. In actuality, the book clubs' monthly newsletters delivered to subscribers included many book reviews on a range of new books. Rather than restricting the market, all of this talking and writing about books might have

....

ix   As to what, exactly, Edmund Wilson found so reprehensible about the monthly book clubs, we can look to an excerpt from "The Milhollands," in which the chapter's narrator argues that once the book clubs "begin recommending the second-rate—let alone the third-rate and the forth-rate, as the Readers' Circle sometimes does—you're not gradually educating people, as Warren claims he is...you're simply letting down the standards and leaving people completely at sea. The most immoral and disgraceful and dangerous thing that anybody can do in the arts is knowingly to feed back to the public its own ignorance and cheap tastes..." Wilson wasn't the only critic. Ezra Pound had been a visiting critic at *H-T Books*, under Irita Van Doren's editorship, until the writer resigned in a fury in 1931. Pound lambasted Irita in a letter dated Dec. 14, 1931: "You know perfectly well that I consider BOOKS like every other god damn American advertising medium, IS engaged in retarding the entrance into America of any and every live thought...You are NOT as stupid as the groveling bugs on some of the other papers, and for that reason you are all the more RESPONSIBLE for the impossibility of keeping in touch with what is BEING thought."

resulted in an expanded market. Contrary to some arguments, members were not forced to buy the monthly selection; they could substitute it with one of the many other reviewed books. It can't be denied, however, that for the lucky author whose book was chosen, upward of 50,000 copies were sold instantly and mailed out to club members. That was a windfall for most authors, who would otherwise never see such sales. In other words, if an author's book was selected as the book-of-the-month, the financial rewards, and the publicity, were unbeatable. *If.*

The rise in mail order book clubs across the 1930s, and the ubiquity of literary journals and book review sections of the big newspapers, garnered a larger critique against the literary critics themselves, namely that literary criticism had devolved into nothing more than salesmanship. In a series of articles for *The Nation* in the fall of 1935, writers Mary McCarthy and Margaret Marshall blasted practically everyone in the trade for their anti-intellectualism, salesmanship, and overall uncritical amiability. McCarthy and Marshall (although it was really just McCarthy writing the pieces; the senior writer, Marshall, had been assigned to the task in an effort to rein-in, or at least keep an eye on, McCarthy and her frankness). McCarthy called out everyone from Henry S. Canby to Burton Rascoe to Clifton Fadiman to William Rose Benét for their collective descent into intellectual laziness. She railed that Canby "attempts no real criticism...He is like an old gentleman wandering down a strange street..."; Rascoe "deals in ready-made superlatives," hugely influential yet exceedingly anti-intellectual; and Benét, "a little slow on the uptake." All of the critics, McCarthy charged, knew a good book when they saw it, but had real trouble identifying a bad one. And what accounted for this state of uncritical criticism? The book clubs. "The tony critics as well as the hack book reviewers" were all in bed with the literary magazines and the book clubs, with a bottom line of increasing sales. McCarthy called Carl Van Doren "an important and serious critic" who intellectually out-ranked the rest of the crowd, but charged that his own critical writing suffered under his editorship at the Literary Guild. According to McCarthy and those in her camp, criticism and salesmanship were not good bedfellows.[120]

By the close of the '20s, Van Doren had recovered from the meager reception of his last two books and had returned to editing at the Literary Guild full-time. In 1930 he published a biography on Jonathan Swift, the Irish author best known for his book *Gulliver's Travels*. This book, *The Portable Swift*, put Van Doren back in the mode of biographer. Not since his doctoral dissertation on Peacock had he written a full-length biographical study. He revealed, "A biographer looks into his heart as a poet does." Perhaps during his separation and the slow breakup of his marriage, Van Doren's soul needed tending, now more than ever. Scholar by training, Van Doren lost himself in the research process.

Poring through original manuscripts, tracking down records left not only by the subject of his study but those who knew him well, scanning the historical record for clues: this is the work of the historian, this is the fun stuff for the biographer on the trail. In an article he later wrote for *Good Housekeeping,* Van Doren described the hunting expedition known as biographical research, acknowledging "A great man moving through public affairs leaves far more traces of himself than we usually imagine. The problem is less how to find material enough than how to put it in order and how to reconcile contradictions in the evidence." Heartily inspired and pleased to be back in the mode of biographer, Van Doren moved from *Swift* to his *Biographical Sketch* of Sinclair Lewis, and in a few years left The Literary Guild to devote himself solely to writing full-time.[121]

In late 1932, during the tail end of the Hoover presidency and the country's bottomless sense of despair and collapse, Van Doren set out on a seven-week lecture tour across the U.S.. He enjoyed the unexpected little things that would happen along any lecture circuit: the variety of entertainments planned for him in cities along the way, catching up with old colleagues or former students, dining with friends he hadn't seen in years. The tour ended in southern California, and all those clichés about the sun and fun and promise of Los Angeles did not disappoint. Van Doren heartily enjoyed himself in southern California, which "swarmed with cousins." He swam in the Pacific Ocean, picnicked in the mountains, spent one night in the desert beyond Palm Springs (Mary Austin territory, and the future site of Elizabeth Marion's wistful desert hermitage). Hollywood proved to be an antitoxin against the spiritual malaise that had plagued him; he found Tinsel Town to be "a good deal like nature… a good deal like human society." At the age of forty-seven, the long ache of his depression lifted.

Jean Wright Gorman, who had introduced Van Doren to Broadway in New York, was now his "chief guide" in Hollywood. After the California vacation, Van Doren felt a subtle, internal shift, in which his life—if not better—had become bigger. Emerging from his own personal depression in the midst of a national one, Van Doren reflected as only a historian might, finding solace and strength in the very *Americanism* of his situation. "After years of prosperity I had felt myself a failure, stopped, disintegrated, insecure…[But] this was America, where thousands of men had come out of similar defeats as a matter of course. I did not know how to doubt that I would emerge and survive. Perhaps it was not mere traditional optimism. Perhaps it was national stamina. I was part of America."[122]

Although Van Doren's personal depression lifted during his time in Southern California, the country was still deep in the grip of the Great Depression, which would fester and demoralize millions of Americans like a contagion across the 1930s. In his essays from this period, Van Doren wrote that where the literature of the 1920s had been primarily concerned with individual freedoms, the literature of the '30s questioned how individuals could come together in any common effort to survive. The '30s was not a time to shout for freedom, it was a time to seek individual and collective modes of survival. Unrest existed everywhere. Van Doren wrote, "Americans, who had always looked forward, would often look back to the golden age of prosperity... It would affect the whole national character. When the past is heavier upon them, their pace is dogged at best. They run onward only when the future pulls, promising them that whatever has happened can happen again, and more."[123]

Van Doren discarded his plans to do another book on American literature. Instead, he would stick to literary reviews, complete his *Anthology of World Prose*, which had been long in the making, and write his autobiography. He lived like a hermit during these years, seeing hardly a soul outside of family. He worked slowly but surely on his autobiography, envying "the sons of bitches who can write fast." He spent weeks at a time visiting his parents and brother Frank in Urbana, making the trek up to Michigan to visit brother Guy when travel permitted. When his father passed away from liver cancer in the fall of 1933, Carl and his brothers pulled together to square away their parents' financial arrangements.[124]

A private man, Van Doren confided only in his closest brother Mark that a divorce from Irita was likely. During the several weeks he spent with his mother during Christmas of 1935, Van Doren gave no indication of personal or marital discord. That stoic Dutch indifference prevailed, and his family would not notice the emotional strain Van Doren was under. It was only after Irita filed for divorce in Reno, and the divorce was granted in February of 1936, that Van Doren finally broke the news to his mother. Divorce might have been a regrettable but understandable fact of life among the New York modernists, but in the Middle West in 1936, this was alarming news. Dora Van Doren would try not to be too unhappy about the divorce and certainly would not reproach her eldest son, although the announcement came as a great shock. His brothers, too, were sorry to see the breakup of the marriage. Irita had filed the claim for divorce under terms of desertion, although with few legal routes to choose from, it was likely the simplest way out.

Indeed, the couple's divorce had been a long time coming, as Carl and Irita had been living apart since 1929. By now, Irita Van Doren had become a leading literary influence in her own right, apart from her status as Mrs. Carl Van Doren. She had been named editor of the *New York Herald-Tribune Review of Books* in 1926. The biographical dictionary *Notable American Women: The Modern Period* describes Irita as one of the reigning cultural influencers of the country, with booksellers across the country closely following *Books'* reviews and stocking their shelves accordingly. Unlike her predecessor Stuart Sherman, Irita never actually wrote reviews or essays for *Books*. She freely admitted she was no writer. Instead, she relied upon her appreciation for literary aesthetics and hired visiting writers to serve as temporary lead critics, bringing on board leading names like Virginia Woolf, Rebecca West, Ford Maddox Ford, and E.M. Forester. Irita was widely known for her southern charm, and those who met her generally admired her, both personally and professionally. Urbanist and essayist Lewis Mumford once told her, "I don't know whether it's your natural Southern sweetness, or my professional respect for your skill as an editor, but I find you very hard to resist, and have almost given up trying to." She charmed practically everyone who knew her.[125]

After her divorce from Van Doren, Irita became romantically linked to businessman-turned-Republican presidential nominee Wendell Wilkie. Irita met Wilkie when he was invited to speak at the *Herald Tribune* Forum in 1937, while she was editor at *H-T's Books*. For the next several years, the pair lived and travelled together and attended the parties of New York literati together. In spite of his status as a married man (there was a Mrs. Wilkie: Edith), Wilkie was a known ladies' man and had alleged affairs with secretaries, writers, movie stars. He was not particularly interested in maintaining a veil of discretion; Wilkie once held a press conference—rather boldly—from Irita's New York City apartment. The message implicit in such a blatant presentation of intimacy did not go unnoticed, but the romantic affairs of a presidential candidate was not necessarily news-worthy information to the press, which in 1940 tended not to delve into the personal lives of political figures, however much they knew. Wilkie and Irita's relationship was not particularly scandalous, as it might have been in another era. But as the Republican National Convention of 1940 approached, President Franklin Delano Roosevelt, incumbent on the Democratic ticket, encouraged his staff to leak word of the affair, saying "[We] can't have any of our principal speakers refer to [the affair] but the people down the line can get it out... actually she's a nice gal but there is the fact."[126]

The affair was in fact not leaked to the larger public, and since Wilkie lost the election to FDR, was never used as fodder for any political or societal intrigue.[x] There was never any official scandal. After losing the election, Wilkie set to work writing *One World*, which Irita edited. His second bid for the White House in 1943 was even less successful; he did not receive his party's nomination the second time around. The year was not a good one for Wilkie, and after a series of heart attacks, he died in 1944. Carl sent his ex-wife a note of condolence following Wilkie's death,

....

x   A series of events put the Republican and Democratic parties in a sort of scandal-avoiding détente during the 1940 presidential election. The matter concerned Wilkie's (R) affair with Irita, and a trove of potentially embarrassing letters between Vice President Henry Wallace (D) and his eastern "guru." The Democrats agreed not to leak word of the Wilkie-Van Doren affair if the Republicans would agree not to leak word of the Vice President's unflattering, and potentially alarming, letters to his guru.

remarking that the "rare personal bond" between Wendell and Irita was palpable and acknowledging that Wilkie, a great man in his own right, was greater still for having had the privilege of knowing her. Irita continued to influence the nation's literary landscape for decades to come, as editor of *Books* and later as literary consultant at William Morrow & Company. She hosted the very popular and successful literary series, *The Book and Author Luncheon*, created in 1938 by the American Booksellers Association. From 1938 until her retirement from *Books* in 1963, she hosted the book forum with authors known and unknown, and the program quickly became a staple of the New York literary world and a standard component of WNYC radio's weekly lineup.

Van Doren used these introspective years to write his autobiography. He spent several months at a time with his parents in Urbana across 1935 and 1936. It might seem curious that a man of only fifty years would choose this age at which to write his memoirs, although Van Doren had, by this time, spent twenty years critiquing the work of other authors. It was time to write his own story. Dividing the book into three worlds: *Pre-War*, *Post-War*, and *New World?*, Van Doren recalled his childhood in Hope; his education at Urbana and Columbia; and his career in literary criticism, which expanded into his essays and perceptions on the whole of American culture.

He wrote about the restlessness of the 1920s, a decade decorated and flavored by that rebellious generation that wanted... what, exactly? Van Doren looked deep into the collective psyche of his generation and proposed: "Ask the romantic Younger Generation what it demanded and it answered: to be free. Ask it free for what, and it did not answer, but drove faster, drank more, made love oftener." The frenetic pace and high feelings of the '20s could not last, however, and by the 1930s, Van Doren described a nation in a profound state of unrest. Unrest everywhere.

His autobiography, which he titled *Three Worlds* and published in 1936, commented on the America he saw as intellectual, critic, and flaneur:

> Americans, who had always looked forward, would often look back to the golden age of prosperity which had built such cathedrals and universities and museums and railway stations and office buildings, such roads and bridges, such institutes and endowments, as could perhaps no more be undertaken. It would affect the whole national character... When the past is heavier upon them, their pace is dogged at best. They run onward only when the future pulls, promising them that whatever has happened can happen again, and more.[127]

Re-entering the social scene from which he had retreated during his depression and separation, Van Doren could now be spotted out on the town among any number of literati who were enjoying the city's diversions from the nation's larger economic and societal woes. Van Doren enjoyed stopping in at the Breevort, a Village hotel and café built in 1845 and a favorite stop for writers, artists, and heads of state. There were parties to launch new books, invitations to dine with H. L. Mencken or James Thurber, and annual requests from Sinclair Lewis to make a summer visit. Critics and publishers such as William Saroyan, Edmund Wilson, Carl Van Vechten, Condé Nast, and Carl Van Doren might be found brushing elbows at the Irving Place Theater in nearby Union Square, where its star attraction, Gypsy Rose Lee, performed a strip-tease unlike any other.

Instead of simply removing her clothes (anyone could do that), Gypsy Rose Lee "swanned languidly across the stage." Her performance accentuated the *tease* over the *strip;* in fact she was once criticized by a fellow strip-teaser for deceiving the public. Rival June St. Clair complained to the press, *"Why, she doesn't even strip!"* Part of Gypsy's act involved telling stories about herself, and she always left more to the audience's imagination than she left behind on the stage.[xi] She was no bimbo; Gypsy Rose Lee was an avid reader, always fascinated by books (she once bought a

....

xi   CVD once wrote in a letter to Gypsy Rose Lee, "I wanted to point out how you are different from all the other strippers I have ever seen. Seeing them is something like getting a peep at a girl on a picnic. Perfectly ordinary experience. But to feel that you are seeing a princess take off her pants: That's something else again."

copy of the weighty *Das Kapital* because she figured it would give her plenty of reading time for her money) and she later became the author of two best-selling mysteries, a play, and her own memoir, which would go on to inspire the 1959 Broadway musical *Gypsy*. Van Doren and Gypsy Rose Lee became close enough friends (he was always attracted to an intelligent female mind) that in 1942 she asked him to be the best man at her second wedding. He accepted gladly.[128]

Following the publication of *Three Worlds*, Van Doren determined to write a book unlike anything he had written before: the seminal biography of Benjamin Franklin. Securing a book deal with Viking Press, Van Doren received a $3,000 advance on the project, the same deal he had secured with Harper's for *Three Worlds* and which, he informed Viking, Harper's had earned back immediately after publication (although sales of *Three Worlds*, after this initial surge, quickly dried to a faint trickle). The Biographer on the Trail travelled up and down the eastern seaboard, spending considerable time in Philadelphia at the American Philosophical Association, which Franklin founded in 1743 and had since become the repository of the Franklin Papers, as well as in the libraries of the Historical Society of Philadelphia and the University of Pennsylvania. He travelled to Boston, Franklin's birthplace, seeking materials stored in the recesses of the Massachusetts Historical Society and Harvard University. Documents and images located in the libraries at Yale and Cornell, the Frick Art Reference Center, and the New York Public Library demanded the training of a sleuth to exhaust every possibility of usable source material. It took "bravery and power" to sustain a biographer on his (or her) quest to map the historical landscape and gather critical morsels from the "underwoods" of the past. For two years, the work required almost daily use of the New York Public Library, its staff and collections.[129]

Looking beyond the critical events surrounding Franklin's work in diplomacy, science, and letters, Van Doren reveled in locating previously unpublished personal details, those tidbits of minutiae that "may seem small matters, but add lifelike touches to the biography." Franklin's own truncated autobiography, first published in 1791, was a starting point for Van Doren, who heartily admired "the only great American man of action who is known particularly as an autobiographer." Believing Franklin's own words absolutely critical to his biography, Van Doren would create a fuller narrative than Franklin had time to do himself when writing his memoirs.

Upon reading early chapters of the manuscript, Van Doren's editor at Viking was concerned that it perhaps contained too many direct quotes from Franklin's autobiography. The editor advised removing, or at least minimizing, any number of the generous passages afforded to Franklin's direct quotations. Van Doren, himself an editor for many years, could not have disagreed more. Certainly the passages in question should not be removed;

rather, everyone else who had read the manuscript had raved about the "amazing felicity and charm of his [Franklin's] words." Van Doren knew that Franklin's own words were critical to any honest and comprehensive account of the life of this "great man of action." Ever judicious, Van Doren allowed that he would consider the matter before the book went to print.[130]

The editor in Van Doren was neither rash nor impetuous, and he likely did take another look at the manuscript. Perhaps he simply took a second glimpse. But no, Franklin's words could not be cut, nor could the manuscript be edited down to a more "readable" length. Here, the biographer and the editor in Van Doren were in complete agreement, even if the result was a biography that ran to over 770 pages. The opening words of the book's preface prepare the reader: "This is a long book." Van Doren argued the book might well have run two or three times as long, as Franklin's life and the documentation thereof was extensive. The writer acknowledged, "It is also difficult, with the new facts at hand, not to let it run beyond a readable length. This book, full as it is, is a biography cut with hard labor to the bone."

This biography goes into detail because Franklin led a detailed life which in a general narrative loses colour and savour. But the chief aim of the book has been to restore Franklin, so often remembered piecemeal in this or that of his diverse aspects, his magnificent central unity as a great and wise man moving through great and troubling events. No effort has been made to cut his nature to fit any simple scheme of what a good man ought to be. Here, as truly as it has been possible to find out, is what Franklin did, said, thought, and felt. Perhaps these things may help to rescue him from the dry, prim people who have claimed him as one of them. They praise his thrift. But he himself admitted that he could never learn frugality, and he practiced it no longer than his poverty forced him to. They praise his prudence. But at seventy he became a leader of a revolution, and throughout his life he ran bold risks. They praise him for being a plain man. Hardly another man of affairs has ever been more devoted than Franklin to pleasant graces. The dry, prim people seem to regard him as a treasure shut up in a savings bank to which they have the lawful key. I herewith give him back, in his grand dimensions, to his nation and the world.[131]

The country's interest in Ben Franklin was unquenchable; a lecture tour at the end of 1937 brought standing-room only crowds, and the book had not even been published yet. Van Doren wrote to his editor, "Franklin has gone in this country as no other subject I have ever spoken on." *The Atlantic Monthly* and the *Saturday Evening Post* had already sought out serialization rights on early chapters of the book. Van Doren, however, held out in the hopes that Book-of-the-Month-Club would pick up the book. This would bring a sizable paycheck for the two years and nearly

$20,000 Van Doren figured he had spent in man-hours on the project. In the spring of 1938, Van Doren requested an additional $2,000 advance (or, if not an advance, an interest-bearing loan would also do) from Viking to see him through until the book's publication date. Viking happily sent the advance, eager to see its author freed from any serious financial worries so that he could finish the task of writing.[132]

In August, one month before Viking published the first edition of *Benjamin Franklin*, Book-of-the-Month Club offered Van Doren a contract for $14,000 to include the book as its monthly selection. This was a serious windfall for any writer, even one of Van Doren's reputation, in the lingering years of the Depression.[xii] When it was released in September, *Franklin* immediately garnered both critical acclaim and commercial success. and within a couple of months Van Doren was in talks with the famed playwright and screenwriter Sidney Howard to bring *Franklin* to the stage. Van Doren met Howard for dinner in New York City to discuss the possibility of a collaboration, wondering out loud how Franklin might be adapted to the stage. Howard was instantly on board, and an agreement was reached. The playwright was

....

xii   For some financial perspective: as literary editor at *Century* in 1922, CVD's annual salary was $5,000. For the first half of 1942, CVD's royalties on *Three Worlds* come in at a meager $6.49 from Harper's. In 1944 CVD earns $350 per program for his radio show, *American Scriptures*, $300 for *Words at War*. Throughout 1944-45 he earns $500 lecture fees on all out-of-town speaking engagements. $14,000 from Book-of-the-Month Club was serious money for a writer.

given exclusive rights to *Franklin* for six months; if no production contract was signed by March 1940, the agreement would be terminated. Looking ahead to a Broadway opening, all proceeds from ticket sales would be split fifty/fifty between Van Doren and Howard.

Howard, who had received the Pulitzer Prize in 1925 for his play *They Knew What They Wanted;* wrote the screen adaptation for Sinclair Lewis' novels *Arrowsmith* in 1932 and *Dodsworth* in 1934; and wrote the screenplay for *Gone With the Wind*, was widely regarded as the hottest screenwriter in Hollywood. But how, exactly, would he put words into the mouth of the great Ben Franklin? Howard shared his artistic trepidation with Van Doren, writing, "The thing that terrifies me the most is writing things for Franklin to say. The old boy combined immortal with dirt farmer simplicity and I am undertaking quite a contract."[133]

Between sales from regular retailers and the Book-of-the-Month Club, which generally guaranteed a subscription list of 50,000 sales, and the Broadway deal with Howard, Van Doren was absolutely giddy over *Franklin*'s success. By the following summer, Howard was busy writing the screenplay from his farm in Tyringham, Massachusetts and all was proceeding apace. In what can only be described as a freak accident, Sidney Howard was killed in August, 1939 when he was cranking the engine of a two-ton tractor. The tractor lurched forward, pinning Howard against the wall of the garage and crushing him to death. With the sudden death of a man still so relatively young, and with no one convinced that another playwright might finish the screenplay, Howard's unfinished draft hung in the balance. Sherwood Anderson's name came up as a possibility to finish the play, but any negotiations failed to reach a definitive conclusion. Meanwhile, if a Broadway play was not to be, Hollywood was interested in producing a film based on Van Doren's *Franklin*.

In February 1940, RKO Studios purchased the rights from Van Doren for $3,000 with plans to produce a film starring the English stage and film actor Charles Laughton. It seems a performance of Van Doren's *Franklin* was never to be, as this latest attempt was thwarted as well when rival production company Warner Brothers claimed subject-matter rights over the material. While the two studios disputed the potential legal issues at hand, any plans for a film adaptation of *Franklin* were effectively put in limbo.

A literary critic and editor across the 1920s, Van Doren had returned to the art of biography with his studies of Jonathan Swift, Sinclair Lewis, and his own autobiography, all published during the first half of the 1930s. Winning the Pulitzer Prize in 1939 for *Benjamin Franklin* capped off a decade which saw a notable shift in his writing projects. While he still wrote critical essays and reviews—in fact, he wrote well over one hundred introductions to other authors' books, including *Thais* by Anatole France; *Billy Budd, Benito Cereno and The Enchanted Isles* by Herman Melville; *Early Tales of the Atomic Age* by Daniel Lang; *Twelve Lives* by Plutarch; *Red Badge of Courage* by Stephen Crane; *Land of Little Rain* by Mary Hunter Austin; and *Selections From the Writings of Thomas Paine*—in his heart Van Doren was a biographer first.

While researching and writing his next books, *Secret History of the American Revolution; Mutiny in January; The Great Rehearsal;* and *Jane Mecom, the Favorite Sister of Benjamin Franklin*, Van Doren's primary interest was in *the people* behind the historical events. In each of these new projects, he relished the small details of his subjects' lives, uncovering tidbits of information that, when strung together, created a full person. While the minutest of details might seem insignificant, this was where Van Doren found the "lifelike touches" that added up to an interesting biography. Most histories, he confided to his friend Julian Boyd, revealed little about the men (or women) themselves. In an era when the Grand Narrative still reigned supreme, Van Doren was interested in uncovering the stories of how particular men and women *lived.* In doing so, he made a concerted effort to tell these stories in the most concise way possible. He labored at getting to the point efficiently and effectively; the critic in Van Doren was not impressed with superfluous prose. Simply put, Carl Van Doren was convinced that "most histories seem too long."

When the announcement came in the spring that Van Doren would be awarded the Pulitzer Prize for *Franklin*, the self-described "biographer first" could not have been more elated. Understanding that a biographer must look into his heart as a poet does, Van Doren surely felt a sense of humble satisfaction with the honor before him. The malaise and soul-searching that had plagued Van Doren earlier in the decade had served the writer well. Edmund Wilson had publically satirized Van Doren's work on more than one occasion and found Van Doren, at his best, as merely "amiable." However, the amiable critic was in fact a formidable biographer. And this formidable biographer was now recognized at the pinnacle of any writer's career: he had been awarded the Pulitzer Prize; he had obtained the highest honor in his field.

CHAPTER 7

→ · ←

THE AMERICANISM OF
CARL AND MARK VAN DOREN

A key feature of Carl and Mark Van Doren's work, and legacies, lay in their roles as interpreters of a collective American identity during the first half of the twentieth century. Indeed, the Van Dorens' sense of *Americanism* highlights an appreciation for "American genius" that was very much a part of the cultural landscape of the modern period leading up to and through World War II. Katherine Woods, a writer for the *New York Times Book Review* and the *Atlantic Monthly* across the 1930s and '40s, described Carl Van Doren as "a figure of vital influence in American letters not only because of his shrewd and brilliant judgment and his gifts in the use of words but because behind judgment and phrase is a mind saturated with its subject- assimilated knowledge not merely of the detail at hand but of all unspoken details that have gone before." Likewise, Mark Van Doren's poetry provided an interpretation of the particularly *American* scene.

As anthologists and editors, Woods saw both Van Dorens as providing valuable influence in creating a collective and uniquely *American* literary and cultural sensibility. If, someday, the names of Carl and Mark Van Doren were to be erased from the American memory, their combined legacy of literary and cultural influence surely would impact the cultural landscape for generations to come. Of this, Katherine Woods was quite certain.[134]

Mark's professional opinion and esteem always meant more to Carl than anyone else's, and the brothers shared their drafts and manuscripts with one another throughout their careers. After earning his A.B. at the University of Illinois, pausing his education when he was drafted into the army during World War I, Mark followed his older brother to Columbia to complete his own doctoral work. From the 1920s through his retirement in 1959, Mark Van Doren was an instructor and then full professor at Columbia, teaching widely-attended courses in the humanities, poetry, and English literature. In the 1930s he and John Erskine established the *Great books* program at St. John's College in Annapolis, a feat that would broaden Mark's reputation as a great man of letters. He would be regarded as one of Columbia's most popular and liked professors, a teacher who appreciated his students as much as they appreciated him. Mark Van Doren once remarked, "I have always had the greatest respect for students. There is nothing I hate more than condescension—the attitude that they are inferior to you. I always assume they have good minds."

Mark Van Doren was brought on board as *The Nation*'s poetry editor in 1920, and later succeeded Carl as literary editor at the magazine. Carl and Mark Van Doren, Mark's friend from Columbia Joseph Wood Krutch, and literary critic Ludwig Lewisohn soon comprised a tight literary circle, held together "by a shared passion for literature as an art so interwoven with life that neither could be understood without the other" and steering a new course at *The Nation* which influenced its creative and critical content for the next many decades. Like Carl, Mark was no fan of the New Criticism that emerged in the 1930s, and seriously challenged the method's insufferable pseudo-scientific dissection of both poetry and prose, insisting its tenets and its methodology were way off base. In the preface to his 1942 book *The Private Reader*, Mark provided a multi-tiered account of what, exactly, was so wrong with this academic dissection of literature. Poetry, he reminded, is not science, and a good critic cannot look to the scientific processes of decoding and dissecting in any attempt to understand the subtle, intangible essence of the art form. Quite frankly, Mark Van Doren insisted that we do not understand very much about poetry and we never will. And yet, ignoring the most obvious divide between poetry and science, the New Critics were attempting to capture and then beat to death that diffusive nature of poetry which can never be succinctly or neatly defined. The New Criticism was doing all it could "to arrest the lyric in its flight," strangling poetry with ill-conceived ideas about psychology, semantics, and definitions, with little heed paid to whether they were truly present in the poems or not. Under the New Criticism, "the encirclement which poetry is undergoing is as dreadful to behold as it is humorless to hear." This New Criticism was bad science, not an art, whereas *good* literary criticism was very much an art form.[135]

While Carl was a biographer first, Mark Van Doren was, first and foremost, a poet. The author of numerous short stories, compilations of literary criticism, and novels, it was poetry that earned Mark the Pulitzer Prize in 1940 for his *Collected Poems*, just one year after Carl had won that prize for biography. Carl and Mark Van Doren are, to date, the only sibling pair to have won the Pulitzer. The mutual respect and admiration Carl and Mark held for each other across their lifetimes was immense. Carl once wrote that Mark "is all that a part of me would rather be than anything in the world." Of Carl's generosity and limitless influence on his own life, Mark wrote that his elder brother "was prodigal, he gave me every thought he had." Mark acknowledged that his older brother was generous to a fault, and while there was a certain largess to Carl's nature, he was also quite sensitive. Mark admired the fact that many who knew Carl counted him as their most cherished friend.[136]

Both Van Dorens were devout adherents to the precepts of liberal education. Both men held intellectual curiosity as the necessary seedbed for any solid education. A true scholar must be most interested not in what he already knows, but in what he will know tomorrow. Equally important, Mark Van Doren understood the necessity for a common foundation of collective knowledge in any modern society. In the preface to his book *Liberal Education*, Mark wrote, "Members of any modern society need to know a great many things in common. How they know them may be an individual matter, but whether they know them can make a fatal difference... The question then presses, if any question does, is what shall everybody know?" Moreover, argued the younger Van Doren, education is not and should never be viewed as a passive process. Education is something that one must work to achieve. It is not something imparted by *authorities*. One's education is, very simply, up to oneself. It takes work. One does not *get* an education. One must *labor* for it.[137]

Mark Van Doren defined a liberal education as a *complete* education. Which does not mean knowing all there is to know; rather this assumes an understanding that the task of seeking a complete education is not impossible. The "Educated Person" is, in fact, an attainable end. He is someone who is committed to reason over superstition. Someone who tries, as best as she is able, to understand the whole of knowledge. Someone who is free to disagree, who does all she can to avoid the bewilderment of one who is not educated. Someone who is free to ask questions—even terrifying ones—and to seek answers. In total, an Educated Person is the Jeffersonian ideal of the Whole Man. No man, or woman, can ever know all there is to know, can never attain absolute wisdom. But he will attain nothing if he does not make the attempt. And with the foundation of democracy resting upon equality in education, a liberal education becomes necessary for the very state of democracy to endure. Van Doren's treatise on liberal education rests on a cornerstone: the benchmark for determining the success of education is not what a person or a population *believes*. The benchmark is how well they *think*.

In his essay "The Kinds of Knowledge," Mark Van Doren wrote, "The nature of man is to want more knowledge than he will ever possess." He argued that thinking, actually, is a difficult task. Thinking can even be dangerous. But this intellectual exercise "wakes us up" and, unlike certain philosophies which speak to the contrary, thinking in fact makes for happy men. Men not "at ease, but happy." Recalling Descartes' infamous revelation *Cogito, Ergo Sum*—"I think therefore I am"—Mark Van Doren encouraged recent graduates to consider his own heavy edict: "Not to have had the desire at all is never to have lived." The poet Alan Ginsburg, who was a student of Mark Van Doren's at Columbia, praised his teacher as "one of the few Gnostic professors at Columbia...he was interested in illuminated wisdom."[138]

This illuminated wisdom translated into a poetic sensibility that was predominantly pastoral in nature, and one that was steeped in the poet's ever-present tendency *to look*. Poems like *After the Drought*, *Morning Worship*, and the book-length *A Winter's Diary* present a clear sense of Mark Van Doren's pastoral leaning and influence of poet William Wordsworth. Mark Van Doren's first novel *The Transients*, published in 1935, bridged the gap between narrative prose and an esoteric poetic sensibility best described as "other worldly." Carl described *The Transients* as "a history of an imaginary divine honeymoon, the story and the essence of all human love at its best... Only a poet like Mark Van Doren, with his intense heart and his lucid mind, could have told a story which burns with so much heat and yet throws off so much light. *When heat and light are mated in a book, the book is literature.*"[139]

Carl always envied what he considered to be Mark's easier time as a writer. While staying with his mother in Urbana during the winter of 1936, Carl hastened to finish his autobiography, pausing to send word to Mark as to his literary progress. "Forgive this lousy typing, I am worn out with hours of pounding this machine. The book is at last going with something of a rush— or what I call a rush. About a normal pace for you, damn you. Love to everybody, Carl." Upon reading the draft copy of *Three World*'s early chapters, Mark assured his brother this was an honest work. Indeed, Carl had created a world on paper with which his readers would surely connect. Deeply moved by Carl's recollections of their Illinois boyhoods and by Carl's ability to recreate his very self on paper, Mark could hear his brother's voice with every sentence, and he recognized the particular tone of Carl's voice embedded in the most personal passages of the manuscript. Readers would likewise hear the voice of an honest man; they would hear him, and they would know him. Mark's praise, at once both professional and deeply personal, meant more to Carl than anyone else's. Buoyed by the jolt of pleasure and satisfaction he garnered from Mark's praise, Carl completed the manuscript and sent it off to his editor at Harper's.[140]

Meanwhile, Mark was in the midst of his own project, his novel *Windless Cabins*. When Mark sent a draft of his manuscript to his literary critic-brother for critical feedback, Carl solemnly gushed that he could not put the manuscript down. Describing *Windless Cabins* as "one of the swiftest and straightest" stories he had ever read, the literary critic—or was he acting solely as brother here?—remarked, "It is a very beautiful book, and very wise, and full of profound metaphysics... I couldn't breathe. No waste. No wabbling (*sic*). The positively shortest line between two points." This was praise enough for Mark, who basked in Carl's "spectacle of generosity." And while Mark declared, "The book is published. It needs no other readers!", it would be a few more years before *Windless Cabins* was officially published by

Holt & Company in 1940. Unlike Carl, Mark had his professorship at Columbia, which generally prevented him from writing full-time.[141]

When Carl left his appointment as an instructor at Columbia to head up the Brearley School in 1916, he happily left the cloistered walls of academia behind him. While he maintained his graduate seminar in American literature through the 1920s, Carl was in no hurry to secure another full-time position at *any* university. When offered a professor of English position at Amherst College in 1920, Carl turned that down, preferring the freedom—professionally, personally, *and* intellectually—he enjoyed as *The Nation*'s editor to the long list of duties required of a full professor. Rumblings of a potential position at Columbia emerged in the spring of 1936, and while Carl was not completely committed to the idea of returning to the colorless climate of academia—a place where, he felt, "time seemed to stand still"—the cash-strapped writer admitted to his brother that he would "grab it around the neck and be a faithful professor" if the appointment came through. For reasons unknown, the Columbia appointment did not go through.

It is likely Van Doren had been on the side of non-academic criticism for too long, he could not—or would not—bridge the ideological or temperamental gap required to make it back over to the "other side." So Carl continued down the time-honored path of writers everywhere: he managed to get by through publisher's advances and small loans from loved ones until the royalties came in. And of course, Carl continued to write literary criticism, book introductions, and magazine articles across the 1930s. These shorter pieces brought with them the bonus of a timely paycheck. The reality of his financial predicament, and those old anxieties he had been harboring since his graduate days, incited Carl to advise his brother, "My boy, stick to your professorship. Living by writing is not too satisfactory."[142]

CHAPTER 8

FOLLOWING HIS HEAD

While readership of popular and literary magazines flourished from the early decades of the century, radio attracted an audience beyond those educated readers who looked to journalists and critics to provide cultural and historical commentary on all matters of contemporary concern. Radio provided a democratization of knowledge even beyond that of print. A growing medium by which the man of letters, including both Carl and Mark Van Doren, shared his literary and historical erudition with the public was through an array of bookish radio programs broadcast across the airwaves from the 1920s through the midcentury. The intimacy of radio created the feeling that these literary experts were right there in your own living room, sharing with you his or her thoughts on important books and their authors. Those literary critics and editors who regularly appeared on radio shows became public experts on culture, true *public intellectuals*: bookish celebrities in the public sphere. More than simple entertainment, a concerted effort to elevate moral standards and encourage character development through an engagement with literature was part and parcel of the programs' production.

Bookish radio shows springing forth across the 1920s, '30s, and '40s followed different formats, but all rested upon the precept that literature, historical analysis, and cultural commentary were necessary to the development of informed citizens. Some of these programs were not much more than the authoritative recitation of passages from great books, others resembled an intimate "fireside chat," while a growing number showcased the learned opinions of one notable critic or panel of public intellectuals. Regardless of the format, each program intended to engage the American public in a conversation surrounding the purpose and meaning of literature.

"Literary Vespers" was one of the earliest book programs for radio when it first aired in 1922. Hosted by Northwestern University professor of English Edgar White Burrill, the purpose of the show was to present "the choicest passages of the world's best literature" to the listening public. Burrill personally meant to encourage his audience to read books that would "build character" ; his broadcasts were intended to inspire and promote strong moral values, he was not there to provide literary criticism.

"Vespers" was based on a series of book talks Burrill had given at New York City's Town Hall Theater, in which he simply recited passages from great books, often accompanied by a musical score, and related them to current events. Burrill's show ran across the 1920s and '30s and continued to follow the recitation format that had made his Town Hall presentations so successful.

The "fireside chat," most famously known to us now in Franklin D. Roosevelt's radio addresses during World War II, was another popular radio show format. These programs relied on the intimacy of personable conversation with literary men and women who knew good books. "Readers Guide," hosted by newspaper critic Joseph Henry Jackson, first aired in San Francisco in 1924 before it was picked up nationally by NBC radio. The program presented an informal conversation about selected books with two or three guests, as if the group was gathered together in one's own living room. Replicating the intimacy of a close conversation, this format drew listeners into a dialogue about important books and their authors, creating a conversation with experts as intimate as a Sunday supper with family and friends. "An American Fireside," with Christopher Morley, Amy Loveman, and Henry S. Canby, took the format one step further and built a show around the premise that the editorial trio had gathered in the offices of the *Saturday Review of Literature* to discuss the upcoming print issue. Here, listeners felt they were granted back-stage access to editorial discussions in-the-making.

The weight of a public intellectual's name went far in attracting and holding a listening audience. One of radio's biggest bookworm celebrities emerged in the persona of "The Town Crier." Literary critic and editor Alexander Woolcott adopted the persona of a bookish historian, whom he dubbed The Town Crier, and was invited into homes across the country through his radio program "The Early Bookworm." The program first appeared on the airwaves in 1925 and was sponsored by several publishing houses, including Simon & Schuster, Knopf, and Macmillan. Woolcott, as The Town Crier, reviewed four new books per episode, each carefully selected by his sponsors in the publishing industry.

Alas, the connection between literary acumen and marketing for direct sales was not incidental to these radio programs. In 1933, CBS radio picked up Woolcott's show and broadcast "The Town Crier" for the next five years. *Literary Digest* reported that Woolcott's voice was, at the time, "familiar to everyone in America who owned a radio." When NBC radio conceived a show in 1939 to rival "The Town Crier," it selected *Atlantic Monthly* editor Edward Weeks to lead its program, "The Human Side of Literature." Weeks approached the wildly successful Woolcott for advice as how to construct his own bookish radio show the audience would tune in for. Woolcott advised Weeks that he must, at all cost, avoid *scripting* the show. The best advice he could give his colleague was his own sure-ticket to success: you do not *write* the episodes, but rather make notes for yourself, and then work out a monologue that *sounds* like casual conversation. You needed someone with "good ears" to springboard your ideas off of, to let you know when your presentation sounded "like talk." Above all, Woolcott warned, Weeks absolutely must not simply read a prepared script, chiding "The curse of radio is professors who read."[143]

One professor who did not simply read on-air was William Lyon Phelps, the man who helped make NBC radio's The "Swift Hour" a hugely popular program. Billed as "an hour of melody, drama, and song," Phelps added literary heft to the program with his book talks from 1934-35. With degrees from both Yale and Harvard, Phelps had spent forty-one years on the faculty at Yale and was a popular speaker on the national lecture circuit, frequently speaking at women's clubs, lecture series, and Chautauqua gatherings and drawing up to 2,000 people at some of these events. As per his status as a public intellectual, Phelps also wrote popular articles for *Scribner's* and *Ladies' Home Journal.* In 1939, newspaper columnist Lucius Beebe wrote that Phelps "has probably done more than any living figure to inculcate the American mind with reverence for the written and spoken word. For nearly four decades he has been the nation's most popular lecturer on literature." *Newsweek* reported that Phelps attracted sixteen percent of the listening audience during the "Swift Hour's" Saturday evening broadcasts. Phelps' credentials as a Yale Man assured the listening public that here was a man of classical education and impeccable literary taste. They could trust him.

Historian and popular author Hendrik Willem Van Loon's voice was equally well known across the airwaves from the 1930s through the '40s. Van Loon created "WEVD University of the Air" in 1933, which aired five thirty-minutes broadcasts per week. Van Loon's radio programs were not book-shows *per se*, and during his broadcasts he talked about larger historical incidents and questions of philosophy, concentrating much of his political opinion on the Nazi occupation of his native Holland and the dangers in Europe leading up to the second world war. The man of letters used radio as his medium of choice to spread his erudition and historical analysis to an American public that he worried had become much too indifferent to the "unspeakable Nazi threat" as the 1930s progressed. Competing shows "The Reader's Almanac," "Between the Bookends," and "NBC University of the Air" each regularly included Carl Van Doren among the shows' literary critic guests across the 1930s and '40s, as did Mary Margaret McBride's popular interview show, "Adventure in Reading." "Of Men and Books," with John Towner Frederick, reviewed newly published books and each week gave *The New York Herald-Tribune Review of Books'* list of best titles. Roughly half of the books Frederick reviewed were not best sellers, however, and he made a concerted effort to introduce his audience to less-publicized books.[xiii]

....

xiii   In a January 1949 episode of Mary Margaret McBride's radio show, when CVD appeared to promote his latest book, *The Great Rehearsal,* Van Loon charged that journalism had become a "victim of literature." Today's journalists, he said, had read too much drama and too much melodrama, and this carried over into their journalistic endeavors, which had become all too sensationalized. The results, he found, were lamentable.

Beyond the single expert-led program were an increasing number of panel programs revolving around books and authors. Each episode of NBC radio's long-running "The Author Meets the Critics," which aired from 1941-54, featured a panel of two or three critics that changed weekly. The format of the program set an author against this panel of critics in "a battle of the books...a no holds-barred literary free-for-all." Recorded at Radio City Music Hall, the program's official sponsor was the Book-of-the-Month-Club. NBC later devised a second program, "Books on Trial," for all intents and purposes identical to "The Author Meets the Critics" and meant to capitalize on the popularity of the original panel program. "Books on Trial" was sponsored by the Literary Guild, and so, like many of the bookish radio programs, was conceived not only to bring a literary education to the American public, but was equally meant to persuade consumers into their local bookstores or to join the sponsored monthly book club.

Into this milieu arose the learned Van Doren brothers, equally credentialed, whose own radio programs aired during the early years of the 1940s. Mark Van Doren described the necessity of studying *Great books* in 1941, as the nation entered World War II and was fighting for "things of lasting value" in the military arena. In light of fascism's spread across Europe and America's engagement in a second global conflict in scarcely twenty years, CBS radio's "Invitation to Learning" presented conversations surrounding those lasting works that had "nourished Western thought" for centuries, some for well over a thousand years. The philosophical and material problems that had confronted writers such as Aristotle, Montaigne, Dante, Da Vinci, and Gibbon were the same problems confronting every person in any century; the longevity of these great works lay in their everlasting pertinence. Further, "Invitation to Learning" and its cohort of bookish radio programs meant to encourage the listening audience to read for themselves the books under discussion. These programs were meant to start a national conversation and keep in circulation the moral, ethical, and philosophical ideals of quality literature, essays, and works of history.[xiv]

Mark Van Doren and Allen Tate, both poets and critics, and Huntington Cairns, primarily an economist, co-hosted the program. The aesthetic and philosophical divide between the poets and Cairns made for tension among the trio right from the start. "Invitation" was created in 1940 to bring St. John's College's *Great books* program to a wider listening audience; Mark Van Doren, along with John Erskine, had been instrumental in developing the *Great books* program at St. John's, and he was a frequent lecturer there. His sons Charlie and John would both attend the college. "Invitation to Learning" quickly amassed one million followers

....

xiv   Mark Van Doren stated the reason Gibbon remained such an important historian stemmed from his approach to history, which was very much like that of a poet. Gibbon had the same sense of imagination as a poet: he did not *explain* history, but *re-created* it.

after its first season, and followed CBS's Sunday afternoon New York Philharmonic broadcasts.

The show was very specifically unscripted and unrehearsed. Each week, Van Doren, Tate, and Cairns discussed *Great books* from among ten categories, which included politics, ethics, religion, fiction, and autobiography. An undercurrent of patriotism permeated the program and was there by design. Mark Van Doren explained the importance of studying these books, these "things of lasting value," as they espoused the very values the nation was fighting for in the present world war.

Unlike other radio programs, "Invitation to Learning" actively shunned the *intimate conversation in your living room* format. Instead, its panel members maintained a purposeful air of remoteness. These men were talking to each other; the audience for this trio did not exist. Mark Van Doren described the premise for the show as "an overheard conversation," in which the three men created and fueled a conversation that interested and excited themselves, first and foremost. Any listener who wished to tune in and overhear that conversation was perfectly welcome; no one would drag him to it, no one would try to entice him to stay.[144]

This was a strictly intellectual pursuit, and Mark Van Doren made no apologies for it. After its second successful season, however, producer Scott Buchanan proposed a restructuring of the program, in which the literary content would be broken down into five distinct fields, each managed by an expert "chairman."

The new plan reeked of that dreaded bent towards *specialization*, and signaled a move away from the generalist approach the show had been founded upon. After hearing the network's plans for the new experiment, Mark Van Doren wrote a letter of protest to Buchanan, in which he lambasted that "'fields' was the opposite of what the program wanted, that departmentalization quite killed the idea, that crossfire was the thing, that the term 'general literature' (by which I found out that he meant fiction) gave his whole case away, and that his chairmen stunk."[145]

Mark Van Doren continued his dissertation against the proposed shift to chairmen and their alleged specializations. He wrote to his co-host Allen Tate, fuming the program was deteriorating before his very eyes, was to be overrun by "experts and stunt men." The revamped format was no longer developing a continuity of ideas from week to week in the way the original had; the verbal crossfire was gone. "So we are both out at last, and equal. I was tired anyway, and I am glad to say to hell with it." Mark and Carl Van Doren were, after all, *generalists* of liberal education who abhorred the ever increasing demand toward specialization, now not only persistent in academia, but increasingly in the public sphere as well.

This trend toward academic specialization that had picked up speed by the turn of the century and had become more and more entrenched across the ensuing decades was, as the midcentury approached, beginning to impact the work of public intellectuals as well. As for the radio program's restructured format, Mark Van Doren was most definitely not on board, and he was fired. Allen Tate was fired as well. In a letter to friend and colleague John Peale Bishop, Tate appeared more bemused than aggrieved, writing—rather curiously—that getting sacked was actually good for Mark because the program was no good for him; it had encouraged in him "the small fraction of Van Dorenism which he shares with Carl."[146]

"American Scriptures" with Carl Van Doren and Carl Cramer, followed the recitation format when it aired from 1943-44, a show very much created to salve the soul of a nation at war. The program consisted of a series of recitations which played during the intermission of the New York Philharmonic's Sunday afternoon concerts, broadcast over CBS radio. Van Doren recorded the scripts which he wrote himself (one wonders if Woolcott cringed at Van Doren's performance as one of the professors who simply read on-air), drawn from passages he and Cramer considered vital to the American political, literary, and patriotic canon. Van Doren's intent for the program was to lift America's wartime spirits by recalling the choicest of heroic ideals and deeds reaching out from men and women of the American past who had survived their own national emergencies "with the faith and fortitude which were now again demanded of the people of this nation." Witnessing two world wars in his lifetime, Van Doren understood the importance of illuminating "what is essential in

American history, character, and aspiration" and hoped a recitation of these documents of national history would serve to unite past, present, and future. From Patrick Henry's "Give Me Liberty or Give Me Death" speech, to Ben Franklin's defense of the young nation's Constitution; from an excerpt of the diary of Narcissa Whitman, one of the first women to cross the continent by covered wagon, to a series of quotations concerning freedom of the press, each episode was delivered in Van Doren's personable yet patrician voice.[147]

NBC radio broadcast "Words at War with Carl Van Doren" during the summer of 1944, also in direct response to the political and military reality of the nation at war. The programs were billed as "dramatizations of the most representative books to come out of this great world conflict." Van Doren, presented as one of the nation's leading literary figures, eminent author, and Pulitzer Prize winner, recorded introductions for each selection, after which a team of studio players presented a dramatization of the text. Patriotic music, recognizable as such to any listener of any decade, marked the solemnity of the program.

"Words at War" was less entertainment, more cultural edification in which Van Doren's listening audience tuned in to hear the reassuring and patrician voice of an intellectual whose wide expanse of knowledge offered a much needed *perspective*. The program provided an important collective experience and a critical ideological message during the summer of 1944, a moment when,

"Our hands and our heads and our hearts are all at war, and so are our words. The free words of free men have always been weapons that tyrants dread, as they dread almost no other." This spirit of democracy and commitment to patriotism underscored the whole of Van Doren's work, in times of war and in times of peace, but his efforts in explicitly patriotic endeavors ramped up quite notably during the second world war.

With the war's official outbreak in September 1939, Nazi Germany's military buildup since Hitler's 1933 rise to power created an alarming political landscape in which America, whether or not it would enter the crisis, was forced to confront its own national identity. As the manifestation of the world's greatest democratic project, the *idea* of America and American patriotic sentiment surged amidst the spread of fascist totalitarianism. This was perhaps the last moment in modern history when patriotism, whether one was Republican *or* Democrat, was lauded as the highest of national virtues. When Doubleday prepared to publish *The Patriotic Anthology* in 1941, it asked Carl Van Doren to provide the book's introduction. This anthology, like other collections of patriotic-themed poetry and prose, included writings dating to the colonial era, through the aspiring nation's war for independence, its infancy as a fledgling yet determined democracy, and through the heartbreak of the Civil War and the Great

War. The anthology included poetry from Henry Wadsworth Longfellow ("Paul Revere's Ride"); Oliver Wendell Holmes ("A Ballad of the Boston Tea Party" and "Old Ironsides"); Katharine Lee Bates ("America the Beautiful"); and Walt Whitman ("I Hear America Singing" and "For You O Democracy"). It included prose from Thomas Paine ("These Are the Times that Try Men's Souls"); Abigail Adams (letters to her husband, John Adams); Theodore Roosevelt ("High of Heart"); and Rose Wilder Lane ("The Defense of Liberty"). These were works of "basic American ideals," which taken together created a canon of work steeped in a patriotic sensibility boiled down from time-honored and essential thoughts and feelings. Carl Van Doren understood that individual citizens might think and feel quite differently from one another, but warned that "unless they agree on the main points of national history and policy, attitude and faith, their nation will sooner or later fall apart."[148]

This did not mean that all patriots must be in agreement or hold similar opinions. Van Doren recalled the conflicts and antagonisms that divided Americans since the earliest days, from loyalists versus patriots leading into the war for independence, to the civil war that divided the nation and threatened to tear it asunder. On the divisiveness of the Civil War, Van Doren wrote, "There were sincerity and heroism on both sides and poets to praise and commemorate each cause...It is perfectly possible for a modern American to venerate Lee as well as Lincoln, Lincoln as well as Lee. They were lofty men who were divided by the temporary passions of their day but afterward united in the hearts of their countrymen."

Would a liberal intellectual, such as Carl Van Doren identified himself, hold claim to a similar position today? In the ensuing decades, the very idea of *patriotism* has become embroiled with charges of inherent and incessant subjugation of Americans by Americans. Where Van Doren wrote, "Patriotism is a fellow feeling that consolidates a nation," he was writing from his own very specific cultural context of 1941. When he wrote, "The United States, most fortunate of nations, can remember its past without lamenting or despairing. Circumstances have almost conspired to show favor to America," he was speaking to a sense of *American exceptionalism* that, in the twenty-first century, has since become brandished with charges ranging from racism and nativism to sexism and cultural imperialism. But if we read deeper, Van Doren tells us:

> The theory of equality may have to be re-examined, not to make men unequal but to make more of them justly accessible to equality. But as to fraternity there must be no falling off either in the principle or in the practice. The future of the human world can be happy only if men are everywhere united in a common brotherhood of resistance to tyrants.[149]

Here, Van Doren acknowledges the democratic project was not yet complete. In the face of global tyranny, in fact, patriotic sentiment and commitment to national solidarity were—are—more critical than ever.

Presently, with the war in Europe heading towards yet another full-scale global conflict, the American future perhaps looked less gleaming than it had long appeared, and yet Van Doren still believed his nation was the brightest on earth. He cautioned that Americans must learn from the "warning examples" of Asia and Europe, and hold fast to the nation's democratic principles and strivings for liberty, equality, and fraternity. *The Patriotic Anthology* assembled the "high thoughts, high emotions, high hopes" that marked American history, an endeavor, like that of brother Mark's focus on *Great books*, necessary to shore up America's collective identity and her steadfastness against tyranny. Van Doren held certain in his estimation that "Whatever difference of opinions there may be in America on this or that point of procedure, there is a profound national unity." Whether you call it patriotism, civic pride, or national identity, Van Doren's sentiment is notable of the pre- and immediately post-war era. It marks the mid-twentieth century, almost quaintly, as a nation many would no longer readily identify with two or three decades later. Against this backdrop arose an array of patriotic-themed literature and radio programs as a means of stiffening the American spine.[150]

Indeed, Van Doren's commitment to patriotic sentiment, both his own as well as the collective sentiment he felt was so critical in uniting the nation, guided his work across his entire literary career, becoming more explicit during times of national emergency such as the Great Depression and the Second World War. His selections for and introductions to *The Patriotic Anthology* (1941) and *The Literary Works of Abraham Lincoln* (1942); his books *The Secret History of the American Revolution* (1941), *Mutiny in January* (1943), *The Great Rehearsal* (1948); and his radio broadcasts for "American Scriptures" (1943) and "Words at War" (1944) were all composed during a decade of great political uncertainty. There are, of course, many ways one can respond to moments— eras or epochs, in retrospect—of great political or cultural challenge. Certainly, dissent and rebellion often peak during times of crises, as voices gather to demand or exact a change to a system viewed as inherently flawed. During the 1920s and '30s, for example, Van Doren's literary criticism focused on modernist writers and their cries to *make it new!*, writers like Sinclair Lewis, Elinor Wylie, Theodore Dreiser, and Edna St. Vincent Millay who challenged the *dull* bourgeois establishment and its dull adherence to traditions that did not speak to the modern condition. Van Doren was admittedly attracted to the new literature pouring forth from the lively rebelliousness of the 1920s and the more serious social concerns of the 1930s. In any era, Van Doren felt that good writers must, if not be actually prophetic, record the "tremors of opinion" permeating the cultural landscape.

This is what Van Doren looked for when he wrote literary criticism. *Is it Alive?* On the surface, it may seem incongruous that Van Doren, who had spent the bulk of his literary career admiring and critiquing the work of writers who essentially challenged the status quo, seems to shift towards a more conservative position with his own patriotic-themed works across the 1940s...as if *patriotism* is a necessarily conservative sentiment. But in fact what we find is Van Doren's ongoing appreciation for writing that captures the subtle sensations as well as the more roiled emotions of the age, whatever they may be. The spread of fascism across Europe and England's declaration of war on Germany created a widespread uncertainty among Americans as to the nation's own political and military positioning. Van Doren's concern with national unity, his understanding that "patriots instinctively cherish common memories and hopes, expressed in words that have come to seem inseparable from them" occupied his mind, and manifested in his published works, across the whole of the 1940s.

As to any potential U.S. involvement in the war in Europe, Van Doren felt the United States must support England against Hitler and his army, but admitted it was relatively easy for a fifty-five year old man to say so. It would be much younger men who would do the going and the fighting. Still, Van Doren would add to the war effort in whatever way he could, "willing to be called on as I may be needed, or of any use." In fact, Van Doren would lend his credentials as a historian and a public intellectual to the War and Victory Loan campaigns and the War Finance Program; through his radio broadcasts; and through his examination of earlier times of national crises, through his books.[151]

Following the success of his biography of Benjamin Franklin, Van Doren turned his historical eye to the events surrounding Benedict Arnold's transgressions against the Continental Army during the War for Independence. Sometime in 1938, Van Doren became acquainted with Julian Boyd, Librarian at Princeton University and historian in his own right. Boyd would serve as Princeton University's chief librarian for twelve years, and later as Professor of History at Princeton, president of the American Historical Association, and president of the American Philosophical Society. Boyd would edit the highly esteemed multi-volume set of Thomas Jefferson's papers after 1950, still today regarded as the most comprehensive collection of Jefferson's papers. When Van Doren and Boyd met, both were working on projects of historical natures and came to depend upon one another as an intellectual sounding board. In the spring of 1940, while Van Doren was writing the manuscript for his working title *Benedict Arnold and the Others*, Boyd was instrumental in trying to put together an academic post for Van Doren at Princeton. Boyd was pleased to propose Van Doren as the inaugural Fellow of the Princeton University Library and was very much looking forward to Van Doren's presence on campus, where he might continue to work on his writing, "here in this delightful spot." Some of the powers-that-be at Princeton lamented a perceived slight of the University in which scholars were favoring the archival collections at New York and Philadelphia over the literary riches at New Jersey's Ivy League university. Boyd very much felt that Van Doren's presence at Princeton could help the university "remove that apparent indifference." Boyd and Van Doren both liked the sound of "Fellows of the Princeton University Library," the librarian excited about the possibility of snagging Van Doren for his name recognition and prestige value.[152]

With Boyd in Princeton and Van Doren in New York, the pair maintained an ongoing interplay of "zigzag arguments" through a lively written correspondence. Van Doren sent chapters of his manuscript on Arnold to Boyd for editing and feedback. After reading the manuscript in full, Boyd suggested Van Doren shift the second chapter to the first and challenged Van Doren to begin with stronger introductory remarks. Express your conclusion right up front, he advised, and don't give in to your instincts to trim the book down. Boyd wrote page after page of editorial advice, asked questions of Van Doren's narrative, and offered suggestions when he felt more information was needed. And while Van Doren was often exasperated by the recommendations of his publisher's editorial staff, the historian was grateful for Boyd's extensive comments and suggestions, writing "I don't suppose anybody ever got a grander compliment than your long and detailed letter this morning seems to me. I doubt if I would write that much to Shakespeare if he sent me his eye-witness account of the Second Coming of Christ."[153]

Van Doren admitted to Boyd, as he often lamented to Mark, that writing was a laborious process for him indeed. If he could write five thousand words a week, taking seven days and nights to do it, he felt he had had a good week. And while it might appear to the reader that his simple, direct prose manifested on the page with a minimal of effort, the truth of the matter was that Van Doren was in a constant search to find the shortest way of saying the most. The words, and their cadence, had to be a precise fit. This caution and toil, however, was a sure sign that a writer was on the right track. Van Doren was certain that "occasional temporary despair and self-doubt are the surest signs that a writer amounts to something. The half-witted grandeur-deluded paranoiac minor boys are always perfectly content. That's the reason they are no good. They never challenge themselves and rip their work to pieces."[154]

Within two months of Boyd's editorial suggestions for *Benedict Arnold,* Van Doren had completely reshaped the manuscript. Taking Boyd's advice, he moved the second chapter to the first and trashed the original first chapter, moving a small portion of it to the third chapter where it more rightly belonged. The whole thing, he felt, now moved at a much faster and better pace. Van

Doren changed the title as well, to *Secret History of the American Revolution*. Beyond the pair's ongoing conversation about the manuscript, a whirl of letters back and forth between Boyd and Van Doren across the first half of the 1940s reveals a professional correspondence unmatched in all of Van Doren's papers: *Enclosed is a letter for your research; did you see this piece in the New Yorker? When can we meet to talk about the Committee on Manuscripts? Will you be attending ____'s cocktail party this weekend? How is your work going on the Jefferson papers? Listen to American Scriptures on the Philharmonic this Sunday; Did you read____? Do you know ____? Would you please return the chapters/carbon/photostat I sent you last month?...*

When Boyd asked Van Doren if he was a member of the American Antiquarian Society (and, if not, he really should be), Van Doren replied no, he was not, in fact, a member of *any* learned society. "It's an odd quirk of mine, I suppose, to be such a lone wolf—or maybe hyena." He had recently resigned from the League of American Writers, citing his preference to avoid "nominal associations with groups in which I shall have no chance— and not much disposition—to be active." Van Doren had not relented in his disinterest in being a part of academia or any academic societies, recalling his earlier remark about societies that ranked professors above poets.[155]

This may explain why, when Boyd advised his friend on a possible position with the Princeton University Press, Van Doren hesitated. Van Doren admitted that he was not very keen on the number of social engagements and incidental activities such a post would most certainly require. He had a good deal of privacy just then, and he preferred to keep it that way. Van Doren was still wary of any post he deemed too closely linked with the ivory tower, writing to Boyd, "I agree with you about academic tenure, and academic societies in general. That's why I hesitate about the P. Press." Since that 1908 letter to *The Nation*, in which the young graduate student Van Doren hinted at the scourge of academia, the critic/historian had barely relented. The lone wolf—or, perhaps, hyena—still preferred to work on his own terms and was not eager to be beholden to academia, its offices or its ideologies.[156]

At the end of 1941, Princeton University announced it was suspending all plans to hire any new professors, or fellows, and so the Library fellowship Boyd had been so eager to secure for Van Doren was lost. Van Doren himself was not terribly disappointed. The historian could not, however, turn down admission to the American Philosophical Society, which elected Van Doren to its membership in the spring of 1942, owing to his promotion of "useful knowledge." That society's intellectual prestige—unlike Van Doren's assessment of the League of American Writers—was enormous, and he was honored to be acknowledged by the society founded by Ben Franklin and presided over by the likes of Thomas Jefferson. And when the National Institute of Arts and Letters again elected Van Doren to its membership in 1944—twenty years after he declined its first invitation—Van Doren did accept the honor. Perhaps being on the "inside" was more palatable to a man approaching sixty than it had been for the young writer still in his thirties.

With the publication of *Secret History of the American Revolution*, reviewed in the *New Republic* as "an interesting and important book," Van Doren had done what he did best. His meticulous attention to research uncovered significant materials not previously published in any account of the nation's most infamous traitor. "Pieced together with the skill of a relentless, but fair, prosecuting attorney," Van Doren had illuminated Arnold's duplicity, along with his wife's apparent complicity, and British attempts to lure other Americans as potential turncoats. While Julian Boyd had encouraged Van Doren to give as much to the story as he possibly could, to make it twice as long, if necessary, some reviewers did not appreciate Van Doren's extensive use of quotations. The *New Republic* found the book's heavy use of direct evidence mildly forbidding, although the book was admittedly no less readable, thanks to Van Doren's skillful use of the pen. *The Nation*, Van Doren's alma mater, applauded the book as a work of solid and austere scholarship, and appreciated the fact that its author let the facts speak for themselves. It would have liked, however, to hear the author's own voice in the narrative, citing Carl Van Doren as one of the few writers who could bridge the gap between "romanced biography" and stuffy dissertations. It had hoped that Van Doren would have chosen to do just that in *Secret History*, instead of relying so much on the source materials themselves.

Too many quotes or not, Van Doren was soon looking ahead to his next project, the story behind a New Year's Day mutiny. During his research for *Secret History*, Van Doren had gained access to a new trove of documents, the Sir Henry Clinton papers housed at Clements Library at the University of Michigan. The collection includes correspondence between Benedict Arnold and John André in the months leading up to the discovery of their fateful treasonous plot. It was during this exploration into the archives when Van Doren came across documents relating to the New Year's Day mutiny of 1781, in which General Henry Clinton figured prominently.

What happened was this: on January 1, 1781, fifteen hundred soldiers from the Pennsylvania Line, all serving under General Anthony Wayne of the Continental Army, enacted a mutiny, killing three officers and deserting the army's winter camp at Morristown, New Jersey. That winter had been especially calamitous for the Continental Army, with unpaid, unfed, and improperly clothed soldiers falling further and further into hunger, disease, and despair. The Pennsylvania Line mutineers insisted their three-year contracts had expired and that the Continental Army owed them back pay. After killing the three officers and abandoning camp, the mutineers were set upon by British General Henry

Clinton's emissaries, sent to entice the men to join the Redcoats and fight against their American brothers. The men would not be turned, however, and instead headed south to Princeton, where they dispatched their own envoys to meet General Wayne and discuss terms for reconciliation of their grievances. The mutineers turned over Clinton's men, who were eventually hanged as spies.

The historian in Van Doren was practically giddy over the chance for the first look at the trove of Clinton's personal correspondence, documents, and maps, all recently acquired and archived at Clements Library. His history would include facts and accounts previously unknown. Van Doren wrote to Boyd, "The story yells to be told...Above all, nobody tells us anything about the men themselves," which was always the cinching factor for Van Doren. His desire to know about the *lives* of men and women prodded the biographer into the archives once again, this time uncovering the key players in yet another series of events involving mutiny, loyalties, and patriotism. Van Doren felt this was "a remarkably patriotic book. It shows our ancestors were, in spite of many temptations, virtuous and devoted to the cause of independence."[157]

Against the backdrop of VE and VJ Day, and caught up in a national surge of patriotism unmatched in U.S. history, Van Doren wrote an article in June, 1945 for *Good Housekeeping* magazine which he titled "Our Two Patriotisms." Van Doren argued that local and national patriotisms can and do co-exist, and that while the two types of patriotic sentiment may sometimes appear to work at cross-purposes, there was certainly room for both in the national landscape. In the essay, he described the United States as a federation of *communities*, and that while there had always been localized murmurings threatening to exacerbate or even tear asunder sectional loyalties, "such temporary local grievances are few and unimportant as compared with the sense of national citizenship which all Americans feel." Van Doren saw patriotic bipartisanship, and not merely in the political sense of the word, as a bridge spanning all cultural subdivisions of America. All of us, he wrote, are *Americans* first.

> Think of the soldiers from the Southern States, whose fathers and grandfathers had hated the very name of Yankee, yet who themselves went to the First World War to the tune of The Yanks Are Coming, and whose sons in the present war read Yank, the newspaper for soldiers from all sections. Think of the Marines who raised a Confederate flag over a fortress taken on Okinawa, and of the cheerful smiles that followed the news everywhere in America. Those Marines, like other Americans, knew that the Stars and Bars would soon come down and the Stars and Stripes rise on its staff.

A close affection for the part, a wide vision of the whole: these are the two patriotisms which any American can cherish without

any conflict between them. Those Americans who do not cherish the both at the same time are the rootless and the discon-
nected, and they are figure, if not of comedy, then of pity...Let
no American imagine that he can love his part of the country
fully without a love for all of it, or that he can love all of it if he
has not begun by loving a part of it first.[358]

The Second World War affected Van Doren beyond its moral,
intellectual, and ideological complexities. As it did with most
Americans, the war hit Van Doren close to home. Where brothers Mark and Paul had served in the first world war, the current
war effort had inducted two of Van Doren's sons-in-law into the
U.S. Army. Carl and Irita Van Doren's three daughters, Anne,
Margaret, and Barbara, were now married women with husbands
of draftable age. Anne, who was a manuscript reader at Harcourt
Brace in the 1930s and had some short stories of her own published, married Jerome Ross in 1942. While "Jerry" was stationed
with the Army in Algiers, Anne accepted an overseas position
with the Office of War Information and moved to London in
the summer of 1944. Barbara, or "Bobby" as she was called by
her family, married Spencer Klaw in 1941 after attending Vassar
College—the only one of Van Doren's daughters to attend college—and lived for a time in San Francisco, where "Spence" wrote
for the *San Francisco Chronicle*. In 1943 Spencer was inducted into
the Army and was posted with the Signal corps at Camp Crowder,

Missouri. Bobby took a temporary position with the Office of War Information in Washington D.C. in early 1943 before joining her husband in Missouri, where she began writing a book on the life and times of an Army wife. Middle daughter Margaret was the only sibling not personally affiliated with the war effort. Her husband, Tom Bevans, worked with a publishing house in New York and Margaret had become a children's book author and illustrator and, later, an editor at the *New York Herald Tribune.*

During her year in London with the Office of War Information, Anne sent regular dispatches to her father, whom she addressed as "Dearest Pooch," describing the city's growing feelings of optimism that the war would soon come to an end. After five long years of war, Londoners were starting to think, and to talk, about a brokered peace. In September, Anne wrote of the "perceptible change" in the air, owing to a forty-six-hour lull in the bombings. The effect of that relative quiet was noticeable. Christmas, however, was difficult; nostalgia and loneliness mingled in the souls of all of the displaced men and women so far from their homes. An increase in cigarette rations, however, was cause for some serious celebration shortly after the New Year, with smokers bartering with non-smokers for the seven packs per week they would not use. News and images of the Nazi atrocities in the concentration camps flooded the OWI in April 1945, when U.S. troops liberated the death camps. Anne described to her father the "horrible details" emerging from the camps, including reports from a young soldier who had been among the liberators. She saw in the lad a look of "genuine shock and horror" arising from all that he had seen in the camps; the interview had been emotional and intense.[159]

If the First World War left a younger generation cynical and unmoored in the wake of that seemingly senseless global conflict, the Second World War raised questions moral, technological, and political to more than one generation of horrified Americans. The Atomic Age had arrived and with it an increased urgency to quell, what seemed to many, like global anarchy.

CHAPTER 9

FOLLOWING HIS HEART

The New York literary circle in the first half of the twentieth century was a very small world. Everyone knew everyone. Literary critics such as Carl Van Doren, Joseph Wood Krutch, Herbert S. Gorman, and Henry S. Canby, along with writers like Elinor Wylie & William Rose Benet, Sinclair & Dorothy Lewis, and Malcom Cowley, all lived within walking distance of one another in Greenwich Village. Many owned summer homes in Cornwall, Connecticut or drove up for weekend visits. It didn't take *six degrees of separation* to complete any given circle amongst the literati. To illustrate: Edmund Wilson wrote a satirical piece about Carl Van Doren and Herbert S. Gorman in the *New Republic*; Van Doren worked with fellow writer/critic Herbert S. Gorman; Gorman married Jean Wright (who wrote a handful of book reviews for the *New York Times*); Jean Wright later divorced Gorman, cavorted with Edmund Wilson, and befriended Carl Van Doren...who then married her.

Norma Jean Wright was born in Cleveland, Ohio on June 14, 1892. The middle child of three girls, Norma Jean left Ohio for New York as a young woman and married writer Herbert S. Gorman in New York City in 1921. Actually a year older than Gorman, Jean habitually shaved a few years off of her birthday and gave 1897 as the year of her birth. The couple lived in Greenwich Village, on W. 12th Street, where Gorman worked as a journalist, poet, essayist, and literary critic. He wrote numerous book reviews and literary criticism for the *New York Times* and the *New Republic*, covering writers such as Sherwood Anderson, Elinor Wylie, and Carl Van Doren. Herbert Gorman and Jean Wright co-edited *The Peterborough Anthology* in 1923, and Jean wrote a handful of book reviews for the *New York Times* in 1923 and '24. Jean, along with writer Mary Colum, had organized the 1922 poetry reading in which Van Doren first met Elinor Wylie.

In the summer of 1931, Jean Wright Gorman travelled by train with Edmund Wilson's second wife, Margaret Canby (no relation to the editor Henry S. Canby) to southern California. Jean and Margaret were friends and drinking buddies, and Margaret was making her semi-annual trip to Santa Barbara, where she shared custody of her young son with her ex-husband. At that particular moment, Edmund Wilson was feeling more than a little concerned about the parting, as his relationship with Margaret had been rocky and her emotional state was troubling. Not long into her stay in Santa Barbara and having parted from Wilson on less than happy terms, Margaret suffered a freak, and fatal, accident. A petite woman who preferred dangerously high heels, she lost her footing and tumbled down a flight of stairs at a party, fracturing her skull. Wilson was devastated and, as one can imagine, overcome with feelings of guilt at the way the couple had parted in New York. Who wouldn't reproach oneself after a terrible parting ends tragically? (*If only my final words to her had not been so full of reproach, if only I had listened, if only I had kept my temper, if only if only if only...*) Shortly after the shocking event, Jean headed from California to Reno, Nevada, where she had planned to file for divorce from Herbert Gorman. The divorce was granted in February 1932, and that summer Jean met up with Van Doren in southern California during his westward lecture tour, the tour in which she served as his guide around Hollywood.

Fast-forward to 1934, and Jean was reportedly in "hot pursuit" of Edmund Wilson back on the east coast. The couple spent a summer weekend at the Cape Cod home of writer Mary Heaton Vorse (not *all* literati summered in Cornwall, even if Henry S. Canby felt the most influential of the bunch did). A colleague and friend of Wilson's, Matthew Josephson, later described the weekend scene in which Jean was draped all over Wilson at a late-night gathering of various writer-friends, Jean muttering "affectionate obscenities" in Wilson's ear. Owing to a silly argument with another of the houseguests, Wilson left in a huff. Jean tried to stop him and Wilson gave her an unchivalrous, and deeply inebriated, shove. Later that night, a perhaps dejected or humiliated or drunk Jean spilled gin in her bed and accidentally set the linens on fire with a cigarette. She paid for the damages, and laughed off the incident as nothing more than typical summer shenanigans.[160]

Sometime after her summer fling with Wilson, Jean re-connected with Van Doren and over the next few years travelled with him to Urbana to visit his family, vacationed with him in Bermuda, and helped type Van Doren's manuscript for his autobiography *Three Worlds*, which was published in 1936. Carl and Jean were married on February 27, 1939 in a quiet ceremony at a friend's home in San Francisco, three years after Van Doren's divorce from Irita was finalized. He was fifty-three years old, she was forty-six, although she admitted to thirty-eight. Where Irita was described throughout her life as a sweet Southern girl, Jean was a party girl who liked gin and cigarettes and running with the literary crowd on free-wheeling jaunts in and out of New York City. She was extravagant where Irita was genteel. Van Doren could not have picked a more different sort of wife for his second marriage. From January through March of that year, Van Doren was busy with another of his cross-country lecture tours, this time travelling with Jean to Wisconsin, Oregon, California, Utah, and Colorado.

In classic Van Doren style, he made a point to keep word of the nuptials quiet. Writing to his friend Victor Chittick in February, Van Doren included a clipping from the morning paper announcing the wedding. He wrote, "Once or twice I came damned near telling you about the marriage, planned only a few days before I left New York, but I reflected that a second marriage is not the first, and who in hell was I to rub other people's noses in my affairs, however fragrant." In a letter to his brother Mark, Van Doren said only, "San Francisco is superb and incredible. More when I see you."[161]

A year after the wedding, Mr. and Mrs. Van Doren were photographed taking a belated honeymoon to Hawaii. While there, Jean sat down for an interview with a Honolulu reporter, who described Mrs. Carl Van Doren as "a little bit of a vivacious brunette." The newspaper article, "Wife Doesn't Review Van Doren's Books—She Helps Write 'Em" included a photo of Jean posing, very fetching and cheerful, in a Hawaiian *holoku*. Jean reported that she did much of her husband's research and typing for his biography on Ben Franklin. She also claimed to be "co-editor," with J. Donald Adams, of the *New York Times Book Review*. The first claim was possibly correct. Jean, after all, had written some book reviews for the *New York Times* and had co-edited *The Peterborough Anthology* with her ex-husband Herbert Gorman. It's true that she was adept at research, composition, and editing.

Her second claim, however, was most certainly false. Jean might possibly have been a *reader* who submitted summaries for the *Times'* book reviews, but the 1940 census indicates "no income" for Jean that year. Her claim to co-editor is more than doubtful. J. Donald Adams, in fact, was a colleague of Carl's ex-wife Irita. Adams edited the *New York Times Book Review* during the years Irita edited the *New York Herald-Tribune Review of Books,* and the two editors participated in several literary fairs and critics' conferences together. J. Donald Adams and Irita Van Doren presided over the series of book and author luncheons sponsored by the American Booksellers Association in 1938, and both served as judges of the 1945 Harper's Prize Novel Contest. In light of Adams' close dealings with Irita Van Doren, it is curious that the new Mrs. Van Doren would publically, and erroneously, attach her name to the esteemed *Times* editor in such a manner. In 1940, however, the chances that a New York reader would stumble across an article in a Honolulu newspaper were quite slim.

There are several indications that Carl and Jean Van Doren's marriage was never an easy one. Jean often suffered from what Van Doren regularly described as sinus trouble, insomnia, or tooth ailments. Not infrequently, he made excuses for his wife's absence at dinners or weekend gatherings. While the couple did spend weekends visiting with Van Doren's close friends the Boyds at Princeton, and with Carl's brother Paul, who lived in nearby Glen Ridge, and Jean had accompanied Carl several times on visits to family in Urbana, there was enough tension to prevent Van Doren from enjoying his family's summer home in Cornwall, which Irita retained after the divorce. In fact, Van Doren had not been to Cornwall in a good many years, that bucolic and literary outpost he so enjoyed throughout the 1920s.

In late 1944, Van Doren's daughter Anne wrote of her concern for her father and the stress his marriage was causing him. She had just heard from her sisters of the latest round of difficulty between Carl and Jean and their recent separation. This was not the couple's first separation; Anne in fact was relieved to hear the news. Underlying the couple's difficulties were some questions surrounding Jean's mental state. Anne practically pleaded with her father to take care of himself first and foremost, and allowed that perhaps, as Carl had said, Jean was not always able to take responsibility for her troubling behavior. Nevertheless, Anne was primarily concerned for her father's wellbeing, not Jean's. She worried about the effects the difficult marriage was having on her pops. Anne, Van Doren's eldest daughter, insisted her father not feel sorry for Jean, nor feel guilty about this latest separation. Jean's general mood of unhappiness was making the two of them unhappy, and Anne hoped her father would be firm and not reconcile with his wife this time. It wouldn't, she felt, help matters anyway. And while Anne had always tried to behave and think charitably towards her step-mother, "as one does about somebody who is sick," some things simply could not be worked out.

Tension and unhappiness had plagued the Van Dorens' marriage for quite some time. Van Doren's heavy travel schedule across 1944 and 1945, which took the author/critic back and forth across the country, from Shreveport and New Orleans, to Oklahoma City, Dallas and Ft. Worth, Kansas City, Chicago and Urbana, Buffalo, Worcester, and back east to Providence, New London, and New York (all of this travel by train or propeller-driven aircraft; either scenario presenting a tiresome itinerary) added to Van Doren's daily stress. A retinal surgery earlier that year had been a frightful ordeal as well. All three of Van Doren's daughters hoped he would remain resolute following this latest separation, move on with his life, and escape the emotional torment this marriage was causing him.[162]

This latest separation would indeed be final. Sometime just before the New Year, Jean travelled to Reno to secure a divorce, which was granted on February 7, 1945, nearly six years after the couple had wed. By June, Jean was dead. According to the death certificate, Jean Van Doren's body was found on June 26, 1945 at an address about a block from Van Doren's 41 Central Park West apartment. The death certificate listed Jean's age as fifty years old (actually, she was fifty-three) and cause of death as "congestion of the viscera: pending chemical examination." When Van Doren later wrote to his friend Victor Chittick, he described that Jean "died tragically from an overdose, accidental, of sleeping capsules, after years of tormenting insomnia." Van Doren's woeful letter of an accidental overdose technically jibes with the death certificate's "pending chemical examination" notation, and his comments over the years as to Jean's insomnia and recurring pains corroborate the likelihood of her use of sleeping pills. Jean's death was certainly shocking and painful to Van Doren and the family. The marriage had not ended well, and those wounds were still fresh.[163]

However, another account of Jean Van Doren's death is more troubling. Edmund Wilson was no particular friend of the Van Dorens, but neither was he interested in incurring charges of libel. And he had dated Jean Wright Gorman, however briefly, back in the '30s, so he had an interest in her fate. A prolific writer, Wilson had kept a lifetime of personal diaries and notebooks and published these writings in decade-long installments. *Edmund Wilson: The Twenties*; *Edmund Wilson: The Thirties*, and so on. Many of these published journals contained uncensored descriptions of his most intimate encounters. There was a lot of sex, and names were named. But Wilson was never sued for libel or slander. Often caustic, he was not in the habit of lying or spreading unfounded gossip.

In the final volume of Wilson's published diaries, *The Sixties; The Last Journal*, Edmund Wilson claimed that Jean Van Doren committed suicide; that she had hanged herself. Wilson recalled a 1960s cocktail party, whose guests included presidential speechwriter Richard Goodwin (Goodwin had been a part of the House

Subcommittee on Congressional Oversight's investigation into the 1950s quiz show scandal which implicated Mark Van Doren's son, Charlie, as among the rigged contestants[xv]). In the journal, Wilson recalled that he and Goodwin and some other party-goers had been talking about the Van Dorens, and Goodwin mentioned something about Jean Gorman's suicide: specifically that Carl had returned home and found that Jean had hanged herself (In reality, and perhaps more frightfully, it was Carl's daughter Bobby who made the horrific discovery). This revelation, amidst an otherwise festive social gathering, gave Wilson quite a shock. He said that he knew Jean had committed suicide—apparently others knew it too—but he hadn't known the grisly details.[164]

Van Doren had been travelling on a lecture tour in mid-June and was scheduled to head back to the city towards the end of the month. The gruesome story, which apparently was already known to many in that circle, aligns within the timetable of Carl's travel schedule and return New York. The official death certificate's "Congestion of the viscera" is a vague post-mortem notation and does not discount death by strangulation. Although Jean had moved back to Cleveland after the divorce and was living in her parents' home, it is unclear what brought her back to New York in late June. Wilson's published account of Jean's suicide was never

....

xv   The reader may recall Robert Redford's 1994 film, *Quiz Show*, which featured Ralph Fiennes as Charlie Van Doren, Paul Scofield as Mark Van Doren, and Rob Morrow as Richard Goodwin.

publically challenged. He was not known to publish false rumors. He had enough of his own colorful experiences to write about.

Anne, living in Italy with Jerry since the end of the war, telegrammed her love and support to her father as soon as she heard the staggering news. In a lengthier letter, she reiterated her shock and surprise, and was primarily concerned with her father's emotional and physical well-being. Anne was firm: he should not torture himself over this, should not reproach himself. He was not responsible. Anne, sadly, felt this ending was inevitable and was probably a more peaceful ending than what might have occurred if Jean had continued in her present state. Anne surmised that Jean was, fundamentally, an unhappy woman. She probably could never be happy. Years later, when friend and colleague Joseph Krutch wrote an homage to Van Doren in *The Nation,* he acknowledged that Carl had experienced more than his share of sorrow and tragedy in his lifetime. Certainly Jean's death had to account for much of that sorrow.[165]

The extant collection of Van Doren's personal correspondence in the year following Jean's death dwindles remarkably. Van Doren was most certainly not in the spirits for the small-talk and incidental ramblings that often go into letters between friends. Equally likely is the very real possibility that many of Van Doren's letters during this time were lost or purposefully destroyed. One does not necessarily want the blackest part of one's life to be saved for posterity. Stoic Dutch indifference or not, no letters remain in Van Doren's papers which might give future readers a glimpse into the private pain and anguish Carl felt in the weeks and months following Jean's death. This was most certainly a determined choice. The busy exchange of letters between Carl and his brother Mark, between Carl and his good friends Victor Chittick and Julian Boyd and Sinclair Lewis, all fall silent. There is very, very little mention of Jean. Practically nothing. To Chittick, Van Doren only wrote, "As to the private tragedy about which you speak so understandingly, it is too agonized and complex to write about, but I'll tell you when I see you."[166]

In September of 1945, Van Doren's friends threw him a birthday party to honor his sixty years. Mark Van Doren, Julian Boyd, Sinclair Lewis, the publisher George Macy, and a gathering of local friends made a grand party for the honored guest, still grappling with the sudden and dramatic demise of his ex-wife. As a souvenir, Macy put together a hardbound booklet, *Now That Carl is Sixty: A Birthday book*, filled with poems on aging and the wisdom of passing years from a variety of writers, including Thomas Moore, Anatole France, and Ralph Waldo Emerson. Adding to the celebratory tone, Van Doren's latest book, *Carl Van Doren: The Viking Portable Library*, had recently come out to laudatory reviews. In his introductory chapter "What is American Literature?" the literary critic was at his most brilliant. The essay gives an intellectual history of American literature as a series of biographies of those authors whom Van Doren found most essential to the literary canon. With writing that is both elegant and erudite, Van Doren covered authors from the colonial period to his own time.

Pulitzer Prize-winning author Annie Dillard once wrote about a well-known writer who was "corralled" by a student after class, asking if she thought he could become a writer. The writer's response was: *Well... Do you like sentences?* As much as Van Doren admitted to his closest friends that he never found writing to be easy, that he struggled with every line to make his point as concisely as possible, he was clearly a man who reveled in a good sentence. Of Thomas Paine, Van Doren wrote, "Within a year he had made himself as much an American as he needed to be." Of Washington Irving's prose, Van Doren praised, "In a soil accustomed to facts, Irving planted fiction," while of James Fenimore Cooper, Van Doren wrote, "in a boredom of which he was possibly not aware, he became a novelist." And while Mark Twain and Henry James were contemporaries, Van Doren astutely described the completely different worlds in which they lived: "The two men belonged to barely overlapping Americas."[167]

Through the essay, originally printed as a "little book" in 1933 and reprinted in 1935 and again for the *Viking Portable Library* in 1945, Van Doren set out to answer the question of, what, exactly, is *American* literature. The literary critic determined, "American literature is the only important literature in the world which is younger than the art of printing." Which tells us two things: firstly, that American literature is the only "important" literature not begun in the oral tradition. It came after the printing press. Secondly, but more provocatively, Van Doren's statement reveals his certainty—and that of his generation and of every generation before him—that there is an objective standard by which litera-ture can, and should, be weighed. There is good prose, and there is poor. There is strong literature, and there is weak. There are seers, and there are poseurs. But fundamentally, and on this point the critic was quite clear, ascertaining the difference is a neces-sary task and one which can, in fact, be determined.

Beginning with the colonial period, Van Doren character-ized the whole of American literature as being primarily con-cerned with bringing the *News from America* from the New World to the Old. Early American writers like Jonathan Edwards and Benjamin Franklin meant to show outsiders how Americans *lived* in America, what is was *to be* an American, and how the American experience was unique and exceptional. These writers meant to show that, unlike their forbearers from the Old World, "free-born Americans would create starting with fresh materials and working to fresh patterns: Europeans might be descendants, but Americans were ancestors." Generally marked by a collec-tive feeling of hopefulness, from the very beginning Americans did more than simply endure their present circumstances, they "embroidered it with magic."

Even when the News from America was not especially good, or fair, or lived up to one's expectations, the early writers—even the pessimists—wrote with the conviction that, even if America was *not* Utopia, was not the golden City on the Hill, that it *ought* to be. Because America, and Americans, were *different*.

The Revolutionary period created writers like Thomas Paine, who was not born an American but after arriving here became "as much an American as he needed to be" and whose political and common-sensical treatise decried, "in a world full of tyrants, America must be an asylum for the rights of man." Paine, who was later derided for attacking the Church with the same ferocity with which he attacked imperial rule, was a critical voice in forging the course of a new nation because his words *rallied the undecided*. His compelling prose ushered forth a mass impetus to act against a tyrannical crown as a *moral obligation*.

American literature was hopeful, was enthusiastic, was heroic, was mythic: was epic. James Fenimore Cooper created the character Leather-Stocking as "a true hero for the American heroic age." Walt Whitman was America's poet, Mark Twain its comedic wit. American philosophy materialized in the writings of Ralph Waldo Emerson, whose "mind was a hive," and from the writings of Thoreau and Hawthorne. The American men of letters from the nineteenth century expressed themselves in words as they expressed themselves in action. They were Men of Action, they were Man Thinking. Van Doren wrote that "Emerson, saying that man was the center of the universe, was seen to be saying that Americans were centers of a universe of which the manifest substance was American." They were heroes all, heroes of action and heroes of the mind.

What they were doing, argued Van Doren, and what solidified this canon of American literature, was that essential function of all good literature: they were making heroes, and those heroes made America. They were myth-makers. But the myths they created were not spun from fanciful yarn. No, these writers had their fingers on the pulse of their times, each skilled at perceiving, reflecting, and distilling the essence of the epoch. They were prophets, they were seers, who transformed into words "what essence they could get out of the yeasty ferment of the times." Which is what Van Doren later wrote about Sinclair Lewis, and Mary Hunter Austin, and Elinor Wylie. Each spoke with the "tongue of faith" in a way that reflected America's changing attitudes toward the ever-changing world.

Across the 1940s, Van Doren wrote a series of articles for the popular women's magazine *Good Housekeeping*, including "A Biographer on the Trail," "Our Two Patriotisms," and "What I Saw When I Was Blind." For two weeks following his surgery for a retinal detachment in July of 1944, Van Doren did not know if he would ever see again, or how much sight he might have left. During his recovery, both eyes were taped shut and covered with a close black mask. He saw only a sporadic flood of white light.

He admitted, "Once, in spite of my naturally steady nerves, I had a sudden fear that the light might become more that I could bear." In his article "Women's Instinct," Van Doren wrote about the cult of women's intuition. For his part, he did not believe women had a particularly magical instinct which men lacked. Women may say they act on instinct, and men on judgment, but Van Doren argued these two were actually intertwined processes. He wrote about the Touro Synagogue in Newport, Rhode Island, the oldest synagogue in the country and recently named a National Historic Site. Van Doren was the emcee of that dedication ceremony and spent a grand time at the Hotel Viking in one of the nation's oldest port cities. In "Out of Order," the cultural critic wrote on the difference between meetings and mobs, asserting "Rules of order are so familiar and habitual to us, and to the people of democratic societies everywhere, that we seldom stop to reflect on what they mean in our lives as citizens. Yet probably no other customary way of doing things exerts a more truly civilizing influence."

Throughout the fall of 1945 and into 1946, Van Doren continued his lecture circuit at a hurried pace, travelling to Buffalo, Philadelphia, Nashville, Atlanta, Oklahoma City, New Orleans, and Chicago. His contract for all speaking engagements earned $500 per lecture, plus travel expenses and a berth in a Pullman car. Crisscrossing the country, Van Doren wrote to Julian Boyd of the frenetic pace for the not-so-young-man of sixty, both boasting and lamenting, "I shall kill myself yet." He regretfully turned down a position in the diplomatic corps, confiding to Boyd that "it almost broke my heart" to do so but felt, for reasons of health, it was simply impossible (Boyd assumed, by "diplomatic corps," Van Doren was referring to something at the Library of Congress, where their mutual colleague Archibald MacLeish was Librarian). By the spring of '46, the speed at which Van Doren had continued to work following an emotional year had taken its toll. For the man who so enjoyed the excitement of the lecture circuit, meeting up with old colleagues and making new friends along the trail, public engagements had become tiresome and stressful.[168]

Some time had passed since Van Doren had last visited Sinclair Lewis, and Red was eager for his friend to come stay at his country retreat in Williamstown, Massachusetts. Red's latest bucolic home, Thorvale Farm, sat among "the most glorious mountain view, the most enticing woods and meadows to walk in...I've seen so little of you, the past couple of years. Let's not lose each other. Ever, *Red*." Nagging bouts of high blood pressure and "nerves," however, forced Van Doren to lay low in Cornwall with Margaret and the grandchildren for the summer. Doctor's orders. It was time to ease up on the "excessive work and strain" this travelling man of letters had become accustomed to. Van Doren's galloping pulse needed a rest.[169]

During his marriage to Jean, Van Doren had avoided the family home at Cornwall. Now, it became his refuge. Located in Litchfield County, it's difficult to imagine a more picturesque

New England landscape. The auto route leaving the city (one could also make the journey by train; the Harlem Line headed straight to Cornwall) was mostly a straight shot up Route 22, through Westchester County and northward through the more remote villages of Croton Falls, Brewster, and Pawling in Putnam and Dutchess counties. In Wingdale, NY, one passed the newly erected Harlem Valley Psychiatric Center, an imposing cluster of austere and uniform brick buildings erected in 1924. The campus presented a foreboding contrast to the otherwise bucolic landscape; one doesn't have to wonder at the hospital's remote location, seventy-five long miles north of the city.

After passing through Wingdale, one made a sharp eastward turn towards Bull's Bridge, one of a handful of covered bridges scattered across the state, and crossed the Housatonic River into Connecticut. From there, Route 7 follows the river north, through the village of Kent and the many cow and horse pastures which creep up into the foothills. The stretch of road contains thirteen miles of the most picturesque New England hills and valleys you can imagine, the Housatonic River crawling slowly past you as it winds its way south through several state forests before releasing its energy into Long Island Sound at Milford. At Cornwall Bridge, the road split, with one fork heading east along Route 4 towards Cornwall. Van Doren, however, would continue north for a few more miles, crossing back over the Housatonic River and winding along its western bank to the covered bridge leading into West

Cornwall. More hamlet than village or town, West Cornwall's toll house, train station, and post office pass in the blink of an eye before ascending the long, winding road of Cream Hill to the Van Doren home.

With its covered bridge, rushing river, sparkling red and orange foliage in the fall and blankets of white snow in the winter, Cornwall was more than a summer encampment for New York's literary intelligentsia; it was the one place where Van Doren could spend great stretches of time with his daughters and their own growing families. In the months following World War II, Anne's husband Jerry had been stationed in Rome, where she found a job working for the magazine *Nuovo Mondo* near the couple's flat in the Via Gregoriana neighborhood. Although the view from the couple's terrace overlooking Saint Peter's Cathedral and the Vatican was impressive, Anne was happy to return home as soon as the State Department took over operations of the Office of War Information and Jerry received a discharge. In New York, he found work writing programs for radio shows, and Anne wrote articles for various print publications. Margaret had become a children's book author and illustrator, and her husband Tom Bevans was a partner at Simon & Schuster. Bobby was an author as well, and her husband Spencer Klaw was with the *New Yorker*. As Van Doren described, writing "somewhat runs in the family." The sons-in-law and Irita Van Doren joined the family on the weekends, while

Anne, Margaret, Bobby and Grandpa Carl held down the fort for the long summer retreat.

At Cornwall, "The roads are wildly twisted and almost impossible to direct anybody over. When people come to visit us we ask them to come to West Cornwall, our railway station on U.S. Highway 7, and telephone us; then we drive down and bring them up...We have little but weather and landscape to occupy ourselves with here on vacation." Van Doren herded the grandchildren, tended to the garden, and was known to take a cycle or scythe to the overgrowth of brush surrounding the property. Late in the summer, Van Doren wrote to Victor Chittick that he would arrive by train for the Reed Writer's Conference that fall, as his doctor had forbidden him to fly due to his "galloping pulse." In October 1946, Van Doren's eyes, fully recovered from the retinal surgery, lighted for the first time on Elizabeth Marion.[170]

By this time, Van Doren's family had become a respected literary dynasty. In addition to Carl and Mark and Carl's ex-wife Irita and Mark's wife Dorothy, Carl's grown children and their spouses were also working in the writing professions. Carl's ex-wife Jean (when she was alive) and Jean's first husband Herbert Gorman were in the writing loop. And while New York City was the locus of all of this literary activity, its tentacles stretched far beyond the metropolitan area, even beyond the Van Dorens' homes at Cornwall, or Edmund Wilson's cottage on Cape Cod, or Sinclair Lewis's farm in Williamstown, or Mary Hunter Austin's retreat at Carmel. These tentacles stretched even to a family farm in the remote town of Spangle, Washington. Elizabeth Marion's growing friendship with Carl Van Doren, the *Man who Knew Everybody*, was not even *her* first time at this rodeo. She too had connections. She was already a part of this interconnected web of writing people. It was a very small world indeed.

To illustrate: Carl Van Doren met Mary Hunter Austin, he as a literary critic, she as an expert in American Indian folklore and writer of the western landscape. Mary Hunter Austin lived for a time in Greenwich Village at 10 Barrow Street, just around the corner from Van Doren's apartment on West 13th Street. Van Doren's good friend Sinclair Lewis used to visit Mary there and they had lovely, folksy conversation. Her upstairs neighbor was Hendrik Willem Van Loon. Van Loon, like Van Doren, was a historian, literary critic, author, and editor. Van Loon and Van Doren were co-editors at the Literary Guild of America; Van Loon was also the creator of the long-running radio program "University of the Air."

He, too, was a man of letters. Born in 1882 in Rotterdam, Van Loon had emigrated to the United States in 1902 to study at Cornell University. He later earned his Ph.D. from the University of Munich and wrote for the Associated Press in Europe during the First World War. The author and illustrator of many books, including *The Story of Mankind*—the first book ever to win the Newbery Medal—Van Loon wrote articles for *The Nation*, *Forum*, and for a time was associate editor of the *Baltimore Sun*. He had an expansive presence on radio shows, including "University of the Air," in which he discussed historical incidents and expounded upon his many philosophical and political opinions, especially as these related to the Nazi occupation of his native Holland and the impending global crisis.

In the years leading up to the Second World War, Van Loon broadcast anti-Nazi speeches over the air waves, a mission dear to his Dutch affinities but one which Van Loon could not be sure the American public sufficiently appreciated. Like Carl Van Doren, this man of letters wore many hats; writing for and speaking on behalf of political causes grew out of the reputation Van Loon had earned as a historian and literary critic. In a letter to Elizabeth Marion, Van Loon made clear the critical nature of his on-air political commentary, and acknowledged he would have little time to devote to the "pleasanter jobs" of literary work so long as he was committed to warning "our indifferent public against the unspeakable Nazi threat."[171]

As is very nearly universally the case, his name has been lost to history with the passing of that era of public intellectual life. But in his day, Van Loon was a man of influence, a respected historian and cultural critic, a voice heard across the radio waves captivating the attention of millions of Americans. Hendrik Willem Van Loon became acquainted with Elizabeth Marion and helped her get her first novel published. Elizabeth Marion later captured the attention of Carl Van Doren, who was enchanted. She wrote to him about retreating to a desert hermitage in a remote corner of the Southwest. Van Doren learned much of what he knew of that western desert from Mary Hunter Austin, and dreamed of joining Elizabeth Marion in neighboring hogans.

How exactly Elizabeth Marion of Spangle, Washington came to be introduced to Hendrik Willem Van Loon is not entirely clear. Most likely she introduced herself via letter. This is what Elizabeth Marion would have done in 1938 as she was seeking a publisher for her first novel, *The Day Will Come*. If the New York publishing world did not have its sights set on Spangle, Washington (and it most certainly did not; the current population of Spangle is only around 240 people, Carl Van Doren had difficulty finding a map that marked the tiny town in 1946), then Elizabeth Marion would have been pro-active in investigating her publishing options. However the first introduction was made, from 1938 to 1944 Elizabeth Marion and Hendrik Willem Van Loon shared a professional correspondence that can best be described as student-mentor. Van Loon introduced Marion to his literary agent, Jacques Chambrun, and to Elizabeth Reilly, a good friend of his who just happened to be an editor at Thomas Y. Crowell Company. These were fortuitous connections for the young writer from Spangle, as Crowell would publish three Elizabeth Marion novels: *The Day Will Come*, *Ellen Spring*, and *The Keys to the House*.

The surviving letters in the Marion-Van Loon correspondence include only those letters from Van Loon himself; Elizabeth's letters have been lost. A curious habit in all of Van Loon's letters to Elizabeth was the ever-present ellipses. Van Loon rarely used any capitalization, and instead of periods marking the end of a sentence he preferred the ellipse. Later, in her letters to Carl Van Doren, Elizabeth Marion similarly did not adhere to the rules of capitalization, and like Van Loon, she regularly employed ellipses instead of periods. This sort of informality could simply have been *de rigeur* in the 1930s and '40s, but it's not likely. This author has not seen the pattern so completely adhered to outside of Van Loon's letters to Elizabeth or Elizabeth's letters to Van Doren. It's curious, the behaviors and mannerisms we pick up along the way. Who really knows what mark of influence he or she will leave upon another...

Writing from his apartment in New York City or from his summer home along the coast of Maine, Van Loon advised the much younger writer from Spangle to hold fast and remain persistent. He too, even at this successful stage of his literary career, was not immune to the dreaded rejection slip. Van Loon assured Elizabeth that even he had "to fight for every book, for every idea, for every damn thing I ever did and I still have to fight, for if I did not have to fight I would write like the rest of them...publishers and editors are stickinthemuds who holler for new ideas and fear them." Van Loon asked Elizabeth Marion about her current writing projects: to whom did she send her work? He liked to help talent when he saw it, good writing was hard to come by and she had a special knack for putting words together. He was delighted to help her in whatever way he could.[172]

Of the many kernels of advice the elder writer offered his would-be acolyte, Van Loon frequently encouraged Elizabeth Marion to get out and see the rest of the country. As Elizabeth was still living at home with her parents, a status not particularly unusual for an unmarried woman in her early twenties at the tail end of the Depression, Van Loon reproached the newly published author for taking her "free board and lodging too seriously." While writing would never make her rich, *per se*, he instructed Elizabeth to stop worrying so much about her bank account; ongoing sales of her novels would likely yield her a nice income. She really needed to get out and see the world.

And while he applauded her native gift for writing, for the life of him Van Loon could not imagine how she acquired or fostered that gift in a backwater like Spangle. She could expand her horizons in any number of places; her destination needn't be so obvious as New York City, Van Loon insisted. Elizabeth might just as well take some time away from Spangle and head to Chicago, where she had been offered an opportunity at the prestigious University of Chicago. Like Carl Van Doren, Hendrik Willem Van Loon was no fan of academia. He had taught for a while at Cornell University after he earned his Ph.D. Rumor had it that while he was a most popular instructor with the students, Van Loon was, on more than one occasion, accused of "lapses in historical accuracy." *Baaah!* Van Loon responded, his fellow scholars were simply peeved by his own obvious popularity. That was the end of Van Loon's academic career; he would spend the rest of his life writing, very successfully, in the public realm. Van Loon advised Elizabeth Marion that in spite of any university's intrinsic weaknesses, by all means yes, she should accept the offer and go to Chicago. There, she would be surrounded by books, intelligent people, and good conversation.[173]

The literary critic in Van Loon cautioned the young novelist against what he found to be some stylistic flaws in her writing. Several of the characters in Elizabeth Marion's books were downright unpleasant. Many of the female characters, especially, were portrayed consistently in unflattering terms. Writing to Carl Van Doren several years later, Elizabeth Marion described the inherent differences she perceived between men and women. As far as she was concerned, "men are—hearty, I think; as a general rule, that is; not always; but women are—I dunno what exactly... not nasty-minded exactly, petty-minded perhaps, reducing all of life to a minute investigation of all the tiny wheels and tubes and internal combustions of bodies, their own and everyone else's..."[174] An excerpt from her second novel, *Ellen Spring,* mirrors these sentiments:

Mother was just like that, Ellen thought. Just as thin and sour and superior...just as ready to make conversation of her mental ills and never knowing they were ills. Or mental either: Fanny Leonard thought and felt and lived with and by her peculiar abortive emotions.

She made no attempt to understand anything except herself, and herself only to confirm to her vanity. All else she ignored, and from the delusions of her conceit came her concept of wisdom. There is never any arguing with such women.[175]

Van Loon appreciated that Elizabeth Marion was currently living amid conditions that were quite likely a hindrance to one's creative or intellectual aspirations. That is, she was stuck in Spangle, surrounded by non-writer types. He could intuit, perhaps in response to something specific Elizabeth had told him, that she was frustrated with the present situation or her present company, and so she created these "nasty" types of characters in her novels as a way of venting.[xvi] However, he warned the young

....

[xvi] Numerous examples from The Keys To The House further illustrate the author's frustrations: "He wished women thought before they spoke. They had a habit of uttering blasphemy as heedlessly as they discussed hats and children." And later, the book's narrator reveals: "I hated myself, and I hated every other woman I saw because I thought she was capable of being what I had been...It was cruel of me, wasn't it? Judging other women by what only I knew of myself..." These sour descriptions of female characters speak to Elizabeth Marion's perceptions of the indolent and self-involved woman. However, a worthwhile woman was the opposite of all of these things: rational, efficient, faithful, industrious (Keys, 16, 238)

novelist that most of her readers had to deal with nasty types of their own, and didn't necessarily want to be reminded of the fact. Van Loon seemed to be advising Elizabeth Marion to tone it down a bit. This sounds a bit like the complaint Mary Hunter Austin made against male editors in general, in that they continually instructed female writers on what they should or shouldn't write about.[176]

If Elizabeth Marion was put off by this criticism, it didn't reflect in the pair's correspondence. Nor did her writing style noticeably change in her subsequent novels. *The Keys to the House*, for example, contains similar character descriptions of the female variety:

> The woman did not, Margaret told herself sourly, smell at all like rosemary, nor did she look like it. She was only an obese slovenly indolent woman who confused busily with industry, who believed that a dime-store cologne bottle was preferable to a bath, who concealed her inherent inefficiency beneath a beaming exterior of cheerful good nature.[177]

Elizabeth Marion found a kindred spirit in Hendrik Willem Van Loon when he announced that what he really needed was a quiet place to write, a sanctuary free from any and all interruptions. He, too, needed a room of his own. "America has never understood what creative work is...yet nobody would come and start and (*sic*) argument with a woman in labor, which is exactly the same thing." This resonated with Elizabeth Marion; he was speaking her language.[178]

Elizabeth Marion and Hendrik Willem Van Loon remained correspondents until his death in 1944 at the age of sixty-two. All three of her novels were published during the years she and Van Loon were acquainted (there is no indication that the two writers ever met). By the time she met Carl Van Doren, Elizabeth Marion had several new writing projects in the works, including many fits and starts, and she was anxious about completing her "opus." She admired Van Doren's clear and concise writing style, knowing very well that it isn't easy to compose sentences that read easily. It's the results that look easy.

A critical component of the entity known as the man of letters, a persona unknown to us today and more than simply a professional scholar or successful writer of broad public renown, was the wide scope in which he, or she, operated. Like that of his contemporaries Hendrik Willem Van Loon, Henry S. Canby, and Stuart Sherman, Carl Van Doren's literary and historical acumen was a useful and highly respected skillset beyond the pages of a literary magazine or biographical text. Leaders from political, civic, and cultural organizations sought out the Pulitzer Prize-winning biographer for his participation in and valued support for their own endeavors. Van Doren's name on the bottom line would lend credence to a cause because his own measured opinion, informed by historical analysis, careful reasoning, and presented with sublime delivery, was valued as *expert*. Historic preservation projects, the U.S. Department of the Treasury, *Americans United for World Government*, and *The Committee of 100: Dedicated to the Creation of an America of Justice and Equality for Our Negro Fellow Citizens* each asked for Van Doren's participation in or endorsement of their campaigns. During the golden age of literary criticism, the man of letters wore many hats.

It seems natural that a man who had written and published essays and books on subjects of historic value would be approached to support historic preservation projects, and so was the case with Van Doren. New York City's Castle Clinton is a fort on the southern tip of Manhattan, originally erected in anticipation of the War of 1812 and serving as a military post for only twenty years before it was turned over to the city and renamed Castle Garden, a site of public and social life, next transforming into an immigration station from 1855-1890, and later housing an aquarium. A storied site to be sure, by 1945 it was a significant historical landmark, one threatened by the midcentury wrecking ball known as urban renewal and the city's incessant march towards modernization. Van Doren undersigned a petition to save the historic landmark, arguing, "Time and the hand of man have destroyed so much of our past that it behooves us all to see that this most notable of the monuments of the old city is preserved for the benefit and inspiration of generations to come."[179]

Van Doren, by this time serving as Vice President of the Society of American Historians, was approached by The Committee for the Preservation of Valley Forge Encampment Area for his assistance in preventing a proposed plan of the Pennsylvania Turnpike Company to extend its eastern terminus through the historic encampment of General George Washington's Continental Army. The Committee argued the turnpike's present plans would "ruin the ideal" of Valley Forge Park, killing the preservation community's own plans to acquire and preserve the entire area as a historic site. As the Turnpike Committee failed to respond to concerns brought before it—this in the era of Robert Moses-style urban renewal, which relied on the powers of eminent domain, rational urban planning, and the razing of any natural or built environment standing in the way of said progress—the newly formed Committee for the Preservation of Valley Forge Encampment Area sought support from renowned experts with weighty names, including Van Doren's, to add heft and credibility to its cause.

On the political front, Van Doren had publically supported the nation's war efforts during World War II with his radio announcements for the Fifth War Loan Campaign, distributed to over eight hundred radio stations across the country. Van Doren's radio message asked Americans to support the troops and the war effort through the purchase of War Bonds, encouraging

Americans to "buy as hard and as well as our fliers and sailors and soldiers fight. Back the Attack—Buy More Than Before!" The U.S. Department of the Treasury offered its gratitude to Van Doren for his support on behalf of the War and Victory Loan campaigns, and in 1946 honored Van Doren with the Treasury Silver Medal Award for his "distinguished service to the Treasury."

Van Doren's political action continued in the days and years following the war, indeed through the end of Van Doren's own life. Shortly after the war ended, and responding to the previously unfathomable civilian death toll wrought by the use of the world's first atomic bombs, Van Doren joined the newly formed political action group Americans United for World Government. Since his promotion of war bonds and the patriotic-themed radio programs during the war, Van Doren's commitment to world peace ramped up strategically in these postwar years. For the organization's pamphlet "How You Can Be More Effective Than an Atomic Bomb," Van Doren wrote:

I am an historian. All that I know about the progress of man convinces me that the only society in which we will ever be able to live in safety must be one which is governed by world law. For that reason, I am joining with AMERICANS UNITED FOR WORLD GOVERNMENT, and others who hold similar views in issuing this statement.[180]

Americans United for World Government hosted a conference at Rollins College in Winter Park, Florida in March of 1946. When Rollins College presented Van Doren with an honorary degree for his work in 1948, the LLD (Law) joined Van Doren's own D.Litt (Literature) and LHD (Humanities) credentials. With its "Appeal to the Peoples of the World," the conference released its mission and agenda directly to the public, bypassing the bureaucratic red tape known as government. The present condition of world "anarchy" was intolerable and unsustainable, what was needed was a condition of global law and order. Signatories of this Appeal included the Chairman of the Institute of Nuclear Studies at the University of Chicago; several U.S. Senators; a Justice of the Supreme Court; Albert Einstein; the President of Standard Oil Company; Nobel Prize winner in Nuclear Physics I.I. Rabi; the discoverer of heavy hydrogen and Nobel Prize winner Harold Uray; and Carl Van Doren. This weighty committee of men of science and public service agreed, "the atomic bomb has enormously increased the destructiveness of war; the conviction that nations cannot be trusted with the sovereign right to make war on their own terms; and the conclusion that nothing short of world government—constitutional federal government—can preserve the peoples and their liberties."[181]

Such a hefty goal: a constitutional federal government to encompass all the nations of the world. The organization's mission and strategy were very different from the national war bond effort Van Doren had participated in, or the radio programs he scripted and recorded in the name of patriotism. AUWG's ideals were utopian and radical. The creation of a federated world government in a global climate filled with international hostilities, ideologically opposed political regimes, and the early stages of a decades-long cold war seems to us beyond unlikely; a system of global law, in a century beset by nationalist rivalries and colonial and postcolonial rule, appears nothing short of outrageous. This was a moment of utopian idealism springing forth from the atrocities of World War II and the realization of man's newly-discovered ability to blow himself, *en masse,* into extinction. Life and liberty had never been so threatened.

The undersigned of the appeal felt the newly created United Nations, an institution established in October 1945 to promote international cooperation and maintain world order in the wake of WWII, was fundamentally unable to achieve the goal of world peace because the sovereign states of the U.N. were bound together merely by treaty, not by world law. The Charter of the United Nations must be amended immediately to include a world government, as the presently conceived organization had not gone far enough.

During the conference at Rollins College, Americans United for World Government spelled out exactly what steps were needed to achieve a world peace in which all people would be able to lead lives of freedom. This mandate insisted the General Assembly of the U.N. be transformed into a legislative branch of world government and the U.N. Security Council be transformed into a global executive branch, authorized to administer and enforce the laws enacted by the General Assembly. Independent courts with jurisdiction and local police departments must be created to prohibit and, when necessary, control any weapons of mass destruction. In addition, a world-wide program of mass education was crucial to developing knowledgeable world citizens. Van Doren wrote, "Only world government, even in the limited terms here advocated, can bring the peace in which the peoples can mature to the full responsibility by which they can realize their destiny as free men." Americans United for World Government was asking for the moon. With global freedom at stake, no concept short of revolutionary could possibly meet the challenge. And yet Van Doren knew that any prospect of a federated world government would require a critical mass of public support; this work belonged to the people as much as it belonged to the experts. He told a reporter from *The Adrian Daily Telegraph*, "Many people say that world government is the only hope, that it is inevitable. Oliver Wendell Holmes once said, 'The inevitable has to be assisted by effort.'" As acute as Van Doren understood the threat of nuclear war and global anarchy to be, he, like astute and thoughtful men before him, understood the necessity of public will in enacting change.[182]

Following the Rollins conference, *World Government News*, of which Van Doren was chairman of the editorial board, announced nominations for individuals and organizations who contributed towards the creation of a world government. Van Doren presided over the winter nominations, held at the Hotel Roosevelt in New York City. Among the nominees were writer E.B. White; Nobel Prize laureate Albert Einstein; former Supreme Court Justice Owen Roberts; and author Emery Reves. When the winners were announced at an awards ceremony in March, 1947, Van Doren presented the honors to Emery Reves for his book *The Anatomy of Peace*; E.B. White and *The New Yorker* for White's editorials; and Ambassador Carlos P. Romulo for his speech before the Political and Security Committee of the U.N. General Assembly.

Adding to his work with Americans United for World Government and *World Government News*, Van Doren was, during this same time, Vice President of United World Federalists, Inc. United World Federalists' mission stated its belief that world peace could only be achieved through a world federal government, whose purpose was to establish a *global* presence of justice, law, and order. UWF's motto, "For World Government With Powers Limited But Adequate to Assure Peace," presented a less forceful mandate than that of Americans United for World Government, however the ultimate goals were similar. Though these organizations today seem a utopian fantasy, the still-fresh images of the atomic bomb's mushroom cloud billowing terrifyingly over the city of Hiroshima convinced many intellectuals, politicians, scientists, and civilians that mankind was on a direct path to its own extinction. Utopian and radical might be the only solution.

Owing to strong personal and professional interests in the push for world government and lasting peace in this new global crisis and cold war, Van Doren wrote the introduction to Daniel Lang's 1948 book, *Early Tales of the Atomic Age.* Through a series of related chapter-stories, Lang's book gave an insider's look into the development of the atomic labs at Oak Ridge and Los Alamos, offering its readers insight into how the enormous secret of these new weapons were kept from the public for so long, and how the scientists who "turned atomic energy loose" felt about the implications of their work. In his introduction, Van Doren applauded Lang's work discussing this "overwhelming theme" as a necessary revelation, one that would "make the public take a sympathetic, co-operative interest in the development of a discovery that marks the beginning of a fateful age. Treatises are not enough; there must also be stories."[183]

Van Doren may have recalled Anne's descriptions of seeing, for the first time, photographs of the atomic bomb explosion over Hiroshima. Writing from her office at the *Nuovo Mondo* in Rome, Anne had reported that everyone who saw the photos viewed them with horror. How could anyone in the world want another war in light of that "terrible discovery?" The historian in Van Doren understood that telling the stories behind the events was critical to any real understanding of where we, the entirety of the human race, might go. He understood that "a knowledge of history and literature was indispensable in affairs." The American public, indeed the global public, required stories, and time, in order to process the full and potential implications of this new and troubling atomic age.

CHAPTER 10

UNDER THE USEFUL TREE

At the close of 1947, Van Doren was still thinking about Elizabeth Marion's desert hermitage in southern California. Earlier that year, his friend and colleague Victor Chittick had compiled a volume of essays, *Northwest Harvest,* which came out of the Reed Writer's Conference. Van Doren was pleased to receive the book, especially savoring the chapter by the woman who had so captured his interest. He wrote to Elizabeth, "With admiration at first reading. With affection at first sight. Yours, Carl." Convalescing from an appendectomy in December, Van Doren was still recuperating in the first months of 1948, and his personal correspondence was his primary connection with the outside world.

Upon hearing of Van Doren's appendectomy, Sinclair Lewis immediately dashed off a letter, exclaiming, "God I hope you're all right!" This disaster never would have happened, Red argued, if Van Doren had agreed to join him on a proposed trip to Italy. Presently, Van Doren was looking forward to a cruise around the islands of Puget Sound with the Chitticks, perhaps later that summer. Wouldn't Elizabeth love to join them? The plans were still in early stages, but the thought of cruising the waters of Puget Sounds, from Whidbey over to Victoria, British Columbia, filled Van Doren with glee. Whether or not details for the private cruise could be worked out, Van Doren was mostly interested in the possibility of talking with Elizabeth Marion face-to-face. It had been over a year since the two met, and Carl thought about her every day. He could still picture her hands as clearly as her face, the two most captivating parts of a person, as far as he was concerned.[184]

You delight me with your surprise at learning that somebody else notices your hands. Bless you, I suspect you of being one of those people who instinctively think of themselves as invisible. I know I do... I don't think I could bear to talk with you if you had gloves on—the same like a veil so far as I am concerned. The hands I hate are those that are hawklike and those that are like soft white worms. The woman's hands that are so often photographed make me sick at the stomach. Limp, without lines of experience, colorless with idleness, and obviously useless. They are supposed to look tempting, I gather, but they look as if they couldn't even make love. (April 15, 1948)[185]

Van Doren was "wild" at having no chance to speak with her about things. It sounds strange coming from a writer, but he confessed, "I talk easily but write not so easily, and I am at a disadvantage when it is all letters." He tried to coax her into visiting New York, with an invitation to head downtown to the Fulton Fish Market and wolf down some oysters. Suddenly addressing her letters, "Dear Carl," instead of the formal "Mr. Van Doren," Elizabeth Marion playfully called him out on the subtle pass he had made, all this talk about hands and what they are good for. She didn't miss the remark about oysters, a known aphrodisiac, either. She had a million and a half things to say and ask; he often teased her and admitted the teasing came only from his fondness for her. Van Doren quite simply found Elizabeth "exciting, engaging, and enchanting." He reveled in her lengthy letters, yet advised her: do not burn the midnight oil. Noting the late hour on her letters, he protectively scolded, "I think you are working too hard, Child. Don't."[186]

Elizabeth sent Carl a snapshot of herself on the farm, promising she would next send the photo of herself that she liked best. "I like it because it's good enough of me and a very good one of my end of the office...which is a junky room, very small, so full of books and papers and photography and houseplants and globes and whatnot that mere people have to be inserted as with a shoe-horn." It was in this small junky room where she saw herself best, and wanted Van Doren to see her there too: a cramped and crowded office surrounded by papers and books, with little room for human guests. This was where she set down to work, this was where she wrote.[187]

Upon receiving the photo of Elizabeth on her farm, Van Doren was especially pleased that he had properly remembered her face, and was delighted the photograph captured her "right hand in plain view." The man was beguiled.[188]

By the spring of 1948, Carl and Elizabeth's increasingly frequent letter-writing had become indispensable for both, living a conti-nent and several decades in age apart from one another. Writing from his apartment, where Van Doren confessed to lately becom-ing "a hardboiled hermit, well insulated in my apartment to which nobody comes without telephoning to ask if it is all right," or from the family retreat in Cornwall, he thought of Elizabeth every day. "Odd I should so often miss you, when I have in fact seen you so little. But you know what I mean, I am sure..." Elizabeth sto-ically but nevertheless lamented her father's habit of retrieving the mail from the Spangle post office only twice a week. When a letter stamped in red appeared on her writing desk, it was a good day indeed.[189]

In each of her own letters to Van Doren, Elizabeth Marion included an astounding array of details describing her daily routine, from the troublesome and loathsome gossip of a visiting aunt, to the cats' daily habits and whereabouts, to her sister's pregnancy, to the rushing of a river after a storm, to the call of the local birds. She wrote about the books she was reading, the errant sons of Abagail Adams and Dolly Madison, and the differing beliefs of Puritans versus Quakers. Still recovering from the appendectomy and dealing with an ongoing "misbehaving heart condition," Van Doren was tired of feeling poorly and deplored his nagging ill health. Elizabeth's wit and love of word-play boosted his spirits no end.

To the biographer-critic, who for years so enjoyed the lecture circuits that brought him to cities and friends across the country, the very idea of speaking to a crowd or attending a committee meeting now filled him with "nerves" and feelings of dread. Confiding only to Elizabeth, Van Doren admitted he flinched at the very thought, "the way you do when you are overstrung and a gun goes off behind you." It was true, even a most reasonable man like himself could succumb to the complex inner-workings of the body and mind— one is human, after all—and the days could be rough. Van Doren shared this vulnerability with Elizabeth alone. While he sometimes remarked on pesky ailments to other close friends or family, those mentions were stoic in tone and he did not elaborate or bemoan his condition. It was only in his letters to Elizabeth where Van Doren truly let his guard down and said, point blank, just how sick he was of it all, how badly he wanted to get on with the business of living and escape what had increasingly become an affliction.[190]

Van Doren's friendship with Victor Chittick had brought him to the Reed Writers Conference in the fall of 1946, and Chittick's retirement party from Reed in the spring of 1948 seemed the perfect opportunity for Van Doren to return to Washington state and to Elizabeth Marion. With a heavy dose of regret, Van Doren wrote to Elizabeth that he was unable to make it out for the event due to his lingering and much regretted health issues. Elizabeth, also invited to the party, was herself uninterested in attending. She did not have a college education, and the thought of being surrounded by professors and their admiring undergrads was not her idea of an afternoon well-spent. Like Van Doren and Van Loon, Elizabeth Marion was skeptical of the milieu of academia and its participants. What undergrads took for sophistication, Elizabeth Marion pronounced, was often nothing more than "misinformation, misconception, and sophistry." She was not interested. Whether she was disappointed that Van Doren could not make the three thousand mile journey to Reed, she did not say.

While a cross-country trip to Portland was out of the question, Van Doren always tried to fit in a summer visit to Sinclair Lewis at his country retreat, currently located in Williamstown, Massachusetts. Perhaps Elizabeth might join him there? He assured her that Lewis "would take to you as Chittick and I did, I have no manner of doubt." Of this, Elizabeth also likely had no doubt. Her relationships with intelligent, creative men had been satisfying for all parties concerned. There was a charming and captivating quality to her otherwise introverted tendency towards the solitary, and the men she had met through professional connections had, to use Van Doren's term, "taken to her" personal brand of opinionated charm. She was the sort of woman, and the sort of writer, whom men might characterize as one who thinks or writes *like a man*. She greatly admired Ayn Rand's *The Fountainhead*, sitting down to read the weighty text only when she had several quiet hours in which to savor the flavor and pace of the book. She was not sentimental, and she deplored the clichéd tendencies of her own sex. In 1948 and having just turned thirty-three years old, she was not looking for a husband; perhaps this freedom from convention added to her allure. When a visiting and very tedious aunt monopolized the household with endless gossip as to the love-lives and romantic encounters of the local gentry, it was all Elizabeth could do to refrain from jumping in and exclaiming that, "nothing on god's green earth could tempt me into the bonds of what is termed holy matrimony...but that would have looked like sour grapes to her, and to me would have looked like treason to a man I once would very much have liked to marry." Perhaps Elizabeth had considered marriage once in her younger years. Presently, she was not interested. She had other things to do.[191]

Air travel in the late 1940s was expensive; a cross-country price tag of roughly $106 in 1950, adjusted for inflation, is nearly $1,000 today. Rail travel wasn't cheap either. Even if the feasibility of a long-distance trip existed for either Van Doren or for Elizabeth Marion, paying one's own way could be prohibitive. Unless you were a person of means, cross-country travel was an infrequent event at best. With the woman he admired living at an unapproachable distance (geographically speaking, although in many ways emotionally as well), Van Doren could only imagine the thrill of escorting Elizabeth Marion on his arm to any number of social engagements. A party at the writer James Thurber's home, or perhaps, the opening of Broadway play, to which a producer personally invited Van Doren and "a beautiful lady," would be so much more enjoyable with Elizabeth on his arm. In fact, Van Doren teased, he might even resort to kidnapping her if necessary. "*Ah*, as you say, *me!*" Teasing aside, the sentiment was heart-felt; his wish would reverberate with any number of infatuated hearts, male or female. Van Doren wrote simply, and plaintively, "I wish you could have dinner with me."[192]

Ah, me!, a phrase Elizabeth used frequently in her letters, had been adopted by Van Doren and became part of their private language. Ellipses began to appear in his letters to her as well; one friend's mannerisms and patterns of speech influence the other's.

On his sixty-third birthday and feeling especially spirited and flirtatious, Van Doren remarked on the photo Elizabeth had sent him a few months back, writing, "I hope you won't mind (says he hypocritically, knowing perfectly well you won't) if I am an observant guy and noticed all the details about you as well as gathered up the total impression. But of course you know this already, being a woman as well as A Writer..." Elizabeth brushed away this note of admiration as "a bit of pleasant blarney." While she allowed these "permitted passes" and wrote that she didn't mind "being teased and informed at the same time, plus flattering references to pulchritude in a degree I hadn't suspected!...maybe so...more likely your rememberer exaggerates things to end...", for her part, Elizabeth admitted to being a truly modest creature.[193]

Even if she were so inclined to match Van Doren's frankness, propriety and modesty held her in restraint. She enjoyed these flirtations, admittedly, but also knew how, in 1948, to pass them off as not serious. She was also somewhat uncomfortable at being the focus of attention, was instead used to going unnoticed. She chose her clothing, for example, "to be as inconspicuous as possible for as long as possible." This, she admitted, was the sad truth. She was a ferocious coffee-drinker, a lover of cats, a reader and a writer, who was more than a little amused at the way men typically reacted towards women. And while she was not interested in most other people's opinions, she was very interested in Van Doren's. She admired him.

In late October of 1948, Van Doren commemorated the two-year anniversary of the pair's first meeting at Reed College, writing "a very pleasant anniversary I find this to be." He was preparing to head south to Huntington, West Virginia and then on to Washington D.C. for speaking engagements. Van Doren was not at all looking forward to the trip, now dodging public engagements whenever possible, but pushed on in the hopes that he would come to dread them less and less each time. The very idea that *he* should suffer so from nerves, at this point in his life, infuriated and embarrassed him. He was ashamed of the affliction, ashamed even to talk about it. And yet he spoke about it to Elizabeth, confessing, "and yet, as you see, I admit it to you. How did you get me this way? Without asking, you pull confidences out of me like corks out of a fizzing bottle."[194]

Perhaps the distance—geographic and otherwise—provided a sense of security and allowed for naked confession Van Doren did not find in more proximate friendships. She was a true confidante. But aside from the forthcoming trip to Huntington, Van Doren was pleased to share with Elizabeth his ongoing research on the private correspondence between Benjamin Franklin and his favorite sister, Jane Mecom. The book, to be published by Princeton University Press, would provide a glimpse into Franklin and Mecom's private lives, revealed through a lifetime of personal correspondence. The historian in Van Doren preferred these subtler facets of the human story to any Grand Narrative, and relished the sleuthing and digging required of the Biographer on the Trail. This sort of work, he wrote, "interests me far more than many subjects that are supposed to be more suitable to history, with all its damned traditional dignity."[195]

Confirming Van Doren's worst fears, the trip to Huntington was a disaster. While preparing to give a lecture at the Marshall College Forum Series, Van Doren was stricken ill and, as there were no rooms available at the local hospital, spent a night in distress at the nearby home of a colleague. After he was finally admitted to St. Mary's Hospital, Van Doren spent several days under care and observation before returning home to New York City by train. Although he had been given a clean bill of health at a checkup earlier in the year, assured by his doctor that his heart was "perfectly sound," the stress brought on by this latest trip and the speaking engagement had proven too much. Recovering at home, Van Doren wrote to Elizabeth on November 15 that, in the simplest of terms, he "blew a gasket. It was the speaking that broke the back." While the *New York Times* printed a report on the author's sudden illness, the news did not reach Elizabeth Marion until she received Van Doren's letter several days later. No, she had not heard that he was ill, she had cheerfully assumed that he was simply too busy to write.[196]

Enough then of the speech-making, Elizabeth concurred, there must be easier ways of gently testing his nerves. He should not write until he was feeling fit as a fiddle, although *she* was happy to write about all things related to the mounting snow in Spangle, her views on cities (New York, in particular), and a curious painting by El Greco. The seriousness of Van Doren's health crisis seems to have been lost in translation; for his part, Van Doren did not wish to rehash the "revolting clinical account" with Elizabeth. But he advised his friend, as young and energetic as she was, to take care of herself, for his sake as well as her own, adding, "I make no mention of all your other admirers. Let them put in their own pleas."[197]

Convalescing from his home at the start of the New Year, Van Doren continued his translation of the Franklin-Mecom letters, a task that can be either thrilling or mind-boggling, depending of course on the penmanship of the writer in question. (Some folks have beautiful and perfectly legible handwriting; a letter written one hundred or more years ago on simple note-paper can read easily and beautifully today. Carl's brother Paul, for example, wrote many letters from his WWI deployment in France, every word remains clear and beautifully composed. Elinor Wylie's handwriting, on the other hand, is practically illegible). The pace of the work is usually slow, although perfect for someone who is housebound. Deciphering the photostats of Franklin's and Mecom's letters to one another, many of the original letters held at the American Philosophical Society in Philadelphia, was slow going during the months following Van Doren's gasket-blowing crisis.

On her end, Elizabeth was anxious to have something substantial to show her publisher, and journeyed to Seattle to meet with a representative from Thomas Crowell, which had published her three novels. Following the most breathtaking views from the airplane, Elizabeth was pleased to learn that Crowell was indeed interested in publishing her next book. The onus was on the author to produce a manuscript, the completion of which still eluded her. Elizabeth Marion was currently working on a story about her cats, the best cats in all of literature, Van Doren assured her. The unfinished story captured the goings-on of the author and her felines, revealing what happens when one moves country people and country cats to town. The Marions had recently moved from the family farm in Spangle to nearby Fairfield, "the last house on the right on the road to Latah," and Elizabeth and her cats were still a bit out of sorts.

Elizabeth, who often asked Van Doren for professional advice as she trudged along through the writing process, had the favor returned when Van Doren announced *he* needed help, "and I mean help, Baby," with an idea that had been slowly germinating. Should he write a short (75,000 words) book on Jane Mecom? The Franklin-Mecom book of letters he was currently preparing for Princeton University Press was geared towards academics and professional historians, not scheduled for mass-market production. Now thoroughly fascinated with Jane Mecom herself, Van Doren had been noodling with the idea of writing a "lively book for the general public" on an interesting woman in her own right. Elizabeth loved the idea; certainly, she insisted, he must do it. From what she could gather from Van Doren's descriptions of Franklin's sister so far, Jane Mecom was far too interesting to be kept in obscurity, or worse, oblivion (or perhaps worse yet, an academic text). With the U.S. Postal Service providing continuity to their ongoing conversation (the nation's first Postmaster General Ben Franklin himself would have been pleased), Carl Van Doren and Elizabeth Marion relied on each other's constant presence, if not geographic and physical, than in spirit and in thought, to discuss all things personal and professional.

Van Doren admitted that he did not simply read Elizabeth's letters, he *ate them up*. Elizabeth cherished his letters as well, which regularly included tidbits of literary history, the origin and meanings of words, and musings on a proposed trip-for-two to the Caribbean or those desert hogans. She wrote:

> Dear me, you are nice, and a great comfort to me...of all the people I know, most of whom <u>can</u> read and write the King's English if only they would, and none of whom is half so busy as you, you are the very only one who finds time to write, and yours always come bouncing back with such alacrity they make me think the postoffice can't be so useless after all... (March 15, 1949)[198]

When Van Doren threatened to cut back on his letters, concerned that his *Dear Elizabeth* was working too hard and burning the midnight oil, he begged, entreated, hell, he ordered her to get more sleep. He insisted she write no more letters to him until she received his next, arguing this temporary but necessary lapse would hurt him more than it would hurt her. But Elizabeth Marion would have none of it. She would write as often as she damn well pleased, thank you very much. *Honestly!*

> Dear Carl—though I've been considering other and less affectionate titles for you—traitor, and rogue, possibly even a whoreson villain, dreadful things anyway—a fine kettle of fish this is and I'll have none of it...hurt you worse than me!...that is a most ancient and disreputable wheeze and you know it and it aint so besides...have you thought what this awful ultimatum will mean? No letters a tall, and all my powers of communication drying up, and nothing to look forward to in the mail?...and leaving me with the last word, so to speak? nobody could stand that!...- and now that you've ordered me around, you can just damnwell sit there and listen while I tell you about today.
>
> *(May 23, 1949)*[199]

Van Doren, duly admonished and realizing the error of his suggested time-out, was pleased that Elizabeth did not heed his ultimatum. He needed her letters as much as she enjoyed his, signing his next, "Affectionately. Solicitously, Carl." When Elizabeth informed Van Doren of an upcoming trip to Missoula, Montana where she was to present a lecture, Van Doren regretted another missed-opportunity to light upon her eyes or hear her speak. He longed to see those hands, which he could still see as clearly as her face. If it was too much when Van Doren asked Elizabeth to describe what she was wearing at the Missoula conference—he had worn-out in his mind the image of her in her outfit at Reed—Elizabeth did not seem put off in the least. She happily provided a description of the "decent," *i.e.* plain, wardrobe she took along to Missoula. This written description satisfied Van Doren's curiosity and desire to the extent that he had no other option. But his *Darling Elizabeth* was mistaken if she though for one minute her "decent" attire was necessarily unflattering, writing, "You are wrong in saying you will now be decent if not ravishing. Those are not antitheses. I suppose I ought not to say that I would rather do than be the second. No? Then I won't. But this is a long rainy day..." He half-heartedly apologized for perhaps speaking too frankly on a hot summer day, but the message was clear. Where Van Doren had once written, "there is a great deal between these crowded lines, and I can trust you to know it," there was no need to read between the lines this time.[200]

The summer of 1949 brought Van Doren back to his annual retreat in Cornwall. If his convalescence following the 1947 appendectomy troubled Van Doren's mind and kept his body to a more sedate pace, recuperating from 1948's gasket-blowing crisis had proven much more difficult. The entire year had been difficult, and Van Doren's summer months in Cornwall were intended "to build up a disturbed nervous system." Laying low meant writing a few magazine articles, which required no outside research and were really just exercises in expository writing, pushing ahead with his work on the Jane Mecom book, baby-sitting a growing brood of grandchildren, and tending the garden. Van Doren admitted to Elizabeth that the year had been pretty grim and solitary, her "merry shrewd letters" all the more precious for it. Ever pragmatic, Elizabeth hoped his family was not working him too hard. At present, she looked forward to his letters, the more the merrier, while she suffered the extended stay of that troublesome aunt. Van Doren could make all the passes, subtle or not so subtle, he wanted; the "loose-chatter" was permitted as long as he kept writing. By the end of the summer, Jane Mecom filled Van Doren's mind almost as much as Elizabeth Marion did. The colonial dame, he admitted, was "in my mind all the time, and the dim Boston ways of her days."[201]

Van Doren had a little secret to share with Elizabeth. *He* was "Bookwright," the anonymous book critic for *The New York Herald-Tribune*. Writing the column for over eleven years, Van Doren assured Elizabeth that no one outside the book trade knew it was he wielding that particular pen. With this revelation, Elizabeth discovered Van Doren's writing was even more prolific than she had known. Meanwhile, a year after her meeting with the Crowell rep, she remained hung up on her own manuscript. Perhaps she was working on too many projects at once. Whatever became of the watchman story? What about the cats?

Van Doren frequently admitted the task of writing never came easy to him. Does it come easy to any writer? Creating something completely original and preferably not dull, from what had been a blank piece of paper? In one of her earliest letters to Van Doren, Elizabeth Marion expressed her admiration for Van Doren's printed words, the clarity and clean diction he was known for. She also knew enough to keep from remarking that Van Doren "made it look so easy." A writer herself, she understood *the results* of Van Doren's literary efforts looked easy. The process, surely, required an intangible mixture of sound familiarity with one's subject matter, conservation of language (one must not rely on jargon), clarity, and a bit of poetry. And patience.

With her opus no closer to completion, Van Doren urged his *Dear Elizabeth* to get down to the business at hand and *write*. The literary critic and personal mentor insisted she must stop over-thinking it. Boiling down decades of his own experience in the writing trade to a very succinct plan of attack, he gently admonished, "You must stop thinking so much and do more acting. A book is an action, not a thought." The prescription was to stop ruminating and *act*. Hendrik Willem Van Loon had, years earlier, offered similar advice when he cautioned that too much time alone with one's thoughts led to useless naval-gazing; Elizabeth would do well to "come east and talk." What exactly was holding up the manuscript we cannot know for certain. The dreaded writer's block? However, Elizabeth Marion reveled in the written word, she certainly had fun with language, and her letters were almost short stories in themselves. She had a special knack for putting words together. So it wasn't for lack of creative output. Elizabeth accepted Van Doren's harangue, *he was right—so right!* She admitted she was all tangled up and flustered with the opus. She had lost her self-confidence, she couldn't see the story clearly in her mind as she once had. She seriously considered putting the opus away and taking a day-job, full time. The world didn't need another ten-cent novelist anyway; the public, she believed, wouldn't care in the least.[202]

Van Doren's lingering health issues, while keeping him close to home ever since the Huntington incident, were not enough to stifle his own creative output. Mailing his final notes on the Franklin-Mecom correspondence to Princeton University Press in November of 1949, he was now free to devote all of his energies to the Jane Mecom book, which would be published by Viking Press and would in fact be Van Doren's final book. The Biographer on the Trail had been slowed down, to be sure, and was feeling far from fit, but far worse than feeling poorly was Van Doren's fear that he might become *dull* on top of it.

To Carl Van Doren or Elizabeth Marion, *dull* was probably the worst thing one could be. In his 1920 review of Sinclair Lewis' *Main Street*, the critic had written, "the principal accusation which Mr. Lewis brings against his village—and indeed against all villages—is that of being *dull*...Mr. Lewis hates such dulness— the village virus—as the saints hate sin." Van Doren had left his position at the Brearley School because he found the Park Avenue scene *dull*. His friend and colleague Stuart Sherman was such a notable man of letters because he was one of the few professors of literature who was *not dull*. Sherman was, rather, "a poet and a wit." Van Doren had praised Willa Cather for "enlist[ing] in the crusade against dulness (*sic*) which has recently succeeded the hereditary crusade of American literature against wickedness." To Van Doren and the modern artists he wrote about, being *dull* was a sinful offense. *Dull* was mediocrity incarnate. No, *dull* would not do, would never do. Feeling particularly low one early December morning, Van Doren took a break from his work on the Jane Mecom manuscript and wrote to Elizabeth, "I am far from well this morning, with symptoms too tedious to mention, I must be brief and probably dull..." With Christmas approaching, Van Doren's usually playful tone to his *Dear Elizabeth* turned serious and tender, and he typed, "Thanks for what you are to me," before adding a hand-written addendum, "and do for me. Yours, Carl."[203]

Even though she was, at present, very concerned the middle section of her own manuscript was *dull*, Elizabeth was anything but dull in her letters. No wonder he found her so charming and amusing; Elizabeth Marion quite simply wrote the most detailed and personable musings on her thoughts and feelings about any number of daily goings-on. She was playful and flirty, challenging Van Doren's latest accusation that she had been shameless and intemperate, responding, "both shameless and intemperate? all at once? me?...blessed if I can remember anything that seemed very much of either at last writing! so I'll just go tck, tck, and hope for the best..." Elizabeth wrote about the books she was reading, the latest was a new photography book by Weegee, as well as the wind and the weather and the multiplying snow in Washington. She begged Van Doren to *please* get a six-gun or bow and arrow or other some-such weapon, and track down the person who invented canasta, and to please murder him—it would be justifiable homicide—as the game was a total time and energy suck, miserable, "simply made to order for people who are sociable and have no need to conserve time and energy...and when even my simple and un-card-sharp-brain can assimilate most of its idiotic foibles?..." She wrote and wrote and wrote. She was his *Bright Eyes* (and he missed those eyes more than she could imagine).[204]

Shortly after the New Year and the ringing in of a new decade, Van Doren felt well enough to attend a party to celebrate the recent publication of playwright-actor Alexander Kirkland's *Naughty '90s Cook Book*. *Look* magazine covered the gathering of literati at the celebrated Barkentin Studio in Greenwich Village.

In its January 1950 issue, *Look* featured a photo-essay of the event, which included a full-page photograph of Mr. Carl Van Doren chatting with book publicist Janice Devine. As the Marion family did not subscribe to *Look,* nor could Elizabeth find a copy at the local drugstore, she asked Van Doren to please send her a copy. She hoped he looked "wise and incorrigible and properly wicked." When the issue arrived, Elizabeth was pleased-as-punch, writing "I like the lines—in your face, I mean; and I like the good blunt honest pose, it looks as if you were probably talking a blue streak." She tacked the oversized photo to her bulletin board on the stove room door so that Van Doren now presided over the room, in absentia.[205]

In addition to the magazine, Van Doren sent a book of poetry for Elizabeth's thirty-fourth birthday, which contained some verse by the English poet Donne. This was a fine and fat volume that Elizabeth could spend days poring through, at her leisure, when she could escape the more mundane necessities of life. She felt compelled to include a particular line from Donne in a thank-you to Van Doren, which seemed especially appropriate under the circumstances: "...and do not forget, incorrigible Sir, *more than kisses, letters mingle Soules: For thus friends absent speak.*" Ah yes, replied Van Doren, all very well and good. But one can't make such a comparison for sure unless one has kisses with which to compare the letters...[206]

Van Doren quite simply *desired* Elizabeth Marion. In every sense of the word. He desired her mind, her wit, and, yes, those lovely hands. He admitted she was his only private correspondent, outside of some letters to his mother. She, uniquely, had his ear, and Van Doren revealed a side of himself that he showed no one else. The pet-names he called her, *Bright Eyes, Proud Beauty, Quicksilver,* were not clichés by any means. The charm of her wit and the speed of her mind intrigued him; he loved her word play, her "recklessness," her turns of phrase. From his lowest days to his friskiest, he turned to her. He confided in her when he wasn't feeling well; he insinuated that he wanted to ravish her. He would have liked nothing more than take her out to dinner, to wolf down some oysters at Sweet's near the Fulton Fish Market, and light upon her bright eyes. He longed for her, and hesitated not for a moment to share his feelings, his passion, with her. "I do love your mind, and don't bother to ask me what else about you, chiefly because I shall not tell you in so many words, and you damned well know already, and for thirty other supreme reasons."[207]

When Van Doren wrote his autobiography in 1935 he had remarked, "I observed happy and unhappy marriages in Urbana, but never a great or tragic love." He remembered his childhood as one sprouting from a pragmatic Midwestern sensibility. But this Dutch stoicism notwithstanding, Carl Van Doren *was* a man of passion. Passion for the intellect, passion for wit, passion for the sort of romantic chemistry that comes around infrequently at best (he *had* felt that with Irita, he would surely admit to himself, once the pain of that divorce subsided). Carl and Elizabeth had met just the one time; this passion was certainly never consummated but instead played out, appropriately so perhaps, in words. On the page. In the mind. When Van Doren wrote playfully, "But keep your eyes out of my mind, Young Woman. Mustn't peep, mustn't touch. Yours, Carl," Elizabeth volleyed back with her own spirited banter. And while she played her cards close to her chest, being the modest creature that she was, she relished the attention, admitting that "vanity is weak and loves it, also its donor."[208]

As Van Doren neared the completion of his manuscript on Jane Mecom, he hinted to Elizabeth there was a surprise for her in the Franklin-Mecom book of letters, just now published by Princeton University Press. An easily overlookable remark, perhaps, but Van Doren wanted to pay a compliment to the woman whom he promised the first copy he received from his publisher. There, in his acknowledgements, Van Doren had included Elizabeth Marion in a list of people whom he wished "to give grateful thanks." Happily, it appeared that Elizabeth's own manuscript was nearly complete as well. She had not thrown in the towel after all, and instead had racked up thirty-five thousand words for the effort. This, Van Doren acknowledged, was "not too bad," and probably quite attractive to publishers, who were looking for books that were neither too long nor too costly to print. Whether or not the opus was finally fit for publication, Elizabeth decided the time had come to meet the demands of reality: she had just accepted a day-job. A writer generally did not get paid, after all, to sit around writing. Ernest Hemingway, F. Scott Fitzgerald, Elinor Wylie, Carl Van Doren, and countless of their peers in the writing professions had all asked—on more than one occasion—to borrow money or receive an advance to tend to those sordid realities like mortgage payments and compound interest. Elizabeth's new position was in the offices of *The Standard-Register*, a local newspaper in nearby Rockford. One hundred dollars a month was a substantial salary to the writer who had taken seasonal administrative jobs in the State House to make ends meet, and Elizabeth admitted to Van Doren "...being both lazy and optimistic and sure that the opus after the next will make my everlasting fortune, I'd rather not work, but oh me, how I do need some cash right now...a dismal subject." She had not given up hope on finishing the manuscript, *any* manuscript, but the reality was there.

Van Doren's enduring support heartened Elizabeth immensely, more than she could possibly say. Did she worry Van Doren would think less of her for taking a day-job? Certainly he did not. He was intensely proud of her, assuring the currently-dejected writer that a good mind is a good mind, and would be good at whatever it set out to do. And he reminded Elizabeth how very much he loved her mind.[209]

Something Van Doren was *not* keen on was a recent proposal to have *his* biography written. A former Columbia student, and apparently a long-time admirer, had recently approached Van Doren about writing a biography of the famous biographer. Van Doren confided in Elizabeth that this left him with quite a "dull situation" on his hands. The former student was a dull man who would work very hard to produce a lousy book. Unfortunate, but there it was. Because, according to the Pulitzer Prize-winning biographer, biography was one of the major arts, and most biographers failed in having any "scrupulous art" in their endeavors. He simply could not go for it. Elizabeth considered and appreciated Van Doren's "polemic dissertation" on the art of biography, but reminded him that *all* of the arts contained more minor than grand practitioners, and he therefore might as well resign himself to being "dully biographied" sooner or later.

In March, that particular moment in the year Elizabeth described as "a snowy cool night; spring has its doubts just now and the pussywillows and blackbirds and the first buttercup of ancient fame get all mixed up with ice and snowstorms and such..." Carl had dinner with Mark and Dorothy Van Doren, and Mrs. Wendell Wilkie. (The literary crowd, we have established, was a very small circle. Wendell Wilkie had been drawn into that crowd through his affair with Irita Van Doren. And while Irita Van Doren and Mrs. Wendell Wilkie were certainly not going to dine together, everyone else remained on good terms regardless of that which was left unspoken in polite company). Edith Wilkie had previously approached (in fact, *insisted*) Van Doren about writing her late husband's biography, which Van Doren declined. Whether this was for professional or personal reasons, he didn't say.

Pushing for a deadline of June 1st on the Jane Mecom manuscript, he was on a roll, feeling very "peart," and knocking out the pages at a better-than-average pace (Van Doren rarely wrote more than seven pages in a day, lamenting "the sons of bitches who can write fast"). Van Doren was looking forward to the completion of the book and confessed to Elizabeth that he, too, could use a paycheck. In a midnight letter—now it was his turn to burn the midnight oil at the typewriter—he admitted he would rather be "under that Useful Tree right now, talking to you instead of writing."[210]

What was this about the *Useful Tree?* Elizabeth could not recall when or where they came up with that imagery, but she liked it. And she liked the latest chapter of *Jane Mecom* Van Doren had just sent, praising, "I think your words not only <u>sound</u> good but <u>are</u> good." She appreciated the sleuthing required of the Biographer on the Trail, especially when it came to navigating gaps in the existing source material. The fact of the matter is, the archival materials a biographer has to work with very much depend upon the actions of persons long-gone. When dealing with correspondence, many letters have been lost, mindlessly neglected, or purposefully burned. Biographer on the trail indeed. Sometimes it can be very hit-or-miss. Elizabeth wrote,

> ...it must be queer and exasperating, the way people save tons of pleasant but non-essential letters, and then carelessly don't save the one important message that somebody like you wants very much two hundred years later...still, that is a long time for anything so elusive as a letter to remain in existence; with only half-way care, words on paper can survive a long time, but think what perils of everyday life can quench them in a twinkling... the wonder is that any of them survive—a millions of them do, and eventually find their ways into books and shelves as mine. (March 19, 1950)[211]

Elizabeth likened Van Doren's divided interests, between herself and Jane Mecom, to "intellectual bigamy," and playfully questioned his fidelity. Van Doren would have none of that—a mark against his devotion!—batting back with, "who are you calling not-so-faithful as all that? Name me a faithfuller correspondent you ever had, and to hell with himherthem!" When Elizabeth intimated that, on the subject of fidelity, it was not of the written/ correspondence variety she had in mind, all bets are off. We cannot assume to know precisely what she was getting at, or how bold she dared to be, but the underlying message is clear. The playful banter between the pair was equally matched on both sides.[212]

Van Doren completed his Jane Mecom manuscript at the end of March, well ahead of his self-imposed deadline. With the bulk of the work now finished, although there would be galley proofs to pore over and illustrations to gather, he was looking forward to his annual summer retreat in Cornwall. Elizabeth plugged away at *The Standard-Register,* proof-reading, editing, and making re-writes during the day, and then writing her personal correspondence late into the night. With each letter received, the lush descriptions of her world shone on Van Doren's days like the brightness in her eyes, a brightness he could only recall in his memory. When he wrote that he admired her shining mind and neat wit and supple understandings, that a good mind is a good mind no matter what it was doing, Van Doren was responding to the several hundreds of pages, by this time, of Elizabeth's unique way with words.

...all the windows are open from the top to prevent Ouiji [cat] from taking a flying dive into the universe, and between roars in the traffic the running of the waters is plain to hear...I stopped to watch it, down at the little bridge on Main Street—just at the bridge the banks jut out a little and drop down a trifle, and the water rushes together in a V-shaped junction with two fringes of foam on either side the V...such a wondrous color it is—but not for water—the fine lush dark-brown of fields, the color of disaster and grief...[213]

Van Doren was invited to speak at a United Nations dinner for the President of Chile in late April. The President was
a great admirer of his work and had asked for him specifically;
Van Doren was pleased for the distraction while he awaited news
from Viking. Anxiously awaited. Much as Elizabeth felt he was
fretting needlessly, even a seasoned and Pulitzer Prize-winning
author could be affected by nervous anticipation while waiting
on the powers-that-be to review and accept his work. From his
apartment overlooking the spring blossoms of Central Park, Van
Doren kept himself busy one beautiful day by writing the introduction to another editor's forthcoming book, the *Limited Editions
Autobiography* of Ben Franklin. With his grandchildren visiting
for the day, running about the apartment and enjoying the curiosity of the building's mail chute, Van Doren was momentarily
able to forget his worries about the delay with Viking. It had been
nearly eight weeks since he submitted the completed manuscript,
surely this was not a good sign. And so when the proofs finally
did arrive on June 1st, Van Doren was heartily relieved, admitting
that Elizabeth was entirely right, there had been nothing to worry
about. It wasn't easy to determine, however, if Van Doren's nerves
were due to a writer's anxiety or something more serious. He had
been afflicted with a "galloping pulse" and pesky "nerves" for
several years now, and what was anxiety, or what was a more serious heart condition, he could not know. Either way, Van Doren
was sick of thinking about it, sick of writing about it.

Elizabeth, meanwhile, had been spending long days at *The Standard-Register*, followed by late nights at her writing desk. She sent Van Doren copies of her column, "Drips from a Leaky Faucet," which he adored and enjoyed, writing, "Sometimes I almost wish you weren't so bright. It's hard to touch you with a new idea...you are probably ahead most of the time already, and one twist of the wrist from me, and there you are away out ahead. Swift Stuff, Betty Marion. The Quicksilver Wench." Elizabeth liked the QW moniker, she almost felt like that "mythical gal" after reading Van Doren's glowing words of praise. Quicksilver, indeed. The days were passing in a whirlwind, and while she would like to write to him every detail of her world, inevitably there were "sixteen billion" things left out. She sensed something intangible, she wanted to slow down time... or did she wish she could grab more of it? She wrote to Van Doren,

> ...time all over the place just out of reach, like the prettiest bauble in the toy shop...when we meet under the Useful Tree, let us put a leash on the bauble and drag it down off the top shelf?... which would be a rather improbable feat, anywhere but under the Useful Tree... (May 25, 1950)

> ...shall we please have Beethoven, in spirit that is, under the Useful Tree? I can't somehow imagine the Tree without the music. (May 31, 1950)[214]

With a twinkle in his eye, Van Doren replied:

Beethoven as such as you like and insist, but just possibly a little Mozart now and then, for grace notes, so to speak. Let's have a long-playing record. Now look at that suggestion: is it insinuating...or boasting? I wrote it in simple good faith.

(June 3, 1950)[215]

While it took Viking eight excruciating weeks to send the Jane Mecom proofs to Van Doren, it took the writer only a week to send his edits back. Exasperated by some "new broom" in the editorial department, Van Doren, who believed one should always write in the fewest but most graceful words possible, was more than a little indignant at this audacious novice who,

has queried some of my most finished sentences with the suggestion they might be clearer or simpler if all reduced, I gather, to some primitive sentence structure; and once or twice they have actually been changed. All are damned well going to be reset at Viking expense. Very few cases of this, however. But it irritates me a little to run into such elementary ideas. Do you think me obscure in my published writings?... (June 8, 1950)[216]

Van Doren would not be rewritten. Certainly not by some "young broom" who didn't know good sentences when he heard them. While there would still be quite a bit of work to do to ready *Jane Mecom* for publication, Van Doren was looking forward to the relative summer quiet of Cornwall. Hot and muggy in the city, cool and raining in Washington, summer was approaching on both coasts and brought wistful reminiscences to both Carl and Elizabeth. Late into the night, fueled by coffee and aspirin, Elizabeth connected with her dear friend:

Dear Carl, Great news on the night - it's raining...a real summer rain, warm after a bitter cold day, sweet-smelling so that Ouija sits in the door and smells till she nearly bursts but will not venture out into it, and steady so that maybe the incipient parched look to our world will go away and everybody's spirits and crops will rise...also a short but fetching letter from you, which raises my spirits if not my crops!... felt logey all afternoon, and dull in the heart for some reason...maybe the cold...

...of course, Mozart, lots of him; for grace...on long-playing records too, insinuating and boastful as that may be!...I do sometimes get a little lonesome for somebody who likes music well enough to listen to it...

...ah me...the nights when I have nothing whatever of any importance to say are almost the worst—nothing to say, no way to stop saying it...a frightful predicament?...the rain chatters on the windows...and either the aspirin or the mental wheels are beginning to revolve rather oddly...I think it may be a little of both, brought on by your remark about 'in the midst of life'...which I hadn't thought of before as having any bearing on what I think and feel right now, but it does somehow—not sure yet, maybe never—very disconcerting to feel things one ought to be thinking and then putting down in black and white! A feeling in its raw state is hardly marketable across the book counter...ah well...

(June 6, 1950)[217]

Van Doren, making his final preparations before heading out of town to Cornwall, recalled that "long rainy day" from the previous summer, when his ardor got the best of him and he confessed to Elizabeth that he would rather *do* than *be* ravishing...With her latest witty response to his "Quicksilver Wench" in a letter before him, Van Doren declared that he alone was "the one man alive who gets most out of what you write or have written or will ever write." Signing, *Love in Love, Carl,* Van Doren dropped one final letter down the mail chute before setting out for Cornwall.

West Cornwall of course

17 June 1950

Sweet to get your welcoming letter here...I have been sleeping like a doemouse since I got here. Mark and his|family drove me up the night of the 13th. His birthday, the 56th, that was. And|the 12th you a year in Fairfield. And the 14th, me ten years at 41 CPW. Anniversaries. Damn this type-writer. It's my new onex I've had for yyar or so, but gone on using the /old|one, which blew up the day I left so I had to send it to berepaired and bring this up. It will take me days to get used to it, all nice and new and heat, with me\used to the old|one\that I can bat hell out of and feel at home with...

...I got a wonderful new scythe yesterday, really what we call here a brush hook, and probably you there too: broad xxx cruel blade with a heavy snathe.)Look at that damned left margin. Or no, don't please. Be easy going and forgiving with me today. I woke this morning thinking variations on the old|saying: I like my xxxx whisky strong and my women weak. Variations. My whiskey straight and my women crooked. My whiskey neat and my women tousled. This last I think my own, and I like|it. Though xxx the whole business has little to do with my own character, I being|no hand for comments on women in the plural. One at a time is enough variety. And now you are the onex I consider singular and|plural enough for all necessary consideration...Very hard rain early this morning, with fancy thunder, which I did not hear, only learned about at breakfast. But you know that rainy days in Cornwall do things|to me. As for today, none|of your business, Bright Eyes. Guess your worst... [218]

Carl, Mark, and Dorothy Van Doren all headed up to Cornwall on Mark's birthday, June 13th. The following week, after only a few days to loosen up the keys on his new and rather sticky typewriter, Van Doren fell ill and checked in to the hospital in nearby Torrington. His next letter to Elizabeth was a short, handwritten scrawl, which simply read:

Sunday I had a slight heart attack (coronary occlusion to you) and here I am laid up in absolute bedrest—for maybe a month, maybe less. I have to write in bed, and very little else. Thank you for the nice S.R.s. More later when I am more able to write. I am much embarrassed at being so useless as this. Yours, Carl
(June 21, 1950)[219]

When she received word of Van Doren's distress on the 26th, Elizabeth Marion tried to lighten the clearly serious situation with a bit of the pair's usual banter, teasing, "I hope your variations didn't get the best of you and all that ails you is that you like whiskey and the women both too much!" Rest and observation, a restricted diet, and a sign on the door stating NO VISITORS amounted to a very slow week, but Van Doren's condition looked hopeful. Mark and Paul were at Carl's bedside, writing to brother Guy in Michigan that their eldest brother was coming along well. The Van Doren brothers had remained a close-knit group, though seldom did all five get together, with Carl and Mark in New York, Frank in Illinois, Guy in Michigan, and youngest brother Paul in New Jersey. A major restriction put upon the ailing Van Doren was an order to remain horizontal, and so any letter-writing was severely limited.

But a writer must write, doctor's orders for complete rest notwithstanding, and Van Doren's only form of communication with his Dear Elizabeth, his Quicksilver, his Proud Beauty, his Beautiful, was maintained through Mark's determination to bring him pen and paper and to deliver Carl's letters as fast as he could write them.[220]

There I was, playing Pan under the Useful Tree, brandishing a Randypandy Heart- and practically forcing it into your young, gay hands! And now look. The heart is rather like old cheese...All this, Quicksilver, is mostly literary. A short-scuffle with the heart, and the doctor already (after a week) says I am out of the woods...

(June 26, 1950)[221]

"Mostly literary" indeed. Van Doren and Elizabeth enjoyed the quick wit and literary turns-of-phrase of the other, even from a hospital bed. Elizabeth assured Van Doren that "the Useful Tree can be anywhere." But the severity of this health crisis was not lost on her, and the confrontation with his possible mortality had her in very low spirits. Very low. She encouraged Carl to get better and hoped he was improving rapidly, attempting to lift his spirits with her regular musings on the day. She sent a clipping of her latest column from the newspaper, wrote of Ouija's shenanigans, and described July 4th festivities in Fairfield. But reality this time was staring her in the face, even from such a great distance. Knowing that Carl was so ill made her terribly lonesome. The Useful Tree, after all, was meant for two.

What is love, after all, if not the desire to see the object of that affection happy, shining, and well; unselfish devotion to the well-being of another. No matter Van Doren's concerns for his own health, he was ultimately concerned for Elizabeth and wanted her to be happy, wanted to say whatever he could to make her eyes shine. Pleased with the clipping of her latest "Leaky Faucet" column, Van Doren praised the novelist-turned-newspaper-columnist for her observations and wit. This latest was the best she had written yet. Always her cheerleader and often a flirt, Van Doren's love for Elizabeth Marion was a tender one. He wrote, "There is nothing that delights me so much as lifting your spirit, with the sudden swift reward of the gleam in your eyes and the light on your [? face?]. The [?] is lovely. So are you. Thanks for both. Yours, Carl." When, a few days later, Van Doren's doctor declared a moratorium on all letter-writing, he insisted in jotting off a quick note. "Really very well, need of absolute rest seems important. Sorry to be so brief. I love to hear from you and [?]. Yours, Carl."222

Elizabeth's letters remained chatty, but her heart had sunk and she could neither keep up her usually cheerful tone nor the playful banter that had characterized her letters over the past three and a half years. Mourning the possible loss of someone who had become so important to her, she wrote, "...and I think that is about all I know tonite...about all I ever know, all by my lonesome under the Useful Tree; wit does not thrive by its lonesome there..." Van Doren's brief letter to his Dear Elizabeth on July 11th was his last:

Several bad days with the ticker, and me pretty horizontal, and required to be silent + sullen. But—I think constantly of the Useful Tree, and send you my love. Carl

(July 11, 1950)223

CHAPTER 11

→ ·· ←

SUCH NOBLE PATTERNS

Carl Van Doren passed away on July 18, 1950, at the age of sixty-four. His brother Mark had been critical in delivering Carl's letters to Elizabeth from the hospital, even writing a letter on Carl's behalf when Carl was no longer permitted, or able, to hold a pen. Distraught at seeing his older brother so frail, the brother of whom he had spent a lifetime in admiration, Mark "said nothing of what was more and more on my mind, the great tree in whose shade I had lived was about to be cut down. It was unthinkable, yet it was true...Since that death the world has been so changed a place that I date most events as after or before it."

The measure of his success is the number of individuals who now think he was their best friend. And he was. For nobody's letters came more promptly when letters were desired; and when we was with anybody it seemed to be true that there was no other person in the world.[224]

Carl Van Doren's bouts with anxiety were not lost on Mark. We don't know for sure, so many decades hence and with subsequent advancements in diagnostic medical technologies, if Van Doren had a specific underlying heart condition which, presenting as a "galloping pulse" and anxiety, fed a vicious cycle of what Van Doren simply understood as "nerves." We do know that anxiety and a rapid pulse troubled Carl Van Doren during the last years of his life. But his stoic Dutch indifference, the cheerful *Heigh-ho!*'s scattered throughout his personal correspondence, and his reassuring laughter presented a dignified and warm figure. He was The Man Who Knew Everybody. Mark Van Doren's praise, "when he was with anybody it seemed to be true that there was no other person in the world" captures the affability and graciousness of Carl Van Doren.

Van Doren's memorial service was held at the Hotel Ambassador in New York City on Sept. 26, 1950, just days after what would have been his sixty-fifth birthday. New York's literary circle came out in full force to honor the great man of letters who, with his passing, presaged the end of an era. The very idea of the *man of letters*, not long for this world, would very quickly become an anachronism. James Thurber, Sinclair Lewis, Clifton Fadiman,

Alred Kazin, Mary Margaret McBride, and colleagues from *The Nation* and *Century* spoke in great admiration of the dignity and historical scholarship of this man so many considered to be his, or her, best friend. Fadiman, who was co-editor at *The Readers Club* with Van Doren, and Sinclair Lewis (under the direction of publisher George Macy), recognized the unique qualities in a man who, even during the golden age of literary criticism, stood apart from all other men and women of ideas who collectively marked an age of public intellectualism, civic pride, and literary appreciation:

> The ancient Greeks, in particular Pindar, evolved the notion of the Noble Example, or <u>paradeigma</u>: that citizen who formed his life on lines so large and spacious in virtue that forever after merely the desire to imitate him was in itself a kind of education. In our day such paradeigmata are rare, in consequence of the the impoverishment of our ideas of politics, which is but the art of living together as men. All the more valuable, therefore, are such noble patterns when they <u>do</u> appear; and such a one was Carl. No one who met him, I do in my heart believe, went away unenlarged; he never acted like a great man, and therefore his example worked subtly and silently on lesser men, like music.[225]

The man who "never acted like a great man" nevertheless left greatness behind. Governor of Alaska Ernest Gruening, who had known Van Doren as a journalist before turning to politics, wrote that Carl Van Doren "carved out a life in which his desire for self-expression found full sway, that he left some enduring literary monuments, that his influence is not ephemeral, and that he made his important contributions to the luster which surrounds the name of Van Doren." Jacques Barzun would have pleased Van Doren with his praise for his mentor's concise use of language and clear, unpretentious prose. Barzun remembered, "I could easily feel: here is a man I have known all my adult life. This great communicability argues a great spirit." Alfred Kazin, who also studied under Carl and Mark Van Doren, simply acknowledged that Carl was "as full of grace as anyone can be."[226]

Elizabeth Marion, although personally invited by Mark Van Doren, was unable to attend Carl's memorial service in New York. After Van Doren passed away, Mark, as literary executor to Carl's estate, returned all of Elizabeth's letters, which Carl had kept among his personal possessions. Now in possession of her letters to him as well as his letters to her, Elizabeth stored away the entire trove. Mark quickly second-guessed his decision to return the letters, and wrote to Elizabeth just weeks after Carl's memorial service, in which he asked her to hold on to the letters, but *please don't burn them*. Some day, he asked, would she please send the entire collection to Julian Boyd at Princeton University Library, who was assembling the Carl Van Doren Papers.

Thankfully, this is exactly what Elizabeth Marion did.

Elizabeth continued writing and editing at *The Standard-Register* and was soon promoted to the newspaper's managing editor. In 1954, at the age of thirty-eight, Elizabeth Marion married Eugene D. Saunders, an employee of the Milwaukee railroad. The marriage was not a happy one, and did not last. In 1959, Elizabeth took a position as copywriter for Spokane's *Spokesman-Review*, the city's paper of record. She was with the *S-R* for twenty years, retiring in 1979. Her apartment on 7th Street in Spokane was, naturally, full of books. Books lined the shelves and overflowed into stacks throughout her home. The magic that books held for Elizabeth Marion in her twenties, those cloth- and paper-bound jewels which shone so brightly "<u>because</u> they're so distant...books do that for me, more than anything else...all the minds, sparkling and mysterious and more everlasting than souls, leaving their welcome testaments on the bookshelves" retained this charm for her throughout her life.

In 1988, Elizabeth suffered a stroke which left her incapacitated. Her younger sister Shirley, the sister Elizabeth had written about so often in her letters to Van Doren, was her caretaker during the last years of her life until she died in 1993. She never published another novel. Some time after 1950, Elizabeth Marion's joy for writing fiction evaporated; the opus, finally and forever, had eluded her. Once she had accepted her fate as a copyeditor, Elizabeth simply and with finality turned her back on ever completing her opus. Unsentimental and ever pragmatic, she did not talk about her three published novels to even her closest friends. Any suggestion that she write another novel was met with disdain. After Carl's death, the muse abandoned her.

But writing *had* been the focus of her life for a great many years, and the life of the mind always animated her spirit. The 1946 Reed Writers' Conference, where Elizabeth Marion had first met Carl Van Doren, had been "an orgy of intellectual glamour" and she never lost the thrill of intellectual life. While Mr. Van Doren's reputation had initially "scared the pants off" of her, in him she knew she had met a truly original human being. Elizabeth wrote, "Mr. Van Doren must meet thousands of people every year, but he makes every single one of them feel that that one is as fine and witty and kind and literate as he is, and I don't know any gift of living that can make more people feel better than they are!... when he makes a speech he just twists an audience easily around his finger and doesn't let them go till he's finished...if then..."[227]

Carl Van Doren's book, *Jane Mecom, the Favorite Sister of Benjamin Franklin*, was published just months after his death. He had lived the full life, at once inside his own head and vibrantly of the world around him. Jacques Barzun, a student of both Carl and Mark Van Doren at Columbia and by the midcentury a formidable man of letters in his own right, along with Lionel Trilling, another early protégée of the Van Doren brothers, took up the baton and left their own profound imprints on the nation's literacy landscape. In his masterwork *From Dawn to Decadence* (published when he was ninety-three), Barzun, like Van Doren, wrote of the *artistry* of practicing history, insisting that "history cannot be a science; it is the very opposite, in that its interest resides in the particulars." Where Van Doren had written that a historian must look into his heart as a poet does, that a biographer must aim to practice a *scrupulous art* in his endeavors, his literary successors Barzun and Trilling codified the art of literary and cultural criticism for their own generation.

Van Doren's "great communicability argue[d] a great spirit." Since the epoch of those great *men of letters*, the intellectual class has cleaved into two: public intellectuals, who have microphones and television cameras but whose thinking, on the whole, falls short of extraordinary; and true intellectuals, hidden from sight behind the ivory tower or institutional walls, whose thinking is first-rate but who toil in relative obscurity. Carl Van Doren embodied that brief moment in our intellectual history where the life of the mind was given wide berth in a truly public forum, an era when the *Man of Ideas* was itself a calling.

Mark composed a poem shortly after Carl's death, which he titled "In Memoriam." With this poem, Mark later said that he was trying to do justice to "the courage and the love which conquered in him the anxiety, the excitement, and the fear. These were as much a part of him as the self-confidence most people envied in a man whose laughter could reassure them as dawn reassures the grass."[228]

Look, till all of his years,
Foreshortened in your gaze,
Become, as under glass,
A few intensest days.

See? The courageous head—
The brown one—the white—
It flickers like a single
Star in densest night.

Listen. But no sound.
Not even glancing here.
The fever in him flashes:
The love against the fear.

Anxiety in this man
Yet could not kill the heart,
That now is burning coal,
And his immensest part.

The panic, the distress—
Oh, brothers, do not cry.
His love alone is climbing
The fences of the sky.

AUTHOR'S NOTE

I come from a writing family. Which isn't to say that we all must write, but many of us have, and still do, and after the joy of putting our words down on paper is satisfied, we then find a way to get those words out into the world.

My grandfather started a literary magazine in the 1930s with his friend from college, and his future wife/my grandmother, who would earn her doctorate in philosophy a few years later in 1941. They named their literary baby *The Fortnightly*, set up shop in North Beach, San Francisco, and wrote in the style of literary criticism that flourished in the '30s and '40s during that golden age. The Great Depression, however, reaching its lowest point, ended that literary production after just one year. My grandfather wrote, "The Depression had subdued us." *Fortnightly* or no, he kept writing. Mostly for himself and for family. He wrote.

My great aunt Lois (Foster) Rather and great uncle Cliff Rather started a home printing press in the Oakland Hills, just east of San Francisco, in the early 1960s. She conducted diligent research at Cal's Bancroft Library and wrote the narratives, which were mostly histories of local persons-of-interest or of California's cultural landscape. Some of the copies have been handed down to me from my family, some I have purchased in used bookstores across the country. He set the type and managed the printing press with one arm (he had suffered a stroke in 1962), and she carved woodcuts and linocuts for the illustrations and learned the craft of bookbinding. In this work of true craftsmanship, the pair hand-numbered each book they had produced themselves. *Bohemians to Hippies: Waves of Rebellion; Gertrude Stein and California;* and *Books and Societies* are some of the Rather Press titles that live on my bookshelf today.

It was my great-aunt Lois, in fact, who first introduced me to the Van Doren literary dynasty when I was much younger. She was pleased to share with me her occasional correspondence with Carl Van Doren from the 1930s and '40s, mostly related to literary and professional interests but also to keep up the family connection between the Fosters and the Van Dorens, both remembering their shared roots as cousins (second-cousins, actually) from the home base of the old Tillotson family homestead. When I made my own trek to Van Doren's Cornwall home at the invitation of

Carl's granddaughter, Susan Klaw, I was continuing a conversation started long before me and my own desire *to know.*

And so we write, and we publish, and we share our stories with the world. I am grateful for the inspiration. In the spirit of the Rather Press: *This book is printed in Spectral, 10.5 pt. font. First print edition, October 2018.*

The Little Red House; Lois Rather, illustration credit. c 1970

ENDNOTES

PROLOGUE

1   "Their writings are conversations" *Three Worlds*, 266
2   *Three Worlds*, 264
3   "Contains not only revelations of the self" Leslie Fielder, *The Art of the Essay*, 4, 487

CHAPTER 1

4   *Jane Mecom*, 240 (italics added)
5   EM to CVD, Nov. 16, 1946 (Box 39 F5)
6   EM to CVD (Box 39 F 1)
7   CVD to EM, Dec 10, 1946 (Box 39 F5)
8   CVD to EM, Dec 16, 1946 (Box 39 F5)
9   CVD to VC, Dec 23, 1946 (Box 39 F5)
10   CVD to EM, Dec 23, 1946; Feb 6, 1947; Feb 28, 1947 (Box 39 F5). The granddaughter CVD refers to here is Joanna, Bobby's daughter.
11   EM to CVD, Feb 11, 1947 (Box 39 F1)
12   EM, *Betty's Chronicles* (unpublished), 12/11/45
13   *Three Worlds*, 8, 24
14   "Like most of his generation" *TW*, 27
15   *TW*, 49, 50
16   Ibid, 1
17   Ibid, 30, 60, 62
18   Ibid, 255
19   "I remember the uprush" *TW*, 81
20   "New York was still less a city" *TW*, 88
21   *TW*, 97

CHAPTER 2

22 EM to CVD, May 19, 1947 (Box 18 F4) (Box 39 F1)

23 CVD to EM, Aug 25, 1947 (Box 18 F4)

24 EM to CVD, Aug 31, 1947 (Box 39, F1)

25 *Keys to the House*, 33, 95

26 EM to CVD, Sept 1, 1948 (Box 18 F5) For a thorough account of *A Room of One's Own*, see Virginia Wolfe's brilliant 1929 essay.

27 CVD to EM, Oct 31, 1949 (Box 18 F7)

28 "Best and Dearest girl," CVD to IB, Dec 1, 1911

29 "There is no general truth..." CVD to IB, Ap 7, 1912

30 CVD to IB, May 17, 1912; CVD to IB July 4, 1912

31 CVD to IB, May 29, 1912; CVD to IB, June 15 1912; "wicked days..." IB to CVD June 26, 1912; CVD to IB, May 28, 1912

32 Chapter VI, *The Devil's Lane*, 1912 (unpublished).

33 "Tremendously good looking," from *Mark Van Doren: Portrait of a Poet*, documentary by Adam Van Doren, 1994

34 *TW*, 95, 107

35 *The American Essay in the American Century*, 70

36 Henry S. Canby, *Alma Mater: The Gothic Age*, 196-8

37 "Another View of the Graduate School" CVD to *Nation*, July 9, 1908

38 "The Scholar-Critic" in *Jacques Barzun Reader*, 89

39 *The American Essay*, 2-3; "There are as few good writers" *TW*, 200-1

40 Ibid, 126

41 Ibid, 113

42 Ibid, 115, 120, 118

43 MVD to CVD, June 30, 1918 (Box 25 F7)

44 PVD to CVD, Nov. 15, 1918, Dec 14, 1918 (Box 29 F1)

45 *TW*, 138, 144

46 "The Revolt from the Village: 1920" *Nation* 10/12/21, 407 (italics added)

47   Ibid, 407

48   Ibid, 407

49   *The Nation* 10/12/21, 410

50   SL to CVD, 10/25/21 (Box 17 F6)

51   *Contemporary American Novelists* (italics added)

52   *TW*, 144

53   "Same general sort as Main Street" SL to CVD, 11/21/21 (Box 17 F6) ; "We have been missing you" 7/29/33 (Box 17 F6)

54   *Sinclair Lewis: A Biographical Sketch*, 7

55   Ibid, 13-14

56   Ibid, 36

57   CVD to HM, (Box 20, F2) ; SL to CVD (Box17 F7)

58   "Touched the literary taste" *TW*, 123. In his autobiography, CVD dates his presence in Cornwall to 1915

59   *American Moderns*, 2

60   Ibid, 89

61   *TW*, 208

62   *American Moderns*, 156; *TW*, 272

63   *TW*, 266. Van Doren's salary in 1922 was $5,000 per year at the *Century*, plus $250 per article written.

64   "Behind the blow" *Many Minds*, 6

65   *TW*, 195

CHAPTER 3

66   Ibid, 195

67   *CAN*, 34-37

68   GA to CVD, June 26, 1922 (Box 14 F5)

69   RH to "The Contributor's Column" (Box 34, F3)

70   *CAN*, 117; WC to CVD, July 30, no year (Box 15, F1) ; TW to CVD, 9/1/36 (Box 15 F9)

71   TD to CVD (Box 15, F9)

72   RF to CVD, Dec 27, 1920 (Box 16 F5)

73   *TW*, 216

74 "Utterly bad" *Three Worlds*, 219 ; *Private Madness*, 27-29
75 *Private Madness*, 38
76 Ibid, 37
77 "Almost nobody knew" *TW,* 220; *Private Madness*, 63
78 "Passed like any other" *TW,* 221; *Private Madness*, 104-5
79 "White queen of a white country" *TW,* 222 ; "To make up for being vain" *Private Madness*, 48; "Laughed about it" *TW,* 236
80 "If I told you" EW to CVD, 8/8/25 (Box 30, F6)
81 *Private Madness*, 82
82 *TW,* 223
83 CVD "Foreword" for Readers Club, c. 1944
84 *New Republic*, 10/7/1925, 176-7 ; "The Friendly Enemy, in *Many Minds*, 203
85 *TW,* 237
86 Ibid, 235
87 Ibid, 233, 235, 240

CHAPTER 4

88   *Earth Horizon*, 71
89   Ibid, 195
90   Ibid, 233
91   Ibid, 312-13
92   Ibid, 324
93   Ibid, 349
94   Ibid, 331
95   Ibid, 319
96   *Many Minds*, 9-10
97   Ibid, 9-14
98   Ibid, 14-17
99   MHA to CVD, April 1, 1923 (Box 14 F5)
100 MHA to CVD, July 14, 1923 (Box 14 F5)
101 *Earth Horizon*, 320, 330

102   Ibid, 367
103   *The Land of Little Rain*, xiii, xiv
104   Ibid, 1

CHAPTER 5

105   *The Roving Critic*, 25
106   Ibid, 27-31
107   Ibid, 148
108   *Many Minds*, 203, 215-16
109   "I knew I had no business," *TW*, 197; "A Note on the Essay," *The New Pearson's* (April 1923)
110   "A Note on the Essay," *The New Pearson's* (April 1923)
111   "The Great and Good Tradition; Stuart P. Sherman: Scourge of Sophomores"
112   SS to IVD, July 4, 1925. From the Irita Van Doren Papers, LOC
113   SS to IVD, July 30, 1926. From the Irita Van Doren Papers, LOC
114   SS to IVD, Aug 15, 1926. From the Irita Van Doren Papers, LOC

CHAPTER 6

115   "Happy and unhappy marriages" *TW*, 7; "The hours of the day ceased to matter" *TW*, 262
116   Ibid, 254-5
117   *TW*, 170-1
118   "The case against the book clubs," Frederick Stokes in the *North American Review*, 07/1929
119   "A Letter to Elinor Wylie," *The New Republic*, 10/7/1925
120   Mary McCarthy and Margaret Marshall, "Our Critics," *The Nation*, 1935
121   "A great man moving through public affairs" "Biographer on the Trail," *Good Housekeeping*, Apr 1945
122   *TW*, 303
123   Ibid, 281

124   "The sons of bitches" CVD to MVD, Aug 20, 1935 (Box 29 F4)

125   *Making of Middlebrow Culture*, 84

126   Charles Peters, *Five Days in Philadelphia*, 35, 176

127   "Ask the romantic YG" *TW*, 174; "Americans who had always looked," *TW*, 281

128   "Swanned languidly across the stage" from *American Rose: The Life and Times of Gypsy Lee Rose*, by Karen Abbott (p. 265)

129   "Rarely does a new historian have the bravery and power to survey and map the field as if he were the first in it." CVD, Introduction to B.M. Fullerton's *Selective Bibliography of American Literature, 1775-1900* (1936)

130   "Life like touches" CVD to DVD (Box 23 F9) ; "The only great American man" CVD to MAB (Box 29, F7) ; "Amazing felicity" CVD to MAB (Box 29 F7)

131   *Benjamin Franklin*, v-viii

132   "Franklin has gone in this country" CVD to HG, Dec 1, 1937 (Box 29 F8)

133   SH to CVD, 1938 (Box 29 F10)

CHAPTER 7

134   Katherine Woods, "The Van Doren Brothers in American Letters," 609, 620

135   "By a shared passion" *TW*, 148; *The Private Reader* (1942)

136   "Is all that part of me" CVD to JB, (Box 20 F1) ; "Was prodigal" *The Essays of Mark Van Doren*, 218

137   Mark Van Doren, *Liberal Education*

138   "The nature of man" from "The Kinds of Knowledge" in *The Essays of Mark Van Doren*, 226; "Not to have had the desire" from "The Joy of Being Serious" in *The Essays of MVD*, 233; "One of the few" *NYT*, Dec 12, 1972

139   "When heat and light are mated" (italics added) No date (Box 8 F2)

140 "Forgive this lousy typing" CVD to MVD 3/28/36 (Box 27 F7); "I hear you talking" (MVD to CVD 5/6/36 (Box 27, F7)

141 "It is a very beautiful book" CVD to MVD, 10/8/36 (Box 27 F8) ; "The book is published" MVD to CVD, 10/9/36 (Box 27 F8)

142 CVD to MVD, 7/22/38 (Box 28 F1).

143 *Writer and Friends*, 20

CHAPTER 8

144 MVD, "High in the Air, But They Don't Talk Down" *New York Times*, 11/16/41

145 Letter reprinted in *The Selected Letters of Mark Van Doren*, 154

146 "The program I said was going to pieces" MVD letter reprinted in *The Selected Letters of Mark Van Doren*; "This will be good for Mark" from *The Republic of Letters in America*.

147 *American Scriptures*, xiii

148 *Patriotic Anthology*, xxiii

149 Ibid, xxvi

150 "Whatever difference of opinions" Ibid, xxiv

151 "Willing to be called" CVD to VC, 1/29/41 (Box 15 F2)

152 JB to CVD, 7/22/40 (Box 20 F1)

153 "I don't suppose" CVD to JB, 2/18/41 (Box 20 F2)

154 "Occasionally temporary despair" CVD to JB, 2/27/41 (Box 20 F2)

155 "It's an odd quirk" CVD to JB, 9/27/41(Box 20 F3); "nominal associations" (Box 17 F5)

156 "I agree with you" CVD to JB, 7/8/41 (Box 20 F2).

157 "The story yells to be told" CVD to JB, 3/18/42 (Box 20,F3) ; "A remarkably patriotic book" CVD to HG, 04/1941 (Box 29 F8)

158 "Our Two Patriotisms," *Good Housekeeping*, June 1945

159 AR to CVD, 9/3/44 ; 12/24/44 ; 1/29/45 (Box 22 F6) ; AR to CVD 4/18/45 (Box 22 F7)

CHAPTER 9

160 Lewis Dabney, *Edmund Wilson; A Life in Literature,* 191-2

161 "Once or twice" CVD to VC 3/15/39 (Box 15 F2) ; "San Francisco is superb" CVD to MVD, Feb 24, 1939 (Box 28 F1)

162 AR to CVD, 11/4/1944 ; 1/7/1944 (Box 22 F6)

163 "Died tragically of an overdose" CVD to VC, 1/18/46 (Box 15 F2)

164 "We talked about the Van Dorens," *The Sixties; The Last Journal,* 108; "Carl's daughter Bobby who made the horrific discovery," personal conversation with Susan Klaw, June 2018.

165 "Perhaps a more peaceful and quiet ending" AR to CVD, 7/9/45 (Box 22 F7)

166 "As to the private tragedy" CVD to VC, 2/13/46 (Box 15 F2)

167 *Viking Portable Library,* 573, 580, 607

168 "I shall kill myself yet" CVD to JB (Box 20 F6) ; CVD to JB, 2/19/45 (Box 20 F5)

169 "The most glorious mountain view" SL to CVD, 5/5/46 (Box 17 F7)

170 "The roads are wildly twisted" CVD to EM, 7/25/47 (Box 18 F4)

171 "When I am off the air" HVL to EM, 3/24/38 (Hendrik Willem Van Loon Papers, Cornell University Library, Box 14 F2)

172 HVL to EM, 3/24/38 (HWVL, Cornell, Box 14 F2)

173 HVL to EM, 1/13/39 (HWVL, Cornell, Box 14 F3)

174 EM to CVD, 3/10/48 (Box 39 F2)

175 *Ellen Spring,* 95, 250

176 "Created a particularly nasty type" HVL to EM, 8/17/42 (HWVL, Cornell, Box 14 F12)

177 *Keys To The House,* 36

178 "America has never understood" HVL to EM, 5/6/38 (HWVL, Cornell, Box 14 F2)

179 *NYT* Letter to Ed, 9/20/45 (Box 21 F5)

180   (Box 14 F4)

181   (Box 33 F6)

182   "Only world government" (Box 33 F6). "Many people say" (Box 34 F7)

183   *Early Tales of the Atomic Age*, 11

CHAPTER 10

184   "With admiration at first reading" CVD to EM, Dec 11, 1947 (Box 18 F4)

185   CVD to EM, Apr 15, 1948 (Box 18 F4)

186   "I talk easily" CVD to EM, Jan 27, 1948 (Box 18 F4); "I think you are working too hard" Apr 27, 1948 (Box 18 F4)

187   "I like it because" EM to CVD, June 15, 1948 (Box 18 F4)

188   "Right hand in plain view" CVD to EM, June 30, 1948 (Box 18 F4)

189   "A hardboiled hermit" CVD to EM, 5/17/48 ; "Odd I should so often miss you" CVD to EM, 4/27/48 (Box 18 F6)

190   "The way you do when you are overstrung" CVD to EM, 5/7/48 (Box 18 F6)

191   "Would take to you" CVD to EM, 5/10/48 (Box 18 F6) ; "Nothing on god's green earth" EM to CVD, 5/8/49 (Box 39 F3)

192   "I wish you could have dinner with me" CVD to EM, 10/11/48 (Box 18 F5)

193   "I hope you won't mind" CVD to EM, 9/10/48 (Box 18 F5)

194   CVD to EM, 10/31/48 (Box 18 F5)

195   "Interests me far more" CVD to EM, 10/31/48 (Box 18 F5)

196   "Blew a gasket" CVD to EM, 11/15/48 (Box 18 F5)

197   "I make no mention" CVD to EM, 12/30/48 (Box 18 F5)

198   EM to CVD, 3/15/49 (Box 39 F3)

199   EM to CVD, 5/23/49 (Box 39 F3)

200   "You are wrong in saying" CVD to EM, 8/12/49 ; "There is a great deal between" CVD to EM, 1/17/49 (Box 18 F5)

201   CVD to EM, 9/7/49 (Box 18 F5)

202   "You must stop thinking so much" CVD to EM, 10/31/49 (Box 18 F5)

203   "I am far from well" CVD to EM, 12/3/49 (Box 18 F8) ; "Thanks for what you are" CVD to EM, 12/13/49 (Box 18 F8)

204   EM to CVD, 1/4/50 (Box 39 F4)

205   "I like the lines in your face" EM to CVD, 2/11/50 (Box 39 F4)

206   EM to CVD, 2/1/50 ; CVD to EM, 2/6/50

207   "I do love your mind" CVD to EM, 3/16/50 (Box 18 F9)

208   "But keep your eyes out" CVD to EM, 3/16/50 ; "But vanity is weak" EM to CVD, 3/19/50 (Box 18, F9)

209   "Being both lazy and optimistic" EM to CVD, 2/27/50 (Box 39 F4)

210   "A snowy cool night" EM to CVD, 3/8/50; "Under that Useful Tree right now" CVD to EM, 3/11/50 (Box 18 F9)

211   "I think your words not only" EM to CVD, 3/14/50 (Box 39 F4); "It must be queer and exasperating" EM to CVD, 3/19/50 (Box 39 F4)

212   "Who are you calling not so faithful" CVD to EM 5/1/50 (Box 39 F4)

213   EM to CVD, 2/27/50 (Box 39 F4)

214   "Sometimes I almost wish" CVD to EM, 6/2/50 (Box 18 F9); "Time all over the place" EM to CVD, 5/25/50 (Box 39 F4) ; "Shall we please have Beethoven" EM to CVD, 5/31/50 (Box 39 F4)

215   "Beethoven as such as you like" CVD to EM, 6/3/50 (Box 18 F9)

216   CVD to EM 6/8/50 (Box 39 F4)

217   EM to CVD 6/6/50 (Box 39 F4)

218   CVD to EM 6/17/50 (Box 18 F9)

219   CVD to EM, 6/21/50 (Box 18 F9)

220   "I hope your variations" EM to CVD, 6/26/50 (Box 39 F4)

221   CVD to EM, 6/26/50 (Box 18 F9)

222   "There is nothing that delights me" CVD to EM, 6/29/50 ; "Really very well" CVD to EM, 7/4/50 (Box 39 F4)

223   "And I think that is about all I know" EM to CVD, 7/13/50 ; "several bad days" CVD to EM, 7/11/50 (Box 39 F4)

CHAPTER 11

224   *The Autobiography of MVD*, 309-311
225   (Box 31, F7)
226   (Box 31 F4; F9)
227   EM to Maude *X*, 11/5/46
228   *The Autobiography of MVD*, 312

BIBLIOGRAPHY

Austin, Mary Hunter. *The Land of Little Rain, Photographs by Ansel Adams, Introduction by Carl Van Doren* (Boston: Houghton Mifflin Company, 1950)

Barzun, Jacques. *A Jacques Barzun Reader* (New York: Harper Collins, 2002)

Cairns, Huntington, Allen Tate, Mark Van Doren, eds. *Invitation to Learning* (New York: Random House, 1941)

Canby, Henry S. *Alma Mater: The Gothic Age of the American College* (New York: Farrar and Reinhart, 1936)

Claire, William, ed. *The Essays of Mark Van Doren; 1924-1972* (Westport: Greenwood Press, 1980)

Columbia University Library, the Mark Van Doren Papers

Cornell University Library, the Hendrik Willem Van Loon Papers

Dabney, Lewis M. *Edmund Wilson; A Life in Literature* (New York: Farrar, Straus and Giroux, 2005)

Farrar, John. "Ten Years of the Book Clubs," *The English Journal,* Vol 25, No 5 (May, 1936)

Fielder, Leslie. *The Art of the Essay* (New York: Thomas Y. Crowell, 1958)

Hendrick, George, ed. *The Selected Letters of Mark Van Doren* (Baton Rouge: Louisiana State University Press, 1987)

Hively, Evelyn Helmick. *A Private Madness; The Genius of Elinor Wylie* (Kent: The Kent State University Press, 2003)

Lang, Daniel. *Early Tales of the Atomic Age; Introduced by Carl Van Doren* (New York: Doubleday, 1948)

Library of Congress

Marion, Elizabeth. *The Day Will Come* (New York: Thomas Y. Crowell Company, 1939)

Marion, Elizabeth. *Ellen Spring* (New York: Thomas Y. Crowell Company, 1941)

Marion, Elizabeth. *The Keys to the House* (New York: Thomas Y. Crowell Company, 1944)

Murray, Michael, ed. *A Jacques Barzun Reader; Selections From his Works* (New York: HarperCollins Publishers, 2002)

Neal, Steven. *Dark Horse; A Biography of Wendell Wilkie* (Lawrence: University Press of Kansas, 1984)

Peters, Charles. *Five Days in Philadelphia; The Amazing "We Want Wilkie!" Convention of 1940 And How It Freed FDR To Save The Western World* (New York: Publicaffairs, 2005)

Posner, Richard. *Public Intellectuals; A Study of Decline* (Cambridge: Harvard University Press, 2001)

Princeton University Library, The Carl Van Doren Papers

Rubin, Joan Shelley. *The Making of Middlebrow Culture* (Chapel Hill: University of North Carolina Press, 1992)

Sheean, Vincent. *Dorothy & Red* (Boston: Houghton Mifflin Company, 1963)

Sicherman, Barbara, Carol Hurd Green, Ilene Kantrov, Harriette Walker, eds.

Notable American Women: The Modern Period; A Biographical Dictionary (Cambridge: The Belknap Press, 1980)

Stokes, Frederick A. "The Case Against the Book Clubs," *The North American Review,* Vol 228, No 1 (July 1929)

Stuckey-French, Ned. *The American Essay in the American Century* (Columbia: University of Missouri Press, 2011)

Van Doren, Carl. *(in chronological order)*

> *The American Novel* (New York: The Macmillian Company, 1921)
>
> *Contemporary American Novelists* (New York: The Macmillian Company, 1922)
>
> *The Roving Critic* (New York: Alfred A. Knopf, 1923)
>
> "A Note on the Essay," *The New Pearson's* (April, 1923)
>
> *Many Minds* (New York: Alfred A. Knopf, 1924)
>
> *Sinclair Lewis; A Biographical Sketch* (New York: Doubleday, 1933)
>
> *Three Worlds* (New York: Harper & Brothers, 1936)
>
> *Benjamin Franklin* (New York: Viking Press, 1939)
>
> *Patriotic Anthology,* Introduced by Carl Van Doren (New York: Doubleday, Doran and Company, 1941)
>
> *Secret History of the American Revolution* (New York: Viking Press, 1941)
>
> *Mutiny in January* (New York: Viking Press, 1943)

The Viking Portable Library (New York: Viking Press, 1945)

"A Biographer on the Trail," *Good Housekeeping* (April, 1945)
"Our Two Patriotisms," *Good Housekeeping* (June, 1945)
"What I Saw While I was Blind," *Good Housekeeping* (Nov, 1945)
"Women's Instinct" *Good Housekeeping* (Feb, 1946)
"Out of Order," *Good Housekeeping* (Oct, 1946)

American Scriptures, ed. with Carl Cramer (New York: Boni & Gaer, 1946)

The Great Rehearsal (New York: Viking Press, 1948)

The Letters of Benjamin Franklin and Jane Mecom, ed. (Princeton: Princeton University Press, 1950)

Jane Mecom; Franklin's Favorite Sister (New York: Viking Press, 1950)

Van Doren, Mark. *The Autobiography of Mark Van Doren* (New York: Harcourt, Brace & Company, 1958)

Van Doren, Mark. "In Memoriam," *The Autobiography of Mark Van Doren*

Washington State University Library, the Elizabeth Marion Saunders Papers

Weeks, Edward. *Writer and Friends* (Boston: Little, Brown, 1981)

Wilson, Edmund. *The Sixties; The Last Journal, 1960-1972* (New York: Farrar Straus Giroux, 1993)

Wilson, Edmund. *Memoirs of Hecate County* (New York: L. C. Page & Company, 1942)

Woods, Katherine. "The Van Doren Brothers in American Letters," *The English Journal*, Vol 29, No 8 (Oct, 1940)

Wylie, Elinor. *Venetian Glass Nephew* (New York: George H. Doran, 1925)

Wylie, Elinor. "Viennese Waltz," *Century* (September, 1923)

Young and Hindle, eds. *The Republic of Letters in America: The Correspondence of John Peale Bishop and Allen Tate* (Lexington: University Press of Kentucky, 1982)

Zeitlin, Jacob and Homer Woodbridge. *Life and Letters of Stuart P. Sherman* (Freeport: Books for Libraries Press, 1929)

ABBREVIATIONS IN NOTES:

AR	Anne (Van Doren) Ross
CVD	Carl Van Doren
DVD	Dora Van Doren
EM	Elizabeth Marion
EW	Elinor Wylie
GA	Gertrude Atherton
HG	Harold Guziman
HLM	H.L. Mencken
HVL	Hendrik William Van Loon
IB	Irita Bradford
JB	Julian Boyd
MHA	Mary Hunter Austin
MVD	Mark Van Doren
PVD	Paul Van Doren
RH	Rupert Hughes
RF	Robert Frost
SH	Sidney Howard
SL	Sinclair Lewis
SS	Stuart Sherman
TD	Theodore Dreiser
TW	Thorton Wilder
VC	Victor Chittick
WC	Willa Cather

Unless otherwise noted, Box and Folder citations in Notes refer to documents contained in the Carl Van Doren Papers, Department of Rare Books and Special Collections, Princeton University Library.

Made in the USA
Columbia, SC
15 October 2018